The human rights of aliens in contemporary international law

RICHARD B. LILLICH

MANCHESTER
UNIVERSITY PRESS

Published by
Manchester University Press
Oxford Road, Manchester M13 9PL, U.K.
51 Washington Street, Dover, N.H. 03820, U.S.A.

British Library cataloguing in publication data

Lillich, Richard B.
   The human rights of aliens in contemporary international law. — (The Melland Schill
   monographs in international law)
   1. Aliens
   I. Title   II. Series
   341.4′84   JX4255

Library of Congress cataloging in publication data

Lillich, Richard B.
   The human rights of aliens in contemporary international law.
   (The Melland Schill monographs in international law)
   Parts of this volume were originally delivered as the Melland Schill lectures at the
   University of Manchester, Nov. 19–20, 1981.
   Includes index.
   1. Aliens.   2. Civil rights (International law)
   I. Title   II. Series.
   K3274.L55   1984   341.4′82   84-15500

ISBN 0-7190-0914-6

Printed and bound in Great Britain by
Biddles Ltd, Guildford and King's Lynn

CONTENTS

FOREWORD

This book appears as the second in the new series of Melland Schill Monographs in International Law. The series is supported by the Melland Schill Fund which was bequeathed to the university by the late Miss Olive B. Schill of Prestbury, Cheshire, in memory of her brother, Melland Schill, who was killed in the 1914–18 war. Professor Richard Lillich, of the University of Virginia, gave the Melland Schill Lectures for 1981 in the Faculty of Law of the University of Manchester, based upon his research for this monograph.

As the title indicates, the book breaks new ground. The work of an international lawyer with an established reputation as scholar and practitioner in the areas of State responsibility, international claims and international human rights law, it offers a penetrating and informative account of the present state of international law relating to the treatment of individual aliens, from the perspective of human rights. Professor Lillich has drawn on some of his previous work, including his 1978 Hague Lectures on 'The Duties of States Regarding the Civil Rights of Aliens', but essentially the present study is a new and illuminating contribution to the literature. He has devoted considerable attention to recent developments in the United Nations, in particular the Draft Declaration on the Human Rights of Non-Citizens, a project which has not yet reached final fruition but which has stimulated wider interest in the treatment of individual aliens, as distinct from the heavy emphasis given in recent decades to issues of foreign investment, expropriation and compensation. The appendix contains texts of this Draft Declaration, as drafted by the Baroness Elles, the United Kingdom representative, and as it currently stands. These texts are not widely available.

Aliens appear in various legal guises, such as refugees or migrant workers, as well as more or less permanently settled residents. The burgeoning crop of international conventions and State practice relating to such categories of aliens, material which seldom receives scholarly attention, is reviewed here. So is the growing body of European Community law on freedom of movement for workers and the self-employed, and other European arrangements such as the European Social Charter, and the Convention on the Legal Status of Migrant Workers. Relevant bilateral treaties are also considered.

Professor Lillich has compared the law governing the treatment of aliens to 'a giant, unassembled juridical jigsaw puzzle', but has warned us not to be misled by the analogy, since there is no fixed number of pieces and no predetermined 'grand design' to be completed. The legal protection from the extensive powers of host countries which aliens may enjoy varies with different international treaty arrangements, overlaying general rules of customary international law. We still lack a comprehensive international legal regime governing the treatment of individual aliens. International human rights law offers the most promising as well as perhaps the most rational approach to such a regime. Professor Lillich has injected careful scholarship and thoughtful evaluation into this debate. His book is a valuable contribution to the Melland Schill series which is bound to be widely referred to as efforts to develop more comprehensive and appropriate legal provisions for aliens continue.

Gillian White
Professor of International Law
Director of the Melland Schill Fund

Faculty of Law
University of Manchester
March 1984

PREFACE

The first draft of this volume, parts of which were delivered as the Melland Schill Lectures at the University of Manchester on 19–20 November 1981, was written while the author was a resident alien in Great Britain during the 1980–81 academic year. As readers of his 1978 Hague Lectures on 'The Duties of States Regarding the Civil Rights of Aliens' will recognise, the present study is the logical outgrowth of the author's long-standing concern to leaven the traditional law governing the treatment of aliens with the emerging international human rights norms found in such instruments as the International Bill of Rights, the Draft Declaration on the Human Rights of Non-citizens, and the Draft Convention on the Protection of the Rights of Migrant Workers.

Anyone approaching the task of describing, much less critiquing, the variegated assortment of legal regimes taken up in this volume must do so with some trepidation. In the first place, well over a dozen of the topics considered are broad enough to warrant separate monograph treatment. Numerous experts in academia, government service, private practice and international organisations, moreover, have had the occasion to familiarise themselves with particular topics in far greater detail than time permits the author of a reasonably short yet fairly comprehensive survey study: hence some readers are reasonably certain to find the treatment of a particular topic either elementary or inadequate. Finally, developments in the law governing the treatment of aliens — broadly defined — are occurring so fast that it is literally impossible, given writing and publication schedules, to be completely up to date. Nevertheless, the need to bring together developments in disparate areas, the better to permit the author and other writers eventually to complete more comprehensive treatments of the human rights of aliens in contemporary international law, surely makes the effort as worthwhile as it has been taxing.

As mentioned above, substantial parts of this volume were originally drafted during 1980–81, while the author was a Sesquicentennial Associate of the Center for Advanced Studies of the University of Virginia and Thomas Jefferson Visiting Fellow, Downing College, Cambridge. To the Master and

Fellows of Downing go his especial thanks, not only for providing him with a set of rooms which enabled him to work without distraction while at the same time enjoying the comforts of college life, but also for the companionship and intellectual support that greatly furthered his work. Grateful acknowledgment also should be made to the Ford Foundation for its support during this period through a grant to the Procedural Aspects of International Law Institute to study 'The Treatment of Aliens in International Law'.

During the summer of 1981 and upon his return to the University of Virginia, the author received additional financial support from the Dana Fund, for which he wishes to record his sincere appreciation, and from the University of Virginia, in the form of two summer research grants from the Law School Foundation. Three research assistants, Ms Margaret Mary Doyle, Class of 1983, Mr Nathaniel D. Chapman, Class of 1984, and Mr Stephen D. Ramsay, Class of 1984, were particularly helpful in editing preliminary drafts, checking footnote material, and shepherding the final draft through the mysteries of the typing pool's word processors.

The author's deepest debt, however, is owed to his former student at the University of Virginia, Stephen C. Neff, Esq., of the University of Edinburgh, for his yeoman work during the winter and spring of 1981 on what became Chapter IV, Chapter V and Chapter VI of this volume. It is of interest to note that Mr Neff, a qualified solicitor and a resident of Great Britain, was ordered to cease practising law and leave the country under a 1980 policy of HMG designed to weed out alien lawyers, but was spared deportation because the author was able, thanks to Ford Foundation support, to hire him as a research associate on a project that, ironically, involved the human rights of aliens!

Finally, the author would like to express his appreciation to the University of Manchester for extending to him the invitation to give the Schill Lectures in 1981, an honour made all the greater by the fact that, aside from the late Professor Quincy Wright, he is only the second United States citizen to have been asked to give these lectures since their inception. Having a long-standing respect and affection for the university, dating back to Professor B. A. Wortley's twice asking him to lecture there during the 1960s, he was doubly pleased when his friend, colleague and collaborator of many years, Professor Gillian White, current holder of the Chair in International Law, offered him the opportunity to deliver the lectures that grew into this volume. It is hoped that — revised, expanded and updated — they will be regarded as a worthy addition to a truly great series.

Richard B. Lillich
Charlottesville, Virginia
December 1983

To aliens, which means potentially to all of us, and to their rights, especially the general norm of non-discrimination, this volume is dedicated.

INTRODUCTION

In few areas of public international law is there more precedent but less consensus than in that governing the treatment of aliens. While the existence of controversy has not been thought either an insurmountable or unhealthy problem in other areas, the question of the rights of aliens seems to be different, probably because controversies involving aliens strike at the very heart of the system of traditional international law established by the Peace of Westphalia, with its dogmatic orientation towards the institution of the nation-State.

Traditional international law — which in this study will mean all international law (both customary and conventional) predating the UN Charter in 1945[1] — was notoriously a 'law of nations' rather than a 'law of peoples'. In such a world the presence of 'objects' called human beings[2] was an annoying problem, a perceived threat, one might say, to the logic of the system. Moreover, these objects proved over many centuries to be singularly adept in crossing the boundaries of the various nation-States for one reason or another, and also singularly inventive at involving themselves — and therefore the expounders of international law doctrine — in difficulties.

Traditional international law treated aliens in a way which, if not enlightened, at least was consistent with its own underlying premises. Rather than recognising that individuals as such were entitled to a certain range of rights *vis-à-vis* States in general (including, incidentally, their own States), traditional international law 'solved' the problem by subsuming individuals into the nation-State network through the bond of nationality. If a State committed a wrong against an individual who was an alien, then that wrong, if unredressed, was translated into a wrong against the alien's State of nationality.[3] Once two States were involved, traditional international law handled the issue through its normal mechanisms (diplomacy, arbitration, and even war).[4] Under what has come to be known as the 'Vattelian fiction'[5] the alien himself had no right which was cognisable by traditional international law against his host State. Instead, he functioned as a sort of juridical lightning rod, channelling the legal ramifications of the original wrongful act from the domestic law level to the plane of international law.

While it is difficult to criticise this traditional approach on the grounds of logic or consistency, it is all too easy to fault it on the grounds of realism and humanity. One need only clear one's mind briefly of the incrustations of the traditional doctrine to appreciate that an injury inflicted upon an alien rarely causes more than a notional injury to his own State. Consider, for instance, a migrant worker from Algeria employed in France who is a victim of racial discrimination in his attempts to locate housing for himself and his family. Only through the use of the Vattelian fiction can such a situation be transmuted into a diplomatic dispute between France and Algeria, perhaps leading eventually to some redress for the worker. Yet, unless the worker's grievance is one of many, Algeria is unlikely to raise an international fuss. Consider the fact that Ghana registered only a feeble protest after Nigeria's mass expulsion in 1983 of literally thousands of Ghanaian workers.[6]

Admittedly, traders and business enterprises operating in foreign countries have often received over-zealous protection from their home governments, at times even to the point of the use of military force on their behalf. It is important, however, that the admitted serious abuses which took place in the era of 'gunboat diplomacy' do not blind one to the facts of contemporary international life. One should bear constantly in mind that today's alien is far more likely to be a migrant worker than an exploitative capitalist.

To be sure, the exploitative capitalist is not an extinct breed (as the behaviour of some multinational corporations frequently demonstrates). The focus of this study, however, will not be upon him. In so far as the capitalist utilises the corporate form, this study has nothing whatever to say about him — the concern here is with the rights of individual aliens. Similarly, this study will have little to say about such matters as the protection of the purely economic interests of individual aliens, in the sense of profit-making opportunities. While economic interests will be considered in Chapters III–VI, they will be interests of an altogether different sort than would appeal to the exploitative capitalist. The issues discussed will be the right to equal pay for equal work, the right to equal conditions of work, the right to participate in trade unions, the right to repatriate earnings, and so forth.

The central thread running throughout this study is that the logic of the traditional international law system protecting the rights of aliens exclusively (if at all) through the medium of the nation-State must give way in contemporary international law — and, in fact, has already begun to do so — to the direct protection of the rights of individual aliens as such. This question of the rights of aliens is inextricably linked to the contemporary international human rights law movement because it poses a clear test of the relevance and enforceability of the international human rights norms which have developed since World War II. These norms, derived and developed from the traditional law governing the treatment of aliens, are now in urgent need of adaptation and application to the situations aliens face in contemporary international life.

What the international community is witnessing today is a major change — the significance of which cannot be overstated — in the way in which the rights of aliens are protected: from the classic system of diplomatic protection by the alien's State of nationality, invoking the traditional international law governing the treatment of aliens, to the direct protection of the individual alien's rights through his use of national and international procedures to enforce a set of reformulated international norms of the sort which the study will elaborate. At the same time, of course, the change involved is far more than a mere procedural one, since it involves a serious restriction — though (as the discussion below will argue) a much needed one — on the broad autonomy which States have traditionally enjoyed in their dealings with aliens. For this reason, as mentioned above, the topic is one of the most heatedly controversial in all of contemporary international law.

Because the subject of the rights of aliens as individuals falls, virtually by definition, outside the ambit of the traditional 'law of nations', surprisingly little systematic work has been done on it by the scholarly community.[7] Yet the topic is a pervasive one indeed, as the following chapters will illustrate. It is like a giant (though as yet unassembled) juridical jigsaw puzzle whose pieces have been found in such disparate areas of the law as the medieval law merchant, the practice of western European States in the headiest days of imperialism, the commercial treaty practice of the nineteenth and twentieth centuries, the arbitration experiences of the post-World War I era, the general international law of human rights which has evolved since World War II, the regional human rights initiatives (most notably the regime of the European Convention on Human Rights), and various other international, regional and even individual State efforts.

The purpose of this volume is to demonstrate how these various pieces of the jigsaw have been gradually falling together, largely unnoticed, over the course of many generations, but especially in recent years, and to give an impression of what the larger (certainly not final) picture looks like. It is not intended to be a complete review of either the traditional or the contemporary law in this area, but rather to show how it is possible, with a little imagination and some diligent research, to piece together legal norms from a variety of sources to create a new body of general international law. Indeed, one might argue that 'reveal' would be a better term than 'create'. In contemporary international law, however, there is no sharp distinction between the two processes. The essential point is that the raw material for a comprehensive treatment of the human rights of aliens in international law is now available, albeit not yet moulded into even a semi-finished product. This volume is a first — but only a first — step in that process.[8]

Notes

1 Similarly, in this study the term 'contemporary international law' will mean all international law (both customary and conventional) of the post-UN Charter period.

2 For a classic statement of the traditional international law view that individuals are objects and not subjects of international law, see 1 L. Oppenheim, *International Law*, 639 (8th ed., H. Lauterpacht, ed., 1955).

3 '[I]f individuals who possess nationality are wronged abroad, it is, as a rule, their home State only and exclusively which has a right to ask for redress, *and these individuals themselves have no such right.' Id.* at 640 (emphasis added).

4 For a more detailed discussion of the background and substance of the law of diplomatic protection of nationals abroad, see text at Chapter I, notes 18−46.

5 See text at Chapter I, note 21.

6 Nor, in contrast to General Amin's mass expulsion of Asians from Uganda in 1972 — see V. Sharma and F. Wooldridge, 'Some legal questions arising from the expulsion of the Ugandan Asians', 23 I.C.L.Q. (1974), 397 — has this recent expulsion been the subject of scholarly protest. The UN, moreover, has even avoided characterising Nigeria's actions as an 'expulsion'. See 'Ghana's returnees', *UN Development Research Organisation News* (May−June 1983), 1, at 1−2.

7 While much ink has been spilt on the 'diplomatic protection of citizens abroad' or the 'responsibility of States for injuries to aliens', even studies in the latter area cover only a small slice of the law governing the treatment of aliens. Moreover, such studies rarely approach the subject from a human rights perspective, as the present writer has attempted to do elsewhere in a highly limited and tentative fashion. See R. Lillich, 'Duties of States regarding the civil rights of aliens', 161 *Receuil des Cours* (Hague Academy of International Law) (1978−III), 329, at 390−408. See also S. Chandra, *Civil and Political Rights of the Aliens* (1982).

8 The present writer and Stephen C. Neff, Esq., currently have in preparation a full-scale treatise tentatively entitled 'The Treatment of Aliens in Contemporary International Law', which they hope will appear by the end of the decade.

CHAPTER ONE

Pre-twentieth-century developments

A. Limited protection of aliens

It is not unreasonable to suppose that suspicion and fear of strangers long predates the emergence of express legal disabilities of aliens. In the very earliest period of human history, anyone outside his own family or tribe may well have been regarded as one to whom the ordinary standards of decency (whatever those standards may have been) did not apply. Concern with questions of this sort, however, belong more to the anthropologist, the sociologist, and the psychologist than to the lawyer. The lawyer's involvement begins only when such beliefs become embodied in legal doctrines of a more or less formal nature.

The first detailed evidence concerning such a body of legal doctrine comes from the ancient Greek city-States.[1] What is most interesting about this early example of the treatment of aliens is that it illustrates with great clarity the point that legal disabilities of aliens are frequently a function not so much (or, at any rate, not exclusively) of real fear or hatred as of the inherent logic of the prevailing political/legal order. The Greeks certainly had a very strong tradition of hospitality and of what might be termed ethnic solidarity, reflected in and enhanced by such institutions as the common worship of the Olympian pantheon and, most notably, in the great pan-Hellenic festivals which are known — somewhat misleadingly — as athletic competitions. At the same time, however, the various Greek city-States manifested what appears, even from the perspective of our intolerant contemporary world, as an extreme harshness towards non-citizens.

The explanation of this apparent paradox lies in the nature of the Greek political/legal system itself. The city-States of the Greek world were not 'mere' political entities as the nation-States of today are. Rather, the city-States were simultaneously religious and tribal associations. A Greek from another city-State, therefore, was not simply a person owing a primary political allegiance to another sovereign. He was more in the nature of a trespasser on private property, or perhaps an atheist intruding into a religious sphere within which he had no status.[2] The religious aspect was particularly important. From the viewpoint of the official cult of the city-State, the alien was literally a non-person. Not only was he unable to participate in its political affairs, he could not marry a citizen, own property, or have access to its legal machinery (since he was unable to swear any oaths in the name of the host State's gods).[3]

Even in a legal/religious order as inflexible as this one, however, it was not long before the pressures of the 'real world' began to nibble away the rigidities of doctrine. The details of this process are not important in the context of this chapter, save for the mentioning in passing of two legal strategies. One involved the unilateral granting by city-States of various kinds of rights to aliens for such purposes as encouraging foreign craftsmen to settle in the city.[4] More relevant to international lawyers, though, is the second device: the concluding of treaties, known as 'isopolities', between various city-States for the mutual granting of privileges of various kinds to each other's citizens.[5]

In the Middle Ages the situation was somewhat different, substantially because Christianity, the prevalent religion in the West, emphasised the inherent dignity and equality (before God, that is) of all human beings. The alien, therefore, was no longer a non-person in the rigid sense that he had been in ancient Greece. It remained the case, however, that persons who did not have a niche in the prevailing feudal order necessarily led very precarious lives. In particular, in a society in which one's social and juridical role was a function of the quality of one's land tenure, logic decreed that those persons who had no such tenurial rights were often effectively beyond the protection of any law.

The situation of the travelling merchant provides a good example. If, as would be likely, his wealth took the form of chattels which he carried with him, then he was peculiarly prey to robbery, since in this period nothing like regular police forces existed. If he was swindled in a transaction, then there might be no court to which he could have access in an era when courts of the various manors were the only form of 'justice' to which the common person could apire.[6] Even if the merchant did have access to such courts, the law regarding contract was so hopelessly underdeveloped in feudal times that his chances of obtaining relief would be slight indeed.[7] Finally, consider the hazard to the merchant of the feudal practice commonly known as the *droit d'aubaine*, the right of a territorial prince to confiscate property left in his territory by a deceased foreigner.[8]

As in ancient Greece, however, the ingenuity and the acquisitiveness of man in feudal society proved the equal, to a modest extent at least, of the various hazards of political/legal/economic life. For one thing, many princes saw that it was to their advantage to encourage trade and so granted various kinds of privileges to merchants. One of the most important of these privileges was the right to hold a fair, which was much more than a simple gathering of buyers and sellers. Indeed, there were very important legal ramifications flowing from the holding of a fair. Certain juridical immunities, for instance, were granted to persons attending the fair, such as exemption from the right of reprisal for crimes committed or debts contracted outside the fair. Even in the fair itself, a special legal order prevailed. Some of these special rules appear slightly quaint today, such as the right to throw dice and play cards, which the rules of the fairs of Cambrai allowed.[9] Of more lasting value, though, was the fact that the fairs were the cradle of the law merchant — that informal law which the merchants gradually articulated for themselves over the centuries and which has subsequently been embodied in most modern legal systems.[10] The development of laws relating to bills of exchange is only one of many examples that could be cited.

As the Middle Ages wore on and the economy of Europe developed, aliens — by which term is meant, in this context, persons outside the feudal system — actually came to be corporately organised. Travelling merchants, for instance, gathered themselves into convoys or caravans, whose organisational structure was quite advanced.[11] Sophisticated cities developed which, like the fairs, became juridical islands in the great feudal ocean.[12] To appreciate the immense significance of this development, one need only recall western Europe's greatest city of the later Middle Ages: Venice, where the merchants were kings, whose wealth (at least in monetary terms) dwarfed that of the emerging feudal monarchies of the cold north.

This rise of the city and development of stable networks of long-distance trade entailed a quantum jump, so to speak, in the legal state of the art regarding the treatment of aliens. Whole mercantile communities began to negotiate with foreign governments for grants of extensive privileges. A notable example is the extensive range of concessions which the Genoese merchants negotiated in 1261 with the Byzantine Empire.[13] The Venetians subsequently proved to be even more successful at this practice, while in the north of Europe similar policies characterised the Hanseatic merchants of the northern German States.

These concessions often involved the granting by the host sovereign of a legal enclave within his society to the alien merchants: they would be allowed to live under their own law, administered by their own courts, free of the host sovereign's jurisdiction. Such concessions were common in the various trading ports of the Middle East. In the north, one of the most famous examples was the grant of the so-called 'steel-yard' in London to the Hanseatic merchant community.[14] This network of concessions eventually evolved into the capitulation system, where the merchants' home State negotiated with the host country, a development to be discussed below.[15]

Before leaving the medieval antecedents of the traditional international law relating to aliens, it is necessary to return briefly to the position of the individual trader seeking redress for injuries allegedly done to him. He might engage, of course, in that most time-honoured, though risky, of remedies, self-help. The dangers involved in such a course of action, however, could be substantial, particularly in a society where ties of kinship and feudal loyalty were strong.

A lone alien might find himself involved in a serious blood feud in a strange country where, to put it mildly, he would be vastly outnumbered. He would also (if he were a Christian) incur the displeasure of the Church, which throughout this period was struggling to limit the everyday violence and savagery of medieval life.[16]

An alternative type of redress available to the alien was to obtain a letter of reprisal from his own prince. The dangers involved would still be very substantial, but the letter of reprisal conferred two advantages over naked self-help. One was that it bestowed at least a measure of legality upon the action taken (although one might doubt whether the victim would be very impressed on this score). The second was that the letter would typically authorise the merchant to take action not only against the actual person who had wronged him, but also against *any* subject of the country from which the alleged wrongdoer came.[17]

This practice of granting letters of reprisal was clearly less than an ideal method of fostering international harmony and good will. Nevertheless, it had one important consequence, namely, it entailed the thesis that a dispute between an alien and a national of a host State was also, in some measure at least, a dispute between their States. This notion had a long — albeit not necessarily a great — future ahead of it. In fact, even today it remains one of the most fundamental features of international law.

B. Rise of diplomatic protection

1. Background of the doctrine

It has been observed that by the end of the Middle Ages two principal methods had emerged for the protection of aliens: the granting of privileges for alien communities *en masse*, as in the case of trading communities in the Middle and Far East; and the system of licensed reprisals by injured aliens embodied in letters of reprisal granted by an injured alien's sovereign. The first (which will be discussed in more detail below) enjoyed quite a long career, lasting indeed well into the twentieth century. It was the second, however, which in the long run had the greater impact on international law, both traditional and contemporary, because it eventually gave rise to the institution which is now known as the diplomatic protection of nationals abroad.

The system — if one can really call it that — whereby each ruler might issue letters of reprisal to his citizens who had allegedly been injured by foreigners was obviously prone to outright abuse in the worst instances, and to the generating of international ill will in the best of cases. Therefore, it began very early to be tempered by the elaboration — through both custom and treaty — of a set of constraining rules which can be said to constitute international law in the modern sense of that term. For example, the letters would sometimes restrict the circumstances under which reprisals would be executed — for instance, the bearer of a letter of reprisal could not attach the goods of foreign merchants found within his own State unless the owner *himself* had been involved in the alleged injury. Also, starting as early as the thirteenth century, the rule gradually evolved that before a ruler would issue a letter of reprisal his aggrieved subject had to demonstrate that his cause was a just one, and also that he had attempted to obtain redress for his injury under the law of the foreign State but had been thwarted.[18] (It is worth pointing out in passing that, although rules of this nature can be said to be substantive international law rules, no international *procedures* existed to administer them. In other words, the aggrieved person made his representations not to an international body, but rather to his own sovereign. One might consider this defect to be a serious one, as indeed it was, but one also should bear in mind that even today, for the international community as a whole, international machinery to make analogous determinations does not exist.)

Beginning approximately in the sixteenth century, therefore, the newly emergent nation-States of Europe were becoming ever more intimately involved in the supervision and protection of the activities of their citizens abroad. It may be recalled that this period also was the age of mercantile theory and practice, based upon the thesis that the economic growth of one country necessarily came about at the expense of other countries. It was accordingly the age of what might be termed baroque protectionism in the international economic sphere, typified by the English Navigation Acts of the 1650s. Amid the welter of restrictions, exclusions, and monopolies of this decidedly pre-*laissez-faire* era, States in general — and the colonial powers in particular — were very loath to see their citizens injured at the hands of foreigners, since a loss sustained by an individual was considered a loss to the nation as well.[19] From our perspective, this period takes on a certain comic-opera aura, best exemplified perhaps by the so-called War of Jenkins' Ear, launched by Great Britain against Spain to avenge an English skipper whose appendage had supposedly been cut off by a Spanish coastguard.[20]

The more serious side of this frenzied activity manifested itself in the development of international legal doctrine to the point where it took express cognisance of the right of the State to protect its citizens abroad. It was the Swiss jurist Emmerich de Vattel who set forth the theoretical underpinning of the doctrine in his classic treatise of 1758 on *The Law of Nations*. '[W]hoever uses a citizen ill,' Vattel stated, 'indirectly offends the State, which is bound to protect this citizen.'[21] With one *caveat*, this statement may be taken as the classic expression of the traditional right of diplomatic protection. The *caveat* is that Vattel rather overstated the matter when he said that the injured party's State was *bound* to protect him. The doctrine as it actually developed was that the State was *entitled* to protect its citizens abroad if it so chose. However, it was under no duty, domestically or internationally, to do so.[22]

Given that the right of a State to protect its citizens abroad had become established in traditional international law, the question then became: what form might this protection take? Actually, in the eighteenth and even most of the nineteenth centuries, this consideration would not have been recognised as problematic at all. Any effective measures, up to and including military force, were lawful, provided, of course, that the injury complained of actually existed. International law at that time was oriented not towards eliminating resort to force in the international community, as is the case now (theoretically, at any rate), but rather towards the gradual elaboration of rules concerning just and unjust causes for war.

To put the matter more bluntly, any injury inflicted upon an alien carried with it the inherent risk that the gunboats of the alien's home State might come sailing to avenge him. In practice, of course, the sensible first step for the injured party's State was to claim redress from the State responsible for the injury in a peaceful fashion, meaning through diplomatic channels. If such efforts failed, then more serious measures could be considered.[23]

One might legitimately question the extent to which the international community had advanced, by this time, significantly beyond the medieval system of issuing letters of reprisal. After all, it remained the case that the aggrieved person submitted his claim (after his exhaustion of local remedies) to his own government rather than to any impartial international body. In that respect there was virtually no advance on medieval practice. One even might regard the diplomatic protection system to be worse for the world than its letter-of-reprisal predecessor, in that the possibility of large-scale suffering and violence was now much greater because the whole armed might of a nation might be involved in redressing a wrong done to a single person (instances of which will be discussed below).

These criticisms are not without justification. By way of mitigation (rather than of defence), one might plead that the new system did have one advantage over the old reprisal system: by involving the State more intimately in the dispute between its citizens and foreigners and their States, it compelled the State to consider more carefully than it otherwise might have when it should intervene — or, in technical terms, when it should espouse its citizen's claim. For example, suppose that State A was in the process of forging a political alliance with State B when news reached it that one of its nationals had been injured by a national of State B and that the courts of State B had given no redress. State A might well decide that under the circumstances it was in its own best foreign policy interests not to pursue a claim against State B. Such 'cases' rarely make the headlines, or even the history books or the law reports.[24] They do, however, find their way into Foreign Office archives, where anyone who can obtain access and takes the trouble can find numerous instances where States have chosen *not* to espouse the claims of their citizens against foreign States. The sailing of gunboats, then, was certainly not an automatic consequence of an injury to an alien.[25]

In response one might object that, while harmony in the international community may be slightly advanced by the non-espousal of the alleged claim, this gain (which might be only a very slight one) is purchased at the expense of the allegedly injured private party. Traditional international law had a logically impeccable if practically unsatisfactory answer to this objection: that the injury, in law, was inflicted not on the alien himself by rather on his State,[26] and that his State, in refusing to act, was simply waiving its own right of redress.

This point leads naturally to a discussion of some of the details of the traditional doctrine of diplomatic protection. There exists a fairly elaborate body of both theory and practice on this topic. This chapter, however, will cover only certain general aspects of it which are relevant to contemporary issues. No attempt will be made to present a comprehensive treatment of the subject.[27]

2. Substance of the doctrine

Although the traditional international law doctrine of diplomatic protection may be logically sound, it is open to serious criticism from the practical point of view, because it often produces extreme hardship or even outright injustice. This criticism will be considered in more detail below.[28] At this point it is the substance of the doctrine rather than its operation that requires description.

Three aspects of the doctrine in particular call for attention: first, the attribution of the injury to the home State of the injured alien; second, the attribution of the wrongful act to the State in which the alien had resided or done business; and, third, the doctrine of exhaustion of local remedies (under the part of the law known as 'State responsibility').

The two types of attribution are, as one might suspect, by no means unrelated. They are both, in fact, logical consequences of the international legal order as it has existed from the Peace of Westphalia until the present day. Since traditional international law was emphatically a law of nations, only nations (States, in more modern terminology) had either rights or duties under it, individuals being regarded as mere objects.[29] Their activities might occasion legal disputes — indeed, when grievances arose from their activities such could hardly fail to be the case — but those activities belong to what one might term the factual substratum of traditional international law. All legal rights and duties belong only to States.

The first aspect of the traditional doctrine of diplomatic protection under consideration here is the attribution of the alleged injury to the State whose citizen suffered it, rather than to the aggrieved individual himself. Since the time of Vattel there has been remarkably little doctrinal change in this regard.[30] The leading authority for this aspect of the doctrine during this century remains the Permanent Court of International Justice, which, in the *Mavrommatis Palestine Concessions* case, held:

It is an elementary principle of international law that a State is entitled to protect its subjects, when injured by acts contrary to international law committed by another State, from whom they have been unable to obtain satisfaction through the ordinary channels. By taking up the case of one of its subjects and by resorting to diplomatic action or international judicial proceedings on his behalf, a State is in reality asserting its own rights — its right to ensure, in the person of its subjects, respect for the rules of international law.[31]

This doctrine carries within it a number of interesting logical consequences. Suppose, for instance, that the individual and the State have different ideas as to whether to bring the claim or, if brought, the strategy to be used in pursuing it. The answer is clear: because the claim belongs to the State, its opinion controls.

More disturbing yet, suppose that the claimant State succeeds in negotiating a monetary settlement with the other State. To whom does that money belong? This question arose in Great Britain in *Rustomjee* v. *The Queen*.[32] The case considered in what capacity the Crown was acting when it concluded a treaty with China providing, *inter alia*, for money to be paid by the Chinese to Great Britain on account of debts owed to British merchants by insolvent Chinese merchants. The petitioner sought to establish that the Crown held the money in trust for him (as he was one of the injured parties). The court disagreed, holding that the Crown's duty to give the money to the actual injured parties was a function of its general 'duty' to govern its subjects wisely, meaning in effect that it was a duty which could not be enforced in the courts. The Crown, according to the court, did not stand in the capacity of either trustee or agent.[33]

(A further notable consequence of the traditional doctrine of diplomatic protection is that it leaves a stateless person entirely unprotected as far as the pursuit of a diplomatic claim is concerned.[34])

This last point may be generalised slightly to conclude that, in the final analysis, the traditional doctrine of diplomatic protection is not really about the rights of aliens as such, but rather about the rights and duties of States. The fate of the individual alien is worse than secondary in this scheme: it is doctrinally non-existent, because the individual, in the eyes of traditional international law, like the alien of the Greek city-State regime, is a non-person.

It is now necessary to consider briefly the other side of the traditional doctrine of diplomatic protection: the attribution of the alien's injury to the State wherein the injury took place. Here the concern is with an area of international law known technically as State responsibility. Like so much of the international law touching on the rights of aliens, it is one of the most controversial subdivisions of the discipline. Without making any pretence of doing justice to the subtleties involved in the concept, one may say for present purposes that the law of State responsibility entails situations in which a State acts in a way deemed wrongful by international law and thereby incurs what would be termed liability in domestic law, but which is called responsibility in international law. State responsibility therefore covers the entire gamut of State conduct: any situation in which a State might conceivably act wrongfully — which is virtually all areas of State activity — could give rise to the invocation of the doctrine of State responsibility. Historically, however, by far the largest amount of case law on the subject of State responsibility has come from the area of treatment of aliens.[35]

One might approach this area of the law by putting one very general question at the outset: is a State responsible for all injuries to aliens which occur within its jurisdiction? The answer to this question obviously is no. Recall in this connection the statement of the Permanent Court of International Justice in the *Mavrommatis* case, which held that the right of diplomatic protection arises when a State's citizen is injured 'by acts *contrary to international law*'.[36] That same standard applies when considering the respondent State. It is not an automatic insurer of the livelihood and well-being of aliens in its territory. In order for a State to incur responsibility, the injury to the alien must have been wrongful under international law.

Sometimes it is the host State itself which actually inflicts the injury upon the alien, say by arresting him without cause, or by mistreating him while in custody.[37] On the other hand, the original injury is sometimes inflicted by a private party independently of the host government, or by an official of the host government acting outside the scope of his authority.[38] In these latter types of case, the responsibility of the host State may arise from the State's failure to prevent or redress the substantive injury.[39]

There is considerable confusion among the publicists — which, thankfully, it is not the task of this author to resolve — concerning when State responsibility arises and what technical labels to apply to its various aspects. In particular, the term 'denial of justice' figures prominently, though none too precisely, in the literature and case law.[40] Some writers take the position that international responsibility never arises upon the commission of the original wrongful act (whether that wrongful act is committed by the host State itself or by a private party), that responsibility can arise only after the host State has been accorded the opportunity to make amends and has failed to do so, this failure being termed 'denial of justice'.[41] This approach, of course, makes the concept of denial of justice virtually coextensive with the entire law of State responsibility for injuries to aliens.[42] Other scholars have taken a narrower view of the concept and have sought to confine it to shortcomings on the part of the judiciary of the host country. The narrowest view of denial of justice, associated particularly (as will be observed below)[43] with the Argentine jurist Carlos Calvo, holds that denial of justice occurs only when an alien is altogether refused access to the courts of the host State, when he suffers extreme delay in having his case heard, or when the court of the host State refuses to render justice after a hearing. The available case law — most notably that of the US–Mexican General Claims Commission — basically supports a broader reading of denial of justice.[44]

One more aspect of the traditional law of State responsibility for injuries to aliens needs to be mentioned: the doctrine of exhaustion of local remedies. Since the denial of justice is grounded, at least in some fashion, upon a State's failure to redress the original injury, it logically follows that the respondent State must first have been given an opportunity to redress the injury. Put differently, the alien must first have brought the fact of his injury to the attention of the proper local authorities in the host country and accorded them a fair opportunity to respond. This doctrine of exhaustion of local remedies was foreshadowed earlier in the medieval convention, noted above,[45] that individuals would not be entitled to letters of reprisal unless they had previously exhausted their local remedies. The rationale for the modern rule is the same as for its medieval counterpart: to avoid unnecessarily stirring up international strife, one should strive to keep conflicts at as low a level as possible and resort to remedies on the international plane only when local ones have proved futile.[46]

Having now outlined in very summary form the basic principles of the traditional law of diplomatic protection of nationals abroad, it is appropriate to consider the many criticisms that have been levelled against it over the years.

C. Challenges to diplomatic protection — the national treatment and Calvo doctrines

The criticism most frequently and vigorously directed against the traditional doctrine of diplomatic protection has been noted earlier: that it amounted to nothing more 'progressive' than the elevation of the old medieval law of reprisal from the individual to the nation-State level. The point has been made, with some justification, that diplomatic protection often passed over, all too easily, into what has been called 'gunboat diplomacy'.

The criticism contains merit. History is full of examples of the use of military force on a massive scale to redress alleged wrongs which, in retrospect, seem quite minor. Probably the most notorious such incident involved a British military action against Greece in 1850, what is known as the Don Pacifico incident. Don Pacifico was a British subject living in Athens whose house had been plundered by a mob in 1847, in consequence of which the British blockaded the Greek coast and captured a number of Greek vessels. This affair was a particularly egregious one for a number of reasons, the most important perhaps being that the alien had not exhausted his local remedies, as the traditional international law rule that had developed by the mid-nineteenth century required.[47]

The most common arena for the fulsome application of the doctrine of diplomatic protection during the last century was Latin America, where there were numerous forcible interventions by the various European powers,[48] as well as by the United States.[49] From the standpoint of international law, the most noteworthy of these incidents was the blockading of Venezuela by the combined forces of Germany, Italy, and Great Britain in 1902–03 on behalf of various persons with claims against the Venezuelan government. This particular event stimulated the articulation by the Foreign Minister of Argentina of what came to be known as the Drago doctrine,[50] which will be discussed in the next chapter.[51]

The use of force for the protection of nationals and their interests abroad sometimes went beyond the relatively brief actions which characterised the Latin American incidents and led to outright war. It will be recalled that one of the reasons which the United States officially gave for declaring war on Mexico in 1846 was the redressing of grievances allegedly inflicted by Mexico on United States nationals.[52] It also will be recalled that one of the disputes which led up to the Boer War in South Africa (1899–1902) concerned the rights of British subjects (the *uitlanders*) in the Boer republics.[53] In short, there is scarcely any area of international law more closely linked with potentially explosive political controversies than this one.

The arguments about diplomatic protection at the doctrinal level have been no less heated. In this respect, it is necessary to distinguish what one might call a moderate critique of the traditional doctrine of diplomatic protection from what one might label a radical critique. A better terminology to use, however, would be an internationalist-oriented critique (instead of moderate), and a nationalist-oriented critique (instead of radical).

The moderate, or preferably internationalist, approach to the problem is basically an attempt to remedy the abuses of traditional diplomatic protection, especially the use of force to protect property interests, while acknowledging the principal reason for its continued need: that at this stage of the development of international law a State must have, as the Permanent Court of International Justice has stated,[54] the right to protect its nationals abroad. The radical, or preferably nationalist, approach, on the other hand, has held that the so-called right of diplomatic protection actually does not (or should not) exist at all (save in the most extreme and exceptional cases), that the doctrine has been nothing but a formula which great powers have used to dominate their less powerful neighbours by the threat or actual use of military force.[55]

Although the concern here is mainly with the radical, or nationalist, approach, a brief word is in order first on one major feature of the moderate, or internationalist, approach — the invocation of the doctrine of proportionality. This doctrine essentially holds that the response of a State to a wrongful act must be proportionate to the alleged wrong. It is now unlawful, therefore, for a State to launch a full-scale war against another State for damage to the property of one of its nationals on the lines of the Don Pacifico incident. While the doctrine of proportionality has come to be recognised as a general principle of international law,[56] in the area of protection of nationals abroad it has been spelled out by various treaties in the twentieth century, which will be considered in the next chapter.[57] In a nutshell, they greatly restrict and in some instances forbid the use of force by a State to protect its nationals in other States.[58]

For the present, the focus is on the more radical, or nationalist, critique of the traditional law of diplomatic protection, whose most articulate spokesman has been the Argentine jurist Carlos Calvo. Calvo's attack on the traditional law was a fundamental one indeed, since he was not content with criticising the practice of diplomatic protection alone, which, after all, was really more of a procedural device than a rule of substantive law. That is to say, the diplomatic protection doctrine stipulated what the rights of a State were once it was ascertained that a violation of a substantive norm of international law had occurred, in the form of an injury inflicted upon one of its nationals abroad. The injury to the alien had to be a violation of international law, as noted above,[59] but the doctrine of diplomatic protection did not itself state what acts were unlawful and what acts were not. This determination was a question of the substantive law governing the conduct of States.

Calvo might have limited his critique to the procedural aspect of the issue, i.e. to the doctrine of diplomatic protection alone, but he did not. Instead he adumbrated two doctrines, one cutting to the very heart of substantive international law, the other directed specifically to diplomatic protection. The first of these doctrines was what might be termed a radically nationalist approach to the question of State sovereignty. Calvo postulated that one aspect of State sovereignty is the right of States to enjoy, on the basis of equality, freedom from any interference whatsoever by other States. Basically this doctrine is a statement of the extreme positivistic view of international law which reigned supreme in the nineteenth century and has its supporters even now. The contention is that no State is ever bound by any rule of international law until and unless it consents to be so bound. The doctrine consequently denies the existence of any permanent rules or norms of substantive international law which bind all States as such.

The second of Calvo's doctrines relates specifically to diplomatic protection. It holds that whenever an alien suffers an alleged injury his only remedies are local ones.[60] Absent a denial of justice, which he defined very narrowly, diplomatic protection is unavailable to an injured alien.[61]

A serious problem with Calvo's position is that it has proved impossible to keep the discussion purely on the procedural plane. To see why, consider the second Calvo doctrine, that aliens must seek their remedies solely on the local level. The question then arises, what if the local courts are unjust? More specifically, what if the local courts discriminate against aliens and in favour of nationals? Does a valid international claim then arise? If so, then diplomatic protection returns in full force and effect, because, as noted earlier,[62] it is an accepted rule of traditional international law that local remedies must be exhausted before diplomatic protection is extended. In order truly to exorcise the demon of diplomatic protection, one would have to hold that a valid international claim does not arise even in cases where the local authorities patently discriminate against aliens.

This last position is a very uncomfortable one to take, however radical, or nationalistic, one's bent. Scholars of the Calvo persuasion have attempted to circumvent the problem by elevating the diplomatic protection debate from the level of procedure to one of substance. They accept that there are circumstances in which States can lawfully act on behalf of their nationals abroad. They then seek to narrow the ambit of that action markedly by reinterpreting the substantive rules of international law. These scholars accept the proposition that, if an internationally wrongful injury is inflicted upon an alien, then the State concerned incurs responsibility, with the alien's home State permitted to seek redress through diplomatic channels. However, they limit the protection the substantive law affords aliens by arguing that an internationally wrongful act occurs only if the local authorities treat aliens differently from nationals.

In its fullest form this 'national treatment doctrine', as it is known in international law, maintains, first, that aliens and nationals are entitled in principle to equal treatment, and, secondly, that once such equality of treatment is granted, the host State has fulfilled its international obligations, even if the alien or his State is dissatisfied with his treatment. What logically follows from this doctrine, of course, is that there can be no universal standard of treatment of aliens; there can be only individual national standards which each State sets unilaterally.[63]

In opposition to this thesis is the doctrine known, appropriately enough, as the 'international minimum standard'. This doctrine takes into account the possibility that the standards prevailing in a given State may be so low that, even if nationals and aliens are treated (or oppressed) alike, the norms of international law will have been violated.[64] It should now be apparent why the Calvo critique of the traditional law governing the treatment of aliens can be characterised as a nationalist approach, in contradiction to the internationalist approach of adherents to the international minimum standard.

The debate between these two schools of international law is as lively today as it has ever been, and so its detailed treatment will be left for discussion in the context of twentieth-century developments.[65] Before proceeding to that aspect of the problem, however, it is necessary to consider the other major development of the pre-twentieth-century law: the use of bilateral treaties for the protection of aliens.

D. Parallel development of bilateral treaty system — capitulations and Friendship, Commerce and Navigation treaties

The discussion above touched upon two developments during the Middle Ages in the area of treaty law: the first was the practice which arose whereby States would agree by treaty to restrict, or altogether to refrain from, the granting of letters of reprisal; and the second was the negotiation by groups of merchants for various kinds of privileges in the foreign States in which they traded. The first of these practices helped to clarify the concept of diplomatic protection, which became a doctrine of general international law rather than exclusively a treaty matter, and so is discussed elsewhere. The practice of negotiating privileges from foreign governments, on the other hand, had a long career ahead of it in the area of treaty law. Its importance merits separate consideration.

As the nation-States of western Europe gradually crystallised out of the Middle Ages' welter of feudal principalities they began to take a more active interest in fostering the well-being of their nationals abroad. The development of diplomatic protection obviously was an important manifestation of this trend. Another was the custom whereby States would negotiate with foreign powers for various privileges, usually relating to such matters as safe passage for religious pilgrims or for commercial and trading rights.

In the thirteenth century, for example, Emperor Frederick II successfully negotiated with the Muslim rulers of Palestine rights of passage for Christians to the shrines of the Holy Land, a far more efficient method than the launching of crusades to achieve that purpose.[66] In terms of contemporary international law, however, a more important precedent was the treaty negotiated in 1535 between the king of France and the Ottoman sultan providing for reciprocal rights of trade and navigational freedom for the two monarchs' subjects.[67] Two points are particularly worth noting about this developing treaty practice. One is that even though many of these treaties were even-handed on their face, granting equal privileges to both sets of subjects, in reality they were often very lopsided. They generally worked in favour of the European powers, whose economic and military strength during this era was at last beginning to exceed that of the Islamic and oriental States. The other point is that these treaties, as all treaties of that period, were between individual sovereigns, rather than between governments or States of the type that exist today.

Because the actual merchants or pilgrims were not parties to these agreements, they were in the position of what English and United States law would call third-party beneficiaries. The way in which the benefits of a treaty were conferred upon merchants and pilgrims was by a grant, under the domestic law of the host State, of the various rights spelled out in the treaty. These grants were, in form at least, unilateral, i.e. they were conferred by sole authority of the host sovereign, usually in the form of franchises (as opposed to anything that modern observers would recognise as statute law). These franchises were usually divided into chapters — *capitula* in Latin — whence came the name 'capitulation'.

Privileges granted in capitulations were sometimes very extensive indeed. They could include such matters as exemption from customs duties and port dues, the right to freedom of religion, and often — and most important — the right to live under the alien merchant's own legal regime rather than that of the host country. Legal disputes which arose within the merchant or alien community would fall under the jurisdiction of the consuls of that country instead of the host State's regular courts.

During the colonial and imperial periods the capitulation system spread widely throughout the Middle East and Asia.[68] Its history is a fascinating one, lasting well into the twentieth century.[69] Space does not permit detailed discussion here, save to note one very unsurprising but important fact: that, like the doctrine of diplomatic protection, the system came to be widely resented by the various countries in which it prevailed. The view came to be held in many parts of the non-European world that aliens (particularly, of course, persons hailing from western Europe) occupied positions of economic and legal privilege, waxing fat off the exploitation of foreign peoples, backed by the too frequent use of military force. While oversimplified, this picture contained enough truth to ensure that issues relating to the treatment of aliens became steeped in political controversy of the most bitter sort. As will be seen in Chapter III, this legacy influences debates on the subject to the present day.[70]

In the case of the protection of aliens by treaty, just as in the area of diplomatic protection, one may find grounds to argue either that the practice was inherently an unhappy one, or that the problems it generated arose from its application. The forces of history, however, proved kinder to the treaty system than to diplomatic protection, for it became apparent reasonably early on that, political and other circumstances permitting, the protection of aliens by treaty could prove to be mutually satisfactory and, therefore, relatively uncontroversial.

During the eighteenth century the practice of concluding commercial treaties on a genuinely equal basis began. These treaties, which came to be called 'Friendship, Commerce and Navigation' treaties (or simply 'FCN' treaties), provided certain rights and privileges to be granted to nationals of the States parties who traded in each other's territory. The treaty between Prussia and the United States of 1784 was one early landmark in this process.[71] The trend continued, and indeed greatly intensified, during the nineteenth century.[72]

The network of FCN treaties, which grew up in the course of the last century, included so many provisions relating to the welfare of alien merchants and traders that one scholar has characterised them as collectively embodying an international Bill of Rights.[73] These treaties commonly guaranteed that each State party would protect the person and property of the other's nationals. They provided for a right of free sojourn; admission to trade and industry, including the right of permanent settlement (the 'right of establishment', in technical terms); protection from discriminatory taxes and similar imposts; free access to courts; freedom to worship; and exemption from military service.

Another innovation in the area of treaty law which originated in the eighteenth century and then became common in the nineteenth was the most-favoured-nation clause.[74] It was a technical device of great importance, because it provided a mechanism for automatically conferring rights of various kinds on nationals of the signatory powers, thereby enabling States to dispense in many cases with the necessity of laboriously negotiating and renegotiating each and every concession with each and every trading partner. The essence of a most-favoured-nation clause was a promise by State A to State B that whatever rights State A might grant to any other country's nationals would accrue automatically to the nationals of State B. Typically, of course, State B, in the same treaty, would make the identical promise *vis-à-vis* State A.[75]

Yet another common type of treaty provision which came into fairly wide-spread use during the nineteenth century was a national treatment clause. As the name implies, it constituted a promise by State A to State B that the nationals of the latter would receive the same treatment while sojourning in State A as the nationals of A themselves received. While the broad tendency of the most-favoured-nation clause was to assimilate all aliens to one another in terms of legal rights conferred by the host country, the tendency of the national treatment clause was to assimilate aliens to nationals of the host country.[76]

An important distinction must be made here concerning the relationship between this national treatment treaty provision and the national treatment doctrine discussed above.[77] It may appear that the conclusion of national treatment treaty provisions was an indication that the international community was beginning to accept the national treatment doctrine as a part of international law. Such is not the case. The national treatment doctrine, it must be stressed, was a contention that (subject to certain very narrow exceptions) aliens, *under customary international law*, could not expect to receive treatment from host countries more favourable than that accorded by such countries to their own nationals. The international minimum standard position, on the other hand, allowed for more favourable treatment of aliens in cases where a given State's practice did not measure up to that minimum.[78] The existence of treaty provisions guaranteeing national treatment, by their very nature, could not resolve this doctrinal dispute about customary international law, because the real issue in that debate was what happened if a given State's standard of national treatment fell short of the international minimum. The issue, put differently, was not whether a national treatment standard was good or bad in itself, but rather whether such a standard was sufficient to protect aliens adequately. That question is one of general doctrine which can-not be settled by the mere existence of national treatment clauses in various bilateral treaties.

In general, the use of treaty law to clarify and develop the law governing the treatment of aliens has been, and remains, of the utmost importance. Its significance so far has been seriously underestimated by the international legal community, although the oversight, it is hoped, will be remedied in the coming years. This cursory review of pre-twentieth-century treaty law, like that of the pre-twentieth-century background of diplomatic protection and the law of State responsibility for injuries to aliens, attempts only to furnish necessary historical perspective on the problems of contemporary international law relating to the treatment of aliens. Against this background the discussion may proceed to the developments of the twentieth century.

Notes

1 See generally 1 C. Phillipson, *The International Law and Custom of Ancient Greece and Rome*, 122–209 (1911).
2 According to Homer, though, aliens were under the special protection of Zeus. *Id.* at 131.
3 *Id.* at 122–5. See also F. de Coolanges, *The Ancient City. A Study on the Religion, Laws and Institutions of Greece and Rome* (1956 ed.), on the critically important role of religion in the political and legal make-up of the classical city-State.
4 Aliens resident in the Greek city-States, who were known as *moetics*, lived under a special legal regime. They generally had no right of intermarriage with citizens of the host city-State, no right to own real property or to hold public office, and no right to use the common lands for, say, grazing purposes. They had to be under the protection of a patron (who, among other things, would represent them in litigation), to pay a special tax, and sometimes to be subject to compulsory military service. On the law relating to moetics generally, see C. Phillipson, *supra*, note 1, at 157–79.
5 A. Nussbaum, *A Concise History of the Law of Nations*, 13 (1947).
6 As the feudal system evolved, it frequently became the case that only persons with free tenure of land had standing to appear before the ordinary public courts of the realm. Those persons with unfree tenure (such as copyhold tenure in England) were left to vindicate their rights, if at all, in the courts of the manor to which they belonged. See generally M. Bloch, *Feudal Society* (L. Manyon, transl., 1961).
7 In English law, for example, actions for what would be termed breach of contract were extremely cumbersome until, with *Slade's* case of 1602, the more convenient and rational form of action of assumpsit began to be available for contractual claims generally.
8 There also was the *droit de détraction*, which was the right of the host country to 'deduct' a certain amount from the value of the estate of a deceased alien upon its removal. The *gabella hereditaria* was a special death duty to which aliens were subject. The *traite foraine* was an export tax levied upon an alien upon his departure from a host country. 5 J. Verzijl, *International Law in Historical Perspective. Nationality and other Matters Relating to Individuals*, 410–11 (1972). English law did not recognise the *droit d'aubaine*, nor did the sovereign protect the alien, as

was the case generally on the Continent. E. Borchard, *The Diplomatic Protection of Citizens Abroad*, 35 (1915).

9 H. Pirenne, *Economic and Social History of Medieval Europe*, 96–102 (1933).

10 W. Ferguson, *Europe in Transition 1300–1520*, at 10–11 (1962). On medieval commerce generally, see J. Mundy, *Europe in the High Middle Ages 1150–1309*, at 153–73 (1973).

11 For instance, the merchandise was bought and sold in common and the profits were parcelled out according to each merchant's original contribution. H. Pirenne, *supra*, note 9, at 93–5. See also J. Mundy, *supra*, note 10, at 154–5.

12 *Id*. at 422–31.

13 *Id*. at 155.

14 On the steel-yard, see E. Cheyney, *The Dawn of a New Era*, 26–8 (1936). The steel-yard (which was located where Cannon Street Station now stands in the City of London) remained Hanseatic property until 1853. F. Heer, *The Medieval World*, 64 (1961).

15 See text at notes 68–70 *infra*.

16 One method used for controlling blood feuds was the proclamation of 'Truces of God', times during which feuding was forbidden. The Third Lateran Council (1179) confirmed a practice which had grown up in France in the previous century by proclaiming such a truce to run each week from sunset on Wednesday to sunrise the following Monday. A. Nussbaum, *supra*, note 5, at 26.

17 E. Aréchaga, 'International responsibility', in *Manual of Public International Law*, 531, at 553 (M. Sorenson, ed., 1968).

18 5 J. Verzijl, *supra*, note 8, at 275.

19 That similar considerations underlie even the modern international law relating to the diplomatic protection of nationals is apparent from the Separate Opinion of Judge Gros in the *Barcelona Traction* case, where this distinguished jurist made the following comments about the injuries suffered by various interested parties when a host State expropriates a corporation in which aliens hold shares: 'The damage to the company is that it is destroyed; the damage to the shareholders is that they are injured in respect of their property through the destruction of the investment; the damage suffered by the State of the shareholders is that one component element of the national economy has undergone spoliation.' *Barcelona Traction Company* case, I.C.J. *Rep*. 1970, 3, at 276–7.

20 C. Carrington, *The British Overseas. The Exploits of a Nation of Shopkeepers*, 83 (1968). The war grew out of rivalry between Great Britain and Spain over what is now the state of Georgia in the United States. Apparently the story of Mr Jenkins' ear being cut off by a Spanish coastguard was untrue.

21 E. de Vattel, *Law of Nations*, 161 (J. Chitty, ed., 1833).

22 E. Borchard, *supra*, note 8, at 356.

23 *Id*. at 445–56.

24 But see *Redpath* v. *Kissinger*, 415 F. Supp. 506 (W.D. Tex.), aff'd without opinion, 545 F.2d 167 (5th Cir., 1976).

25 See R. Lillich, 'Forcible self-help by States to protect human rights', 53 *Iowa L. Rev*. (1967), 325, at 328 and n. 17.

26 'In legal principle, the responsibility of a state ... is to the state of the alien's nationality and gives that state a claim against the offending state. Although the claim derives from injury to an individual, once espoused it is the state's claim [and] can be waived by the state ....' Am. Law Inst., *Restatement of the Foreign Relations Law of the United States (Revised)*, § 713, comment b, at 211 (Tentative Draft No. 3, 1982).

27 On the law of diplomatic protection generally, see E. Borchard, *supra*, note 8; F. Dunn, *The Protection of Nationals. A Study in the Application of International Law* (1932); H. Neufeld, *The International Protection of Private Creditors from the Treaties of Westphalia to the Congress of Vienna. A Contribution to the History of the Law of Nations*, 94–114 (1971).

28 See text at notes 47–53 *infra*.

29 1 L. Oppenheim, *International Law*, 639 (8th ed., H. Lauterpacht, ed., 1955).

30 *Id.* at 636–7.

31 *Mavrommatis Palestine Concessions* case, [1924] P.C.I.J., ser. A, No. 2, at 12.

32 [1875–76] 1 Q.B.D. 487, aff'd, [1876–77] 2 Q.B.D. 69.

33 A similar case, reaching the same conclusion, was *Civilian War Claimants Ass'n Ltd* v. *R.*, [1932] A.C. 14.

34 E. Borchard, *supra*, note 8, at 591.

35 See R. Baxter, 'Reflections on codification in light of the international law of State responsibility for injuries to aliens', 16 *Syracuse L. Rev.* (1965), 745, at 756–7.

36 See supra, note 31, at 12 (emphasis added).

37 See, e.g., *Kalklosch* case (United States v. Mexico), 4 R.I.A.A. 412 (1928); *Tribolet* case (United States v. Mexico), *id.* at 598 (1930).

38 See, e.g., *Mexico City Bombardment* case (Great Britain v. Mexico), 5 R.I.A.A. 76 (1930); *Caire* case (France v. Mexico), *id.* at 516 (1929).

39 Some publicists take the view that the theoretical basis of the State's liability in this type of case is an implied complicity between the State and the primary wrongdoer. See J. Brierly, 'The theory of implied State complicity in international claims', 9 *B.Y.I.L.* (1928), 42. On the other hand, there is support for the view that the State's failure to redress the primary wrong is analytically distinct from that primary wrong. The holding in the *Janes* case supports this latter view: 'The culprit is liable for having killed or murdered an American national; the [host] Government is liable for not having measured up to its duty of diligently prosecuting and properly punishing the offender. The culprit has transgressed the penal code of his country; the State ... has transgressed a provision of international law as to State duties.' *Janes* case (United States v. Mexico), 4 R.I.A.A. 82, at 87 (1925).

40 An excellent survey of the various schools of thought on denial of justice may be found in O. Lissitzyn, 'The meaning of denial of justice in international law', 30 *A.J.I.L.* (1936), 632. See also A. Freeman, *The International Responsibility of States for Denial of Justice* (1938).

41 While this position has a certain logical elegance to it, it has little clear-cut support in the case law. See, e.g., *Chattin* case (United States v. Mexico), 4 R.I.A.A. 282 (1927), where the view is expressed that State responsibility can arise upon the commission of the primary wrong, provided that it is the State which commits that wrong.

42 For very broad views of the concept of denial of justice, see C. Eagleton, 'Denial of justice in international law', 22 *A.J.I.L.* (1928), 538; G. Fitzmaurice, 'The meaning of the term "denial of justice"', 13 *B.Y.I.L.* (1932), 93.

43 See text at notes 60–1 *infra*.

44 A. Feller, *The Mexican Claims Commission 1923–1934*, at 175 and n. 9 (1935).

45 See text at note 18 *supra*.

46 See R. Lillich, 'The effectiveness of the local remedies rule today', 58 *A.S.I.L. Proc.* (1964), 101.

47 On the Don Pacifico incident, see J. Ridley, *Lord Palmerston*, 374–89 (1971).

48 As more or less random examples of the many forcible interventions by European powers in Latin America for the protection of their nationals' interests one could

cite the following: the use by France of a naval detachment against Haiti in 1825 to compel it to pay an indemnity to descendants of French planters of the later colonial period; the bombardment by France of the Mexican city of Vera Cruz in 1838, which produced 3 million francs for various French claimants; French blockading of Argentina (sometimes in conjunction with Great Britain) from 1838 to 1840 and again from 1845 to 1850; and the bombardment by Spain of the ports of Callao (Peru) and Valparaiso (Chile) in the 1860s. J. Rippy, *Latin America. A Modern History*, 335–6 (1958).

49 For a list of forcible interventions by the United States during this period, both in Latin America and elsewhere, see M. Offutt, *The Protection of Citizens Abroad by the Armed Forces of the United States* (1928).

50 J. Fagg, *Latin America. A General History*, 628 (3rd ed. 1977).

51 See text at and accompanying Chapter II, note 3.

52 E. Borchard, *supra*, note 8, at 455.

53 J. Fisher, *The Afrikaners*, 137–42, 150–6 (1969).

54 See text at note 31 *supra*.

55 This approach has been articulated most forcefully by Judge Padilla Nervo of Mexico. See, e.g., his Separate Opinion in the *Barcelona Traction Company* case, I.C.J. *Rep.*, 1970, 3, at 246.

56 On the applicability of the doctrine to the protection of nationals abroad question, see D. Bowett, *Self-defence in International Law*, 105 (1958).

57 The Porter Convention of 1907 was the first of these treaties. See text at Chapter II, notes 2–3.

58 Article 2(4) of the UN Charter, which prohibits the threat or use of force by States in general, makes forcible self-help impermissible in most protection of nationals' situations. It may still be used, however, when the lives of nationals are threatened and their safety and evacuation are its *raison d'être*. See R. Lillich, *supra*, note 25, at 334–7. See also L. Green, 'Rescue at Entebbe – legal aspects', 6 *Israel Y.B. Human Rights* (1976), 312.

59 See text at note 31 *supra*.

60 Essentially the Calvo thesis was that denial of justice occurred only when the alien was denied access altogether to the local courts when attempting to redress his wrong, or when he suffered extremely long delays in having his case heard, or when local courts, having heard his case, refused to pronounce judgment. Most of the formulations of the traditional doctrine of denial of justice, on the other hand, were broader. See text at note 43 *supra*.

61 The most complete exposition of the Calvo doctrine by the proponent himself appears in 1–6 C. Calvo, *Le Droit international théorique et pratique* (5th ed. 1896). On the development of the doctrine, see F. Dawson and I. Head, *International Law, National Tribunals and the Rights of Aliens*, 13–15 (1971). See also A. Freeman, 'Recent aspects of the Calvo doctrine and the challenge to international law', 40 *A.J.I.L.* (1946), 121.

A 'Calvo clause' is a provision — whether of contractual, statutory, or even constitutional origin — whereby an alien purportedly waives his 'right' to diplomatic protection by his home State, thereby confining himself to local remedies (save in the narrowly defined case of denial of justice). See generally D. Shea, *The Calvo Clause* (1955). See also R. Lillich, 'Duties of States regarding the civil rights of aliens', 161 *Recueil des Cours* (Hague Academy of International Law) (1978–III), 329, at 371, pointing out that the Charter of Economic Rights and Duties of States, adopted by the UN General Assembly in 1974, is an obvious attempt to substitute the national treatment doctrine and the Calvo doctrine for the substantive and procedural norms generally applicable under traditional international law to wealth deprivations.

62 See text at notes 45–6 *supra.*

63 On the origins and purposes of the national treatment doctrine, see F. Dawson and I. Head, *supra,* note 61, at 6–7, 14–15.

64 The classic statement of the international minimum standard — or, actually, the classic statement that such a standard exists in international law — came from United States Secretary of State Elihu Root in 1910: 'There is a standard of justice, very simple, very fundamental, and of such general acceptance by all civilized countries as to form a part of the international law of the world. The condition upon which any country is entitled to measure the justice due from it to an alien by the justice which it accords to its own citizens is that its system of law and administration shall conform to this general standard. If any country's system of law and administration does not conform to that standard, although the people of that country may be content or compelled to live under it, no other country can be compelled to accept it as furnishing a satisfactory measure of treatment to its citizens.' E. Root, 'The basis of protection to citizens residing abroad', 4 *A.J.I.L.* (1910), 517, at 521–2. For an application of the international minimum standard by an international tribunal, see the *Neer* case (United States *v.* Mexico), 4 R.I.A.A. 60 (1926).

65 See text at Chapter II, notes 8–21, and Chapter III, notes 31–40.

66 H. Mayer, *The Crusades,* 227–9 (J. Gillingham, transl., 1965).

67 A. Nussbaum, *supra,* note 5, at 54.

68 See E. Borchard, *supra,* note 8, at 432–4.

69 See generally S. Liu, *Extraterritoriality. Its Rise and its Decline* (1925). During the first half of the twentieth century the capitulation regimes in various parts of the world were dismantled — e.g. in China by the Kuomintang government in the 1920s, in the territories of the old Ottoman Empire by the Treaty of Lausanne of 1923.

70 Witness the heated discussion of Garcia-Amador's reports to the International Law Commission. See text at Chapter III, notes 37–9.

71 A. Nussbaum, *supra,* note 5, at 129.

72 *Id.* at 199–203.

73 *Id.* at 200. The dynamic interplay between these various treaties and the evolution of the international minimum standard for the treatment of aliens in the nineteenth and early twentieth centuries has been assessed by another scholar in the following terms (*à propos* of rules relating to the protection of the property of aliens): 'During the nineteenth and early twentieth centuries, these principles [relating to the protection of property rights of aliens] came to be generally accepted. Only in the case of new States and States with a bad record on the fringes of the Western world was it still thought necessary to embody these standards expressly in treaties of commerce, establishment and navigation. As the leading commercial nation, Great Britain took the lead in this work of consolidating the minimum standards of international law. Through the automatism existing in any system of interlocking most-favoured-nation treaties, the benefits thus obtained for British merchants were liberally generalised, and this network of, on the whole, declaratory treaties gave even greater precision to the minimum standard of international law on the protection of property abroad.' G. Schwarzenberger, *Foreign Investments and International Law,* 23 (1969). For a thorough and imaginative discussion of the relationship between treaty practice and the progressive development of customary international law, see R. Baxter, 'Treaties and custom', 129 *Recueil des Cours* (Hague Academy of International Law) (1970–I), 25.

74 The earliest known instance of the modern type of most-favoured-nation clause

is to be found in the Treaty of Nijmwegen of 1679. H. Neufeld, *supra*, note 27, at 29, 110. Another notable early instance of the most-favoured-nation clause was the Commercial Treaty of Utrecht of 1713 between Great Britain and France — in that case, however, the presence of the provision caused the British Parliament to decline to ratify the treaty. A. Nussbaum, *supra*, note 5, at 127–8.

75 The practice of the United States was more conservative than that of most countries, since its treaties usually contained an element of reciprocity. *Id.* at 201–2. Problems relating to the most-favoured-nation clause continue to occupy the attention of international lawyers: in 1978 the International Law Commission completed drafting a set of articles on such clauses. See Ushakov, 'Most-favoured-nation clause', *ILC YB* (1978–II), 1.

76 A. Nussbaum, *supra*, note 5, at 202.

77 See text at note 63 *supra*.

78 See text at note 64 *supra*.

CHAPTER TWO

Pre-United Nations developments of the twentieth century

A. Restrictions on forcible self-help

The discussion in Chapter I of the abuses which attended the traditional doctrine of diplomatic protection of nationals abroad noted that the moderate (or internationalist) approach to the problem consisted, basically, of retaining the concept of diplomatic protection while at the same time mitigating its less attractive features. One might say that this approach attempted to tame the dragon rather than slay it. The present discussion will indicate some of the ways in which this taming took place.

The most caustic criticism levelled against the diplomatic protection doctrine undoubtedly concerned the use of force by States in recovering debts owed to their nationals by other States. A particularly striking instance of this practice was the Venezuelan blockade of 1902–03 mentioned in Chapter I.[1] This aspect of the problem received attention at the Hague Peace Conference of 1907, from which emerged the Convention respecting the Limitation of the Employment of Force for the Recovery of Contract Debts, more commonly known as the Porter Convention.[2]

The Porter Convention was an important limitation on the doctrine of diplomatic protection, yet it was not as decisive a step as some States had advocated. A number of States were in favour of adopting what became known as the Drago doctrine (named after the Argentine Minister to the conference), which absolutely prohibited the use of armed intervention for the collection of public debts.[3] The Porter Convention, on the other hand, provided only that, before the creditor State could use force, it had to request the debtor State to submit to arbitration. Then, if the debtor State refused to do so, or if, having done so, it later refused to give effect to an arbitral award, the creditor State could resort to force. The Drago doctrine, with its absolute prohibition on the use of force, would not have allowed forceful action in either of those two instances.

Until the adoption of the UN Charter in 1945, Article 2(4) of which prohibits the threat or use of force by States in general and hence absorbs the Drago doctrine into contemporary international law, little more developed in the way of direct legal limitation on the use of force in the diplomatic protection area. Nevertheless it is important to note two significant extradoctrinal developments. One was the greatly altered political atmosphere in which international legal debates have been conducted in this century, contrasted with earlier times. The second was the challenge thrown down by revolutionary governments to the traditional norms of international law, especially those norms governing the treatment of aliens.

Only a few points need be mentioned concerning the altered political context. Of prime importance was the emergence of new world powers outside the traditional European circle. The most obvious examples were, of course, the United States and Japan, both of which established their credentials as world powers in what was the universal political currency of the era: military success. Around the turn of this century both engaged in highly successful wars against European States (Spain was defeated by the United States, Russia by Japan).

Other occurrences also indicated to discerning observers that the world of twentieth-century politics — and hence law — was going to differ significantly from that of past times. The setbacks Great Britain suffered in the Boer War, for example, were a rude shock to Victorian complacency. The Boxer rebellion served as an indication that China also was growing restive under the thumb of the European States. Incidentally, both these struggles directly involved issues of the rights of aliens, the Boxer rebellion in particular being directed against foreigners in China. Even in India, the showcase of British imperial glory, signs of danger were appearing, which intensified after the Amritsar massacre of 1919.

Another major factor in the changing political balance was the serious weakening of Europe following the bloodletting of World War I. After the murderous spectacle of a continent-wide civil war which left some 12 million dead, any claim on the part of the European States to a special insight into the standards and practices of civilised nations rang very hollow indeed.

It is hardly surprising, then, that this political decline of Europe should be reflected in the evolution of new norms of international law, the second of the extradoctrinal developments noted above. The emergence of a revolutionary socialist government in Russia was one landmark. The vast programme of nationalisation of foreign-owned property, without compensation, which the Bolshevik government undertook presented the first major challenge in practice to the nineteenth-century idea of the sanctity of private property.

Probably even more significant, from the standpoint of international law, than the Soviet nationalisations, however, were the Mexican actions of the 1930s. The nationalisation by Mexico of oil interests owned by United States corporations sparked a sharp debate in diplomatic channels between those two countries about the international legal norms applicable to such circumstances. The United States conceded the right of Mexico to nationalise the property of aliens if it wished, but insisted that Mexico must pay 'prompt, adequate, and effective' compensation. Mexico disagreed, holding instead to the doctrine of national treatment discussed above. That is, it contended that so long as the United States corporations were treated the same as Mexican nationals there was no violation of international law.[4]

Needless to say, the above debate did not lead to a definitive resolution of this ever-controversial subject. What it did signify, for present purposes, was that new forces were surfacing in the world which questioned some of the most sacrosanct nineteenth-century norms of international law. With the advent of revolutionary governments espousing radically new conceptions of fundamental rights and duties, it was inevitable that the received wisdom of the nineteenth century as to the treatment of aliens would be subject to severe challenge. That challenge, of course, continues to this day.

B. Failure of the League of Nations to codify the law of State responsibility for injuries to aliens

One of the foremost twentieth-century innovations in the field of international law has been the attempt, on a variety of fronts, to reduce its all too amorphous body of principles, which had developed gradually over the years, into definitive, concise written form. Although the practice of treaty-making has existed since time immemorial, until the twentieth century it functioned primarily as a mechanism dealing with specific problems between two or more States, on a largely *ad hoc* basis. The present century, in contrast, has witnessed the harnessing of the treaty mechanism to articulate fundamental legal norms on a universal basis.

Before such a programme was feasible, certain changes in attitude and perspective were necessary on the part of the international community. Above all, the various nation-States had to consider themselves as truly a community of equals and not as members of a private club characterised by restrictive membership requirements and by informal status distinctions. In the early part of the nineteenth century this club went under the title of the Concert of Europe. It gradually broadened its membership as various nations demonstrated in some fashion their eligibility for membership of what might be dubbed a supranational Masonic lodge. The formal enrolment of Turkey in 1856, for example, was an event of some note in the club's history.[5]

It was only with the Hague Peace Conferences of 1899 and 1907 that the universalist approach began seriously to take hold in international law. At the risk of some inevitable oversimplification, the modern era of international law-making may be dated from those two seminal gatherings.[6] Indeed, from these conferences emerged the first sizable body of multilateral conventions purporting to lay down legal norms of a universal character. Most of the early Hague conventions related to arbitration between States and, more particularly, to rules relating to the conduct of war. As the twentieth century progressed, however, work also began on the codification of other aspects of international law, including the treatment of aliens. The most notable codification attempt in this area was undertaken by the League of Nations. Before discussing that unsuccessful effort, however, it is worthwhile noting earlier parallel activity on the regional level in the Americas.[7]

The very first International Conference of American States, which met in Washington in 1889–90, adopted a Recommendation Concerning Claims and Diplomatic Intervention. The Latin American States were in the majority and, because they had been the foremost advocates of the national treatment doctrine, the recommendation adopted that view. Aliens were to be entitled to equal civil rights with nationals; but States were held to have no obligations or responsibilities to foreigners, other than those obligations and responsibilities which they owed to their own citizens.[8] The recommendation was not a treaty and had no binding force.

At the Second International Conference of American States, in Mexico City in 1902, the Latin American States took the further legal step of adopting a Convention Relative to the Rights of Aliens. The title is slightly misleading, as the convention did not contain a list of rights to which aliens were to be entitled; it was not comparable, for example, to the UN Draft Declaration on the Human Rights of Non-citizens, which will be discussed at length in Chapter III.[9] Rather, the convention concerned itself with the question of the responsibility of the State for injuries to aliens. This approach, of course, was quite consistent with the traditional view that individuals were only objects and not subjects of international law. In any event, the convention adopted the national treatment approach in the area of substantive law, while on the procedural side it confined the exercise of diplomatic protection to cases of denial of justice, unusual delay, and (more vaguely) cases of 'evident violation of the principles of International Law'.[10] In short, it adopted the Calvo approach.

The American States accorded further attention to the question of the rights of aliens at their Sixth International Conference, at Havana in 1928, in two different instruments: the Code of International Law (commonly known as the Bustamante Code),[11] and a new Convention on the Status of Aliens.[12] The Bustamante Code provided for equality of treatment between aliens and nationals with regard to civil rights and to 'individual guarantees'.[13] The Convention on the Status of Aliens related to certain special concerns regarding the treatment of aliens, such as liability for military service, liability for extraordinary contributions and forced loans, enjoyment of 'essential civil rights',[14] and involvement in political activities.

The final major development in the Americas before 1945 was the adoption by the Seventh International Conference of American States, meeting at Montevideo in 1933, of a resolution on 'International Responsibility of the

State'. This resolution was concerned mainly with the treatment of aliens, covering much the same ground as had the 1902 convention adopted in Mexico City. The resolution, however, contained more emphatic wording than the convention on the subject of diplomatic protection, making it lawful only in cases of 'manifest denial or unreasonable delay of justice which [was always to be] interpreted restrictively, that is, in favor of the sovereignty of the State in which the difference may have arisen'.[15]

There is room for controversy as to just how much weight ought to be attached to these American developments. On the one hand, there is no doubt that the American States had generated the most impressive body of statements up to that time on the subject of the treatment of aliens and the doctrine of diplomatic protection. On the other, it could be argued that the standard embodied in their pronouncements did not even represent the consensus of the region, since the United States (as might well be imagined) did not support the positions adopted. On the whole, the better point of view is that these first efforts at codification or restatement served more as authoritative statements of the views of one important segment of the international community — the Latin American States — than as statements of general or even regional international law.

One major attempt by the international community as a whole was made before 1945 to codify the law relating to the treatment of aliens. It took place under the auspices of the League of Nations in the late 1920s, culminating anticlimactically at the First Conference on the Progressive Codification of International Law, held at The Hague in 1930.[16] After a decision by the Council of the League of Nations in 1927 to hold a codification conference, considerable debate ensued as to which areas of international law it would be best to codify. Three topics were ultimately chosen, one of which was 'Responsibility of States for Damage done in their Territory to the Person or Property of Foreigners'. In 1929, the year before the conference met, there were preliminary meetings. In Geneva a preparatory committee met and drew up thirty-one bases of discussion for the conference's consideration. An International Conference on the Treatment of Foreigners also took place in Paris. However, its failure to reach agreement on that subject was an ill omen for what was to follow.[17]

As it happened, the Hague Conference did not reach agreement on the topic of State responsibility for injuries to aliens. The conference committee entrusted with the topic had time to consider only ten of the thirty-one bases of discussion. While it did produce ten draft articles, there was little agreement even on them, and hence the League's codification effort may be said to have failed.[18]

This failure of the League is reminiscent of its inability to develop a comprehensive and widely acceptable body of law on the rights of refugees.[19] In neither case did the fault lie in any timidity exhibited by the League itself.

If anything, the League can be said to have been overly bold and to have bitten off more than it could chew. With the failure of a later attempt by the United Nations to deal with the question of State responsibility for injuries to aliens, to be discussed in Chapter III,[20] this area of international law still remains uncodified. It is likely that this state of affairs will continue for some time to come. This probability does not mean that the outlook for the progressive development of the law relating to the rights of aliens is bleak, but rather that such development will take place by a different mechanism from that of codification. It will come about — and indeed already has done so to a greater extent than is generally appreciated — in conjunction with the development and application of international human rights law, a phenomenon that will be discussed extensively in Chapter III.[21]

Before focusing on that subject, it is necessary to return briefly to the developments in bilateral treaty law which, as observed above, had been proceeding largely independently of the debates over State responsibility and diplomatic protection. After noting the progress achieved from 1900 to 1945 in the treaty area with respect, *inter alia*, to migrant workers and refugees, the discussion will proceed in the next chapter to a description and analysis of the status of aliens under contemporary international law.

C. Continued parallel development of bilateral treaty system

The practice of guaranteeing various rights to aliens (rights usually of a commercial or economic sort) in FCN treaties has continued apace during the twentieth century, without any startling new developments. However, there have been some innovations. Initially, the capitulation system, a by-product of the colonial and imperial eras, has been dismantled. Another development — one with great potential for the future — was the negotiation of bilateral and multilateral agreements concerning collective, as opposed to individual, movements of persons. International movements began increasingly to be planned, and were not always as spontaneous as had been the case in earlier periods.

The demise of the capitulation system merits only a brief note. The system was abolished formally in Turkey in 1923, with the conclusion of the Treaty of Lausanne,[22] while in China it was phased out over a course of years in individual agreements negotiated by the Kuomintang government with the various capitulatory powers.[23] Other such capitulation arrangements also came to a welcome end.[24]

A more important development during this period, in terms of its impact on the future of international law, was the concern manifested in numerous treaties over the collective movements of persons. To be sure, treaty provisions of this nature had existed before the twentieth century — a notable example being the Treaty of Utrecht of 1713, which provided for the transfer of the

French population from what is now Nova Scotia in Canada to Louisiana.[25] Only in the twentieth century, however, had the technology of government and administration reached the point of sophistication that such movements could occur on a large scale in a reasonably orderly fashion. A major impetus in this direction, as in so many others, was World War I. During this conflict the belligerent powers had subjected their populations to a degree of regimentation without precedent in modern times. Not only the military forces themselves but, ultimately, entire populations were effectively conscripted for the war effort, incidentally providing proof of Churchill's dictum that '[t]he wars of nations will be far more terrible than the wars of kings'.[26]

Treaties concerning collective movements of persons are basically of two types: first, concerning exchanges of entire populations;[27] second, concerning the migration of labour. Only a very brief discussion of the two phenomena is necessary at this stage, since the first is really only tangential to the general question of the human rights of aliens,[28] and the second is extremely modest in scale during the period under consideration, as compared to post-1945 developments.[29]

The necessity for population exchanges arose following the break-up of the great multinational empires at the end of World War I, especially the Ottoman Empire. In 1919 Greece and Bulgaria negotiated a voluntary exchange of populations,[30] ultimately involving some 85,000 persons.[31] By arrangement with Greece, the League of Nations assisted in the resettlement of persons transferring to that country.[32] The League also rendered assistance of a somewhat different kind to Bulgaria, by helping it raise a loan for resettlement purposes.[33] Another exchange, involving Greece and Turkey, occurred four years later, in 1923. This exchange, however, was compulsory.[34] Eventually some 1·3 million Greeks left Turkey to settle in Greece, while some 400,000 Muslims from Greece went to Turkey.[35]

During World War II population transfers of hitherto undreamt-of proportions took place, largely as a result of the policies of Nazi Germany. Jews from all over Europe were herded into concentration camps and eventually to horrifying mass slaughter. Also, civilian workers and prisoners of war were imported into Germany and subjected to forced labour: this process took place on such a scale that by the end of the war approximately half the 'German' work force were foreigners.[36] Additionally, Germany negotiated a number of treaties with various central European States which allowed voluntary emigration of ethnic Germans from those countries to Germany.[37] The difficulties which the international community encountered in sorting out the chaos after the war will be discussed briefly in Chapter III.[38]

The other type of treaty providing for the collective movements of persons is more central to contemporary issues of human rights of aliens: the conclusion of bilateral agreements for the influx of migrant workers. Judging from a survey of the treaties registered with the League of Nations and later with the United Nations, it was only after 1945 that such treaties became common, although the pre-1945 period did contain some indications of future trends. Early efforts in this regard were treaties which France negotiated with Poland in 1919[39] and with Czechoslovakia in 1920.[40] These agreements established a system whereby employers of either State applied to their own government for permission to recruit labourers in the other country. Such recruitment then occurred under supervised conditions. For example, the country where the recruitment took place would make the final decisions as to which workers were hired. Also, the contracts of employment had to be in a form acceptable to the two States parties.

Neither of these treaties contained detailed provisions on the rights to which the migrant labourers were entitled once they arrived in the host country. There were provisions that they were to receive equal pay with nationals of the host country for the performance of equal work, which provisions of course were of the utmost value in principle. (Whether they necessarily were in practice is another question, since it may have been that the migrants performed a type of labour at which few nationals worked, in which case there would have been no standard by which to measure equality.) The treaties further provided that the migrants were to receive the benefit of the laws of the host country — i.e. they were not to be confined to what might be called a juridical ghetto, living under a totally different legal regime from nationals. The treaty with Poland contained a most-favoured-nation provision, something which will recur in other contexts. Under that provision, each State party was obligated to treat the migrant workers of the other State no less favorably than it treated the migrants of any third country. The important question of the right of remission of wages earned in the host country was not settled in either treaty, but instead was left for later resolution.

In short, these treaties were a very modest beginning as far as systematic protection of the rights of migrant workers is concerned. The major developments in this field took place after 1945.[41] In fact the problem of the human rights of migrant workers and their families remains one of the most important and lively areas today in the law governing the treatment of aliens.[42]

D. Early developments in international law relating to refugees

The discussion earlier in this chapter mentioned some of the important changes caused by World War I in the general political setting in which international law developed. The war had other effects as well, however, one of which was the generation of an entirely new juridical category of alien — the refugee.[43] A refugee, briefly, is a person who leaves his or her country of nationality, whether voluntary or not, and is unwilling to return there because of a well founded fear that he or she would be subjected to persecution upon return.[44] There was, of course, nothing at all novel about aliens abroad fearing to return home. What was new in the twentieth century was the idea that such persons should be in some way the concern of the international community as a whole rather than being left, as previously, totally at the mercy of the country in which they took refuge.

One legal development which foreshadowed the evolution of an international law relating to refugees was the custom, which gradually became more widespread in the nineteenth century, that host countries would not extradite persons within their jurisdiction if the State requesting the extradition was seeking to prosecute the person in question for a political offence.[45] Although that principle has been embodied in many bilateral and multilateral treaties on extradition, the prevailing view today is that it remains a matter of optional State practice and is not required by customary international law.[46]

While the situation of refugees is broadly analogous to that of persons whose extradition is requested for political purposes, there are significant differences as well. Refugees are likely to materialise in substantial numbers, whereas extradition cases by their very nature involve individuals. Also, extradition cases arise, by definition, when the requesting State has taken the initiative in seeking to obtain jurisdiction over a person living in another State. Problems with refugees, in contrast, usually involve a host State's unwillingness to allow such persons to remain in its territory, a position it is perfectly entitled to take, in principle, under traditional international law.[47]

This last point brings up a final distinction between the cases of refugees and of political offenders in the extradition context. In the case of extradition, the prevailing view is that there is no underlying traditional international law on the subject; i.e. absent a treaty, there is no legal duty on the part of a host State to extradite a person.[48] In the case of refugees, however, there is an underlying traditional international law doctrine of the very clearest sort: a State is not under any legal obligation to allow aliens to enter or to remain in its territory.[49] Thus the basic problem in extradition law has been to build a system of conventional international law out of nothing but scattered State practice. The basic problem in refugee law, on the other hand, is to devise ways to curb or restrain States in the exercise of what is undoubtedly, in principle at least, their legal right to refuse entry to or subsequently expel aliens (whether they be 'refugees' or not).

International concern — not yet law — relating to refugees began with the activities of the League of Nations following World War I.[50] The League's approach, in certain ways, appears strangely cautious from the modern perspective, yet in other ways its efforts were more ambitious than the UN's efforts today. On the side of apparent caution, the League never assumed responsibility for refugees in general during the entire period of its existence. It always confined its work to particular categories of persons — four groups, to be precise: Russians (of whom some 1·5 million became refugees during the years 1918–22);[51] Armenians (about 300,000 refugees scattered throughout the Middle East);[52] various Christian minorities from the disintegrated Ottoman Empire (approximately 30,000 refugees in all);[53] and Germans (over 400,000 after 1933).[54] In addition to these four groups, which fell under the protection of the League's formal machinery for refugee protection, a special bilateral arrangement was made between the League and Greece, as noted above,[55] for the settlement of persons affected by its voluntary population exchange with Bulgaria in 1919.

This cautious approach on the part of the League should not be surprising in light of the novelty of the very idea of international concern for refugee problems. The major inspiration for the League's work on behalf of refugees was the successful operation of the High Commissioner for the Repatriation of Prisoners, who helped to repatriate over 400,000 German and Austrian World War I prisoners from Siberia.[56] From that effort, there grew a concern on the part of the League for Russian problems generally, one of which was the presence of large numbers of Russian refugees in other countries. This initial concern with Russians led the League gradually, in the course of the 1920s, to broaden its concern to include the other groups already mentioned.

The evolution of a specifically legal, as opposed to humanitarian, role in the care of refugees on the part of the League also evolved during the 1920s. One of the League's major initial successes was the devising of identity and travel documents for refugees, known informally as 'Nansen passports', after the League's first High Commissioner concerned with refugee matters.[57] An important further step came in 1928, when an international conference on refugee problems agreed that the League's High Commissioner should be allowed to exercise quasi-consular functions for Russian and Armenian refugees.[58]

The next development occurred in 1933, when the League drafted a Convention Relating to the International Status of Refugees.[59] Here the bolder aspect of the League's efforts came to the fore, in the form of a requirement that States parties surrender one of their most hallowed legal prerogatives: the right to deny foreigners entry to their territory. The convention provided that a State party had to admit a refugee into its territory if the refugee was coming direct from the State at whose hands he feared persecution. The later United Nations Convention, as will be noted in Chapter IV,[60] does not go anywhere near as far.

Perhaps the very boldness of the 1933 convention was its undoing — only eight States ever ratified it.[61] For this reason, it is not necessary to dwell at any length on its provisions. It is enough simply to note that it provided for the guarantee of certain civil rights to refugees and also limited the right of States parties to expel refugees. The present UN Convention and Protocol also contain provisions of this sort, which will be considered in Chapter IV.[62]

In 1938 a second refugee convention was drafted under the League's auspices. This convention specifically addressed itself to the status of refugees from Germany[63] (later extended to include refugees coming from Austria).[64] It was even less successful than the 1933 convention, however, attracting only three ratifications.[65] Clearly, much work remained for the future in the area of the rights of aliens who happened to be refugees.

Notes

1 See text at Chapter I, notes 50–1.
2 200 *Brit. Foreign & St. Papers* (1906–07), 314. On the Porter Convention's background, see G. Scott, 'Hague Convention Restricting the Use of Force to Recover on Contract Claims', 2 *A.J.I.L.* (1908), 78.
3 The original statement of the Drago doctrine appeared in an instruction from Drago to the Argentine ambassador to the United States of 29 December 1902, reprinted in 1 *A.J.I.L., Off. Doc. Supp.* (1907), 1.
4 See the exchanges of notes between the US Secretary of State and the Mexican Minister of Foreign Affairs of July, August, and September 1938, in 5 *U.S. Foreign Rel.* (1956), 674–702.
5 On the Concert of Europe, see generally F. Bridge and R. Bullen, *The Great Powers and the European States System 1815–1914* (1980).
6 For a lively account of the two Hague Conferences, see B. Tuchman, *The Proud Tower. A Portrait of the World before the War, 1890–1914*, at 229–88 (1966).
7 For brief summaries of the American codification efforts, see R. Dhokalia, *The Codification of Public International Law*, 133–40 (1970). Concerning the codification in the Americas of the law of State responsibility for injuries to aliens, see F. Garcia-Amador, 'International responsibility', *ILC YB* (1956–II), 173, 178–9 and 226–7.
8 *Id.* at 226.
9 See text at Chapter III, notes 43–74.
10 Convention Relative to the Rights of Aliens, reprinted in *id.* at 226.
11 For the text of the Bustamante Code, see *The International Conferences of American States 1889–1928*, at 327–70 (J. Scott, ed., 1931).
12 Convention Regarding the Status of Aliens in the Respective Territories of the Contracting Parties Adopted by the VIth International Conference of American States, 1928, 132 LNTS 301, reprinted in *The International Conferences of American States 1889–1928, supra*, note 11, at 415–16.
13 Article 2, *supra*, note 11, at 327.
14 Article 5, *supra*, note 12, at 415.
15 F. Garcia-Amador, *supra*, note 7, at 226.
16 On codification efforts by the League of Nations generally, see R. Dhokalia, *supra*, note 7, at 112–33. On the League's efforts to codify the law of State responsibility for injuries to aliens specifically, see F. Garcia-Amador, *supra*, note 7, at 177–8.
17 For the text of the draft Paris convention, see LN Doc. C.36.M.21.1929.II, at 7. See also A. Roth, *The Minimum Standard of International Law Applied to Aliens*, 71–2 (1949).
18 The ten draft articles are reprinted in F. Garcia-Amador, *supra*, note 7, at 225–6. These articles were worded so vaguely as to provide no clear endorsement of either the international minimum standard or the national treatment doctrine. As set forth in draft Article 2, the international legal duty of host States was basically 'to assure to foreigners in respect of their persons and property a treatment in conformity with the rules accepted by the community of nations'. This formulation, of course,

leaves unresolved the question of what the rules accepted by the community of nations are or how they are to be determined.

19 See text at notes 50–65 *infra*.

20 See text at Chapter III, notes 31–42.

21 See text at Chapter III, notes 1–30.

22 Treaty of Peace, 1923, 28 LNTS 11. Article 28 provided for 'the complete abolition of the Capitulations in Turkey in every respect'. The United States was not a party to this treaty; its capitulations remained until 1931.

23 Beginning after World War I and continuing into World War II, China negotiated an end to the many 'unequal treaties' to which it had been subject since the 1840s. See Q. Wright, 'The end of extraterritoriality in China', 37 *A.J.I.L.* (1943), 286.

24 See, e.g., R. Young, 'Recent American policy concerning the capitulations in the States of the Middle East', 42 *A.J.I.L.* (1948), 418.

25 Under the Treaty of Utrecht of 1713, wherein France ceded what is now Nova Scotia to Great Britain, the French residents (the Acadians) were to be given the choice of either swearing allegiance to the British government or of being removed. In the event, Great Britain did not bother to expel the Acadians until the 1750s, during the Seven Years War, at which time the expulsions caused a great deal of controversy. W. Eccles, *France in America*, 107–8, 185 (1972).

26 Quoted in F. Northedge and M. Grieve, *A Hundred Years of International Relations*, 336 (1971).

27 See generally A. de Zayas, 'International law and mass population transfers', 15 *Comp. Jur. Rev.* (1978), 3.

28 In population exchange treaties, there are typically provisions for changes of nationality so that persons who move do not remain aliens in the State to which they are transferred. See, e.g., Article 7 of the Convention Concerning the Exchange of Greek and Turkish Populations and Protocol, 1923, 32 LNTS 75.

29 See text at Chapter IV, notes 34–72, Chapter V, notes 42–52, and Chapter VI, notes 5–37.

30 Convention between Greece and Bulgaria Respecting Reciprocal Emigration, 1919, 1 LNTS 67. During the pre-world War I turmoil in the Balkans there had been a number of voluntary population exchange agreements between the various States. See S. Ladas, *The Exchange of Minorities. Bulgaria, Greece and Turkey*, 18–23 (1932).

31 Some 55,000 moved from Greece to Bulgaria, while some 30,000 moved the opposite way. Precise figures are very difficult to ascertain, since this treaty did not really begin the exchange process, but rather served to regulate population movements which had been going on for some time. J. Simpson, *Refugees. Preliminary Report of a Survey*, 13 (1938). On the Greek–Bulgarian population exchange process generally, see S. Ladas, *supra*, note 30, at 27–331.

32 Protocol Relating to the Settlement of the Refugees in Greece and the Creation for this Purpose of a Refugee Settlement Commission, 1923, 20 LNTS 30.

33 S. Ladas, *supra*, note 30, at 591–7.

34 See Convention Concerning the Exchange of Greek and Turkish Populations and Protocol, *supra*, note 28.

35 J. Simpson, *supra*, note 31, at 9. On the Greek–Turkish exchange generally, see S. Ladas, *supra*, note 30, at 335–588.

36 M. Proudfoot, *European Refugees 1939–52. A Study in Forced Population Movement*, 86 (1955). See generally E. Homze, *Foreign Labor in Nazi Germany* (1967).

37 See J. Schechtman, 'The option clause in the Reich's treaties on the transfer of populations', 38 *A.J.I.L.* (1944), 356. On the World War II population transfers

generally, see J. Schechtman, *European Population Transfers 1939–1945* (1946).
38 See text at Chapter IV, notes 2–6.
39 Convention between France and Poland Respecting Reciprocal Emigration, 1919, 1 LNTS 337.
40 Convention between France and Czechoslovakia Respecting Reciprocal Emigration, 1920, 3 LNTS 139.
41 See text at Chapter IV, notes 34–57, Chapter V, notes 42–52, and Chapter VI, notes 5–37.
42 See, e.g., the UN's current efforts to draft a general convention on the human rights of migrant workers and their families at Chapter IV, notes 58–72.
43 The concept of refugee may be said to have existed in a rudimentary form in customary international law, although more as a logical outgrowth of the law relating to territorial asylum and diplomatic protection than as an express juridical category in its own right. 1 A. Grahl-Madsen, *The Status of Refugees in International Law*, 42–3 (1966). As early as 1832 the term appeared (as an adjective rather than a noun) in a piece of French domestic legislation, the *Loi relative aux étrangers refugies qui résideront en France*. It was generally understood that the term 'étrangers refugiés' referred to persons who did not enjoy, for one reason or another, the diplomatic protection of any State. *Id.* at 95.

   This emphasis on lack of enjoyment of diplomatic protection persisted throughout the League of Nations era. See, e.g., Resolution (2) of the Arrangement Relating to the Issue of Identity Certificates to Russian and Armenian Refugees, 1926, 89 LNTS 47, and Resolution (2) of the Arrangement Concerning the Extension to other Categories of Refugees of Certain Measures Taken in Favour of Russian and Armenian Refugees, 1928, 89 LNTS 63. It was only after World War II that the legal community began to emphasise fear of persecution as an important, if not absolutely vital, condition of refugee status.
44 The most widely accepted definition of 'refugee' today is that contained in Article 1(A) of the UN Convention Relating to the Status of Refugees, 1951, 189 UNTS 137, as amended by the Protocol Relating to the Status of Refugees, 1967, 606 UNTS 267, reprinted in R. Lillich, *International Human Rights Instruments*, 280.1 (1983). A refugee is 'any person who … owing to a well-founded fear of being persecuted for reasons of race, religion, nationality, membership of a particular social group or political opinion, is outside the country of his nationality and is unable or, owing to such fear, is unwilling to avail himself of the protection of that country; or who, not having a nationality and being outside the country of his former habitual residence, is unable or, owing to such fear, is unwilling to return to it'.
45 The first State which began systematically to include in its extradition treaties a provision excluding extradition for political offences was France, starting in the 1830s. Some States, such as Great Britain, have made the political offence exception a part of their domestic legislation. See the Extradition Act, 1870, 33 and 34 Vict., c. 52, Section 3(1): 'A figutive criminal shall not be surrendered if the offence in respect of which his surrender is demanded is one of a political character. …' See also the Fugitive Offenders Act, 1967, 15 and 16 Eliz. II, c. 68, Section 4(1)(a), for an analogous provision relating to Commonwealth countries. On the political offence exception in international law generally, see I. Shearer, *Extradition in International Law*, 166–93 (1971); T. Carbonneau, 'The political offense exception to extradition and transnational terrorists: old doctrine reformulated and new norms created', 1 *ASILS Int'l L.J.* (1977), 1; B. Wortley, 'Political crimes in English law and in international law', 45 *B.Y.I.L.* (1971), 219.
46 I. Brownlie, *Principles of Public International Law*, 315 (3rd ed., 1979), notes that

some courts 'have abstracted from existing treaties and municipal provisions [on extradition] certain "general principles of law"'. The two aspects of extradition law concerned are double criminality and speciality. Concerning political offences, the author makes the much weaker claim that '[e]xtradition may also be refused ... if the offence alleged is political'. *Id.* See also the similarly cautious comment in S. Oda, 'The individual in international law', in *Manual of Public International Law*, 469, 522 (M. Sorensen, ed., 1968), that 'the principle of non-extradition of political offenders has been generally approved'. It is somewhat surprising that forceful claims have not yet been advanced to the effect that non-extradition of alleged political offenders is now a rule of customary international law.

47 1 L. Oppenheim, *International Law*, 692 (8th ed., H. Lauterpacht, ed., 1955). Oppenheim did concede, however, that '[a]lthough a State may exercise its right of expulsion according to discretion, it must not abuse its right by proceeding in an arbitrary manner'. *Id.* Somewhat more precise is the conclusion stated in the *Boffolo* case (Italy *v.* Venezuela), 20 R.I.A.A. 528, at 537 (1903), that '[a] state possesses the general right of expulsion; but ... [e]xpulsion should only be resorted to in extreme instances, and must be accomplished in the manner least injurious to the person affected'.

48 See, e.g., D. Greig, *International Law*, 408 (2nd ed., 1976).

49 See 1 L. Oppenheim, *supra*, note 47.

50 See generally L. Holborn, *Refugees. A Problem of our Time. The Work of the United Nations High Commissioner for Refugees, 1951–1972*, at 3–22 (1975). See also L. Holborn, 'The legal status of political refugees, 1920–1938', 32 *A.J.I.L.* (1938), 680.

51 L. Holborn, *Refugees. A Problem of our Time, supra*, note 50, at 3.

52 *Id.* at 3–4.

53 *Id.* at 4.

54 *Id.* at 13.

55 See text at note 32 *supra*.

56 L. Holborn, *Refugees. A Problem of our Time, supra*, note 50, at 6.

57 *Id.* at 8–10.

58 *Id.* at 10–12.

59 Convention Relating to the International Status of Refugees, 1933, 159 LNTS 199.

60 See text at Chapter IV, notes 25–6.

61 The eight States were Belgium, Bulgaria, Denmark, Egypt, France, Italy, Norway, and Czechoslovakia.

62 See text at Chapter IV, note 31.

63 Convention Concerning the Status of Refugees Coming from Germany (with Annex), 1938, 192 LNTS 59. This agreement replaced the Provisional Arrangement Concerning the Status of Refugees Coming from Germany (with Annex), 1936, 171 LNTS 75.

64 Additional Protocol Concerning the Status of Refugees Coming from Germany, 1939, 198 LNTS 141. A resolution of the Council of the League of Nations extended the arrangements to cover Sudeten Germans as well. L. Holborn, *Refugees. A Problem of our Time, supra*, note 50, at 22, n. 26.

65 The three States were Denmark, France, and Great Britain.

CHAPTER THREE

United Nations developments

A. UN Charter

The UN Charter, adopted in 1945, is the primary source of many of the most fundamental norms of contemporary international law, such as the principle of sovereign equality of States (Article 2[1]), the general prohibition against the threat or use of force by States (Article 2[4]), the principle of non-intervention in matters within the domestic jurisdiction of States (Article 2[7]), and the inherent right of self-defence (Article 51).

Several articles of the Charter are concerned with the subject of human rights,[1] although none expressly with the rights of aliens. Regarding human rights generally, the most important provisions are Articles 55 and 56. The former states that the UN shall promote 'universal respect for, and observance of, human rights and fundamental freedoms for all without distinction as to race, sex, language or religion'. The latter commits individual member States (as opposed to the organisation itself) to take joint and separate action in co-operation with the organisation for the achievement of these purposes. One also should note Article 1, which asserts that one of the major purposes of the UN is the 'promoting and encouraging [of] respect for human rights and for fundamental freedoms for all without distinction as to race, sex, language, or religion'.

These statements, obviously, are very broad and general in nature. Although there has been much scholarly debate as to their juridical impact,[2] this discussion need not consider that question in detail. What is more relevant for present purposes is to determine how much light these general provisions shed on the subject of the human rights of aliens.

From a strictly textual viewpoint, the answer is: very little. Only four characteristics are singled out in the Charter as being areas where it is *not* permissible to introduce distinctions between persons in the application of the human rights provisions: they are race, sex, language, and religion. Nationality is not mentioned. Thus, in contrast to the Universal Declaration of Human Rights (as the discussion below will reveal),[3] it is not crystal-clear that these four specified areas are merely examples of impermissible distinctions.

Yet without being an enthusiastic adherent of the 'teleological approach' to treaty interpretation one may interpret the Charter in such a fashion without much fear of contradiction.[4]

Taking a policy-oriented approach, one may also argue that inherent in the very concept of human rights and fundamental freedoms is the principle that discrimination against aliens is not permitted save in certain narrowly defined spheres, i.e. participation in a State's political process. This argument, attractive as it is, nevertheless cannot be expected to be entirely persuasive absent a serious effort to define the meaning of 'human rights and fundamental freedoms' in a much more comprehensive and far-reaching fashion than the Charter itself attempts to do.

Thus, to ascertain the additional protection which post-Charter international law affords aliens generally, one must look beyond the Charter itself to the subsequent UN initiatives which, since 1945, have progressively developed the content of the international human rights clauses (e.g. the Universal Declaration of Human Rights, the two UN Covenants, and various other UN efforts which will be discussed below).

B. Universal Declaration of Human Rights

The Universal Declaration of Human Rights[5] is the Magna Carta of contemporary international human rights law. The array of civil and political rights which it guarantees, while certainly not definitive, is comprehensive enough that if ever fully realised the legal and political climate in most States would be improved beyond recognition. Its thirty articles, moreover, are written in the very simplest style, free of the technical or rhetorical language which so often characterises international legal documents.

The concern here is not with the Declaration as a whole, but rather with its impact — if any — on the question of the human rights of aliens in international law.[6] In that context, two areas of dispute are especially important: first, to what extent does the Universal Declaration speak to the treatment of aliens? Second, what is the precise legal status of the Declaration in contemporary international law?

Regarding the first point, like the UN Charter's provisions, the text of the Universal Declaration says nothing expressly about aliens. The question, therefore, is whether aliens fall under its general provisions. Judging from the plain and ordinary meaning of the words used — an interpretory method very dear to the hearts of common-law lawyers which was adopted by the Vienna Convention on Treaties[7] — one would have to conclude that aliens are indeed covered. The reason for so concluding is that the language of the Declaration is couched in universal terms which either state affirmatively that 'everyone' shall be entitled to such and such a right, or provide, negatively from the viewpoint of States, that 'no one' shall be subjected to a particular deprivation.

One also should note that its preamble proclaims the Declaration to be a 'common standard of achievement for all peoples and all nations', there being no express indication that each nation is obligated to apply the 'common standard of achievement' only to its own nationals. Additionally, one also might note that Article 1, which sets the tone of the entire Declaration by affirming that '[a]ll human beings are born free and equal in dignity and rights', clearly embraces aliens as well as nationals.[8]

Any argument, therefore, that the Universal Declaration does not extend to aliens has this initial substantial hurdle of sheer commonsense interpretation to overcome. It is scarcely surprising, therefore, that no scholar has made a plausible claim to that effect. It is true that Article 2 of the Declaration, maintaining that '[e]veryone' is entitled to all the rights and freedoms set forth, adds that this entitlement is 'without distinction of any kind, such as race, colour, sex, language, religion, political or other opinion, national or social origin, property, birth or other status'. In other words, it omits nationality from the list of bases on which discrimination is specifically forbidden. This omission is not fatal, however, because the list clearly is intended to be illustrative and not comprehensive.

The only rights and freedoms mentioned in the Universal Declaration and not available to aliens, therefore, are the ones in which the right itself is formulated in such a way as to apply only to nationals. For example, Article 13(2) holds that everyone has the right to return to 'his' country. This provision guarantees every person the right of entry on to the territory of the State of which he is a national, leading to the conclusion that the article does not grant an alien the right to enter any State of which he is not a national.[9]

Another article in which the concept of nationality is relevant is Article 21, which guarantees everyone the right to take part in the government of 'his' country and also the right of equal access to public service in 'his' country. An alien, in other words, may not claim political rights in his host country on the basis of the Universal Declaration (although, of course, technically he is covered by Article 21 in that he retains his political rights in his home State).

It is possible to offer a more 'progressive' interpretation of Articles 13 and 21 than has been advanced above. One could contend, for instance, that the expression 'his country' does not refer exclusively to the State of the alien's nationality. One could argue for a more sociological, as opposed to juridical, interpretation of those words and conclude that, for any given person, 'his country' refers to the one with which he has the most substantial real connections, whether through family ties, residence, economic activity, or whatever. Under such an interpretation, one might then read Articles 13 and 21 to grant aliens rights in host States.

Although this argument has its attractions, for reasons more of strategy than of logic it probably is best not to advance it, at least at the present stage of development of international human rights law. Such an argument requires introducing a certain artfulness into debates about the meaning of the Universal Declaration which could detract from its cardinal strength of forcefulness-through-simplicity. It would probably be a mistake to open the door to casuistry in debates about the Universal Declaration, as, even in its very plainest and simplest interpretation, it contains guarantees which are very far-reaching indeed. Moreover, as the discussion below will demonstrate,[10] there are other mechanisms available for the promotion of such 'progressive' ends.

The second point regarding the Universal Declaration mentioned above — its legal status — is more open to dispute than the coverage of aliens. It is also an issue more related to jurisprudential questions concerning the sources of international legal norms in general, rather than of norms which pertain to aliens specifically. The discussion, accordingly, will touch only briefly on this issue.

The basic obstacle faced by aliens claiming rights under the Universal Declaration is that the Declaration is not a treaty, but only a resolution of the UN General Assembly. Although General Assembly resolutions do not automatically have the force of international law, in certain circumstances they may become international law over the course of years. Whether a trans-mutation from mere resolution into binding international law has occurred is determined, broadly, by the degree of acceptance by the international legal community of the norms contained in the resolution.[11] The process is one of juridical osmosis, there being no identifiable instant at which a resolution suddenly bursts forth as a binding legal norm. As the process is necessarily a gradual one, disagreement will often occur over whether, at any given time, the magic point has been attained.

In the case of the Universal Declaration, there is fairly persuasive authority which maintains that that point has been reached, at least with respect to many of the rights guaranteed by the Declaration.[12] It has been invoked so frequently in the thirty-five years since its adoption, and in such varying contexts (from domestic and international court cases to State practice to the constitutions of various States)[13] that certainly its key provisions may now be said to represent customary international law.[14]

In short, the Universal Declaration is a highly significant instrument for the protection of aliens, even though its text does not specifically refer to them. Such a powerful legal weapon should certainly not be ignored in efforts to protect the rights of aliens.[15]

C. The UN Covenants on Human Rights

The adoption of the Universal Declaration of Human Rights in 1948 was the first step in the development of what has come to be known as the 'International Bill of Rights'.[16] This term is a collective reference to four instruments: the Universal Declaration; the International Covenant on Civil and Political Rights;[17] the International Covenant on Economic, Social and Cultural Rights;[18] and the Optional Protocol to the International Covenant on Civil and Political Rights.[19] The latter three instruments were concluded in 1966 and have been in force since 1976.

In contrast to the Universal Declaration, there has never been any question that the two Covenants and the Optional Protocol are binding legal agreements, in the full sense of the term, for States which have ratified them.[20] The provisions of the two Covenants are accordingly drafted in a much more 'legalistic' fashion than the articles of the Universal Declaration: they spell out in greater detail what the nature of the rights concerned is, and in some cases they contain provisions which allow States parties to restrict the rights in question under certain specified (but often very broad) circumstances, such as the preservation of public health and morals and the protection of national security.[21]

Most noteworthy for present purposes, however, is the fact that, unlike the Universal Declaration, the two Covenants contain provisions which relate specifically to aliens. Generally, however, both instruments make use of the very broad formulations contained in the Declaration: statements abound that 'everyone' is to have this or that right, or that 'no one' is to suffer such and such a detriment. The Covenant on Economic, Social and Cultural Rights differs only slightly, in that its provisions commonly take the form of statements recognising 'the right of everyone' to benefits of various types. The question of whether provisions of this nature apply to aliens or not is, therefore, basically the same as in the case of the Declaration.[22] The arguments in favour of including aliens in these categories, on the strength of the plain meaning of the text, also applies here and thus need not be restated.

A very brief survey of the two Covenants for provisions relating to the human rights of aliens follows.[23]

1. Civil and Political Covenant

The International Covenant on Civil and Political Rights, as just noted, generally follows the form of the Universal Declaration by providing protection for 'everyone' in a variety of specific contexts. Its terminology is less consistent, however, than the Declaration's. For instance, sometimes the reference is to 'all persons', or to 'accused persons', or to 'men and women of marriageable age', or to 'every child'. This variation in phraseology, however, is of no significance. Therefore, as in the case of the Declaration, the inescapable conclusion is that aliens are generally covered.[24]

Further evidence that the Civil and Political Covenant applies generally without discrimination to both aliens and nationals may be found in Article 2(1), which states that the rights set forth in the Covenant are to be granted to all persons within the territory, and subject to the jurisdiction, of the State party 'without distinction of any kind such as race, colour, sex, language, religion, political or other opinion, national or social origin, property, birth or other status'. Nationality is not mentioned expressly among these grounds ('national origin' refers to a person's descent, not to his juridical nationality). Nevertheless, nationality would appear to fall into the category of 'distinction of any kind'. Also, the list of impermissible grounds of distinction is obviously illustrative and not exhaustive.

Another non-discrimination provision of the Covenant which merits consideration is Article 26, which reads as follows:

All persons are equal before the law and are entitled without any discrimination to the equal protection of the law. In this respect, the law shall prohibit any discrimination and guarantee to all persons equal and effective protection against discrimination on any ground such as race, colour, sex, language, religion, political or other opinion, national or social origin, property, birth or other status.

In the absence of any authoritative interpretation, it is difficult to say with confidence just what this article means. It may refer to non-discrimination in the *application* of the law (e.g. aliens should not be subject to harsher penalties than nationals upon conviction of criminal offences). On the other hand, it may refer to non-discrimination in the *substantive* law (e.g. if a State decriminalises homosexuality, then it must do so for aliens and nationals alike). The better view would be to regard Article 26 as referring to the substance as well as the application of the law, to the extent that the substance of the law relates to civil and political matters. Having reached such a tentative conclusion, one must await further clarification of this point as decision-makers interpret the Covenant in coming years.[25]

The Covenant contains one article, however, which clearly excludes aliens from its scope: Article 25, which guarantees various political rights to '[e]very citizen'. These rights are the following: the right to take part in the conduct of public affairs, either directly or through representatives; the right to vote; and the right of access to public service. It must be stressed, however, that Article 25 does not categorically exclude aliens from the exercise of all political rights in host countries. The article provides only that nationals *must* be allowed these rights; States parties are left perfectly free to grant them to aliens if they so choose.[26] In this regard, mention should be made of Article 5(2), which states that countries may not restrict or derogate from rights which they have chosen to grant on the ground that the Covenant itself does not require the granting of such rights. Thus aliens who are fortunate enough to live in States which have granted them certain political rights have some measure of protection under the Covenant.

Another noteworthy point regarding the availability of political rights to aliens is that Article 25 refers only to the specific rights mentioned above. The denial of these rights certainly does not mean that aliens are excluded altogether from meaningful political activity. They remain free to support candidates, to speak in public on their behalf in election campaigns, to work in campaigns, to contribute to political causes, and so forth.

A second article of the Civil and Political Covenant which specifically affects aliens is Article 12, which concerns freedom of movement within countries. This right is guaranteed only to persons lawfully in the territory of the State party. The distinction, therefore, is not really between aliens and nationals, but rather between *illegal aliens*, on the one hand, and nationals and *legal aliens* on the other.

Article 13, the last article of the Covenant to be considered here, is of cardinal importance for aliens, since it concerns the rights to which they are entitled when host States are taking expulsion proceedings against them. These rights are strictly of a procedural nature — that is, Article 13 does not give aliens any substantive, affirmative right to stay in a host country — but such rights are of great value nonetheless. Expulsion of an alien is lawful only pursuant to 'a decision reached in accordance with law'. The alien must be allowed to present arguments against his expulsion, to appear before the competent authority, and to be represented before that authority. A State party may derogate from these last rights only 'where compelling reasons of national security ... require'. It is a sad comment on contemporary international affairs that aliens have had ample need for the protection of this article in recent years.[27]

2. Economic, Social and Cultural Covenant

The International Covenant on Economic, Social and Cultural Rights may be treated succinctly. In general, it is less favourable to aliens than its counterpart. Presumably this restrictive approach stems from the fact that its provisions typically concern matters where the State's affirmative action is required, such as providing educational opportunities or social security. Since questions inevitably arise concerning the allocation of scarce economic resources, it is hardly surprising that States tend to give their own nationals first priority. The Covenant, in fact, expressly allows such preference to developing countries: Article 2(3) permits them to determine — apparently unilaterally — to what extent they will guarantee the Covenant's various economic rights to non-nationals.[28] Non-economic rights, however, are not prejudiced by this provision.

Also arguably less favourable to aliens, in comparison to the analogous provisions of the Civil and Political Covenant, is the general non-discrimination provision of Article 2(2): it prohibits 'discrimination of any kind as to race, colour, sex, language, religion, political or other opinion, national or social origin, property, birth or other status'. Nationality, as in the case of the Civil and Political Covenant, does not figure in the list. In contrast to Article 2(1) of the Civil and Political Covenant,[29] however, this list of impermissible grounds of discrimination is not contextually illustrative, although neither is it expressly stated to be exhaustive. On balance, though, one is led to the conclusion, no matter how reluctantly, that the Economic, Social and Cultural Covenant does not embody a general norm of non-discrimination against aliens, as does the Civil and Political Covenant. Yet it must be emphasised that this conclusion is not tantamount to stating that international law now authorises discrimination against aliens in these areas. All one may conclude is that *this particular instrument* is not in and of itself the source of such a general norm of non-discrimination. One must look to particular provisions in this Covenant or search elsewhere, as the discussion below will do,[30] to find particular manifestations of the norm.

Having now briefly analysed the most general human rights initiatives to emerge from the UN, the discussion may proceed to consider those international instruments which relate specifically either to aliens in general or to particular categories of aliens.

D. International Law Commission codification efforts

The failure of the League of Nations' attempt to codify the law of State responsibility for injuries to aliens has been noted in Chapter II.[31] The League's lack of success, however, did not mark the end of the international legal community's effort to codify international law. With the establishment of the UN in 1945, its International Law Commission (ILC), set up in 1949, has been entrusted with this mission on a continuing basis.[32]

At its inception, the ILC had to decide which of the many areas of customary international law would first receive its attention. It is of more than merely historical interest that, in the list of twenty-five possible topics which it considered in its initial meetings, the subjects of State responsibility and treatment of aliens appeared separately.[33] Such an approach is the correct one, notwithstanding (as noted in Chapter I)[34] that most international precedents on State responsibility come from the treatment of aliens area.

Of still greater importance for the future development of the treatment of aliens as an autonomous subject in international law was the recognition, again at the inception of the ILC's work, that there would necessarily be some interplay between the subject of the treatment of aliens, on the one hand, and the developing body of international human rights law, on the other. In particular, the ILC was aware of the possibility of substituting international human rights norms, of general applicability, for the international minimum standard of traditional international law, thereby side-stepping the as yet unresolved debate over the minimum standard and national treatment approaches.[35]

In the event, the ILC decided in its early years not to turn its attention either to State responsibility generally or to the treatment of aliens. Indeed, even to this day the Commission has never dealt with the problem of the treatment of aliens as such. State responsibility, on the other hand, was placed on the ILC's agenda following a request by the UN General Assembly in 1953 to codify the topic.[36] In the course of the ILC's initial study of the subject, the question of the treatment of aliens reared its ever-controversial head.

The topic of the treatment of aliens came to the ILC's attention under the rubric of State responsibility because the ILC's rapporteur on State responsibility adopted a narrow approach to his topic. Dr F. V. Garcia-Amador, a noted Cuban jurist, appointed rapporteur for State responsibility, produced a total of six annual reports on the subject, one per year for the period 1956–61.[37] As is customary with rapporteurs, he was left relatively free to approach the subject as he thought best. Changes in approach, if any, would occur after the full Commission's consideration of the rapporteur's work.

In Garcia-Amador's case the Commission, after years of vacillation, eventually disapproved of his approach, which was to divide up the vast topic of State responsibility into discrete areas and then to codify each of these areas, rather than to consider a single body of principles for the whole State responsibility field. Since the law of State responsibility for injuries to aliens, a large part of treatment of aliens law, was the richest in case law, the rapporteur chose it for his initial codification attempt, rather to the chagrin of many Commission members.

From the standpoint of the actual codification of either State responsibility generally or of the law governing the treatment of aliens in particular, Garcia-Amador's efforts ended in failure. More fruitful, however, was his pioneering attempt to fuse the norms relating to the treatment of aliens to the emerging norms of international human rights law, applicable to aliens and nationals alike. His solution to the old *impasse* between the international minimum standard and the national treatment doctrine was to contend that, in light of the development of international human rights law, the dichotomy between them had become obsolete. What had once been termed the international minimum standard had now been subsumed under a general body of international human rights law, which protected nationals and aliens alike. The alleged privileged position of aliens under traditional international law, therefore, was a thing of the past. Since the new human rights norms protected all persons equally, the old international minimum standard and national treatment positions had been synthesised.[38]

Garcia-Amador's innovative approach produced a very tidy resolution of a very knotty problem. Unfortunately, several generations of fierce legal/political controversy could not be put to rest so easily, particularly since his argument was less than airtight. In the first place, the argument depended on the old international minimum standard collapsing completely into the new human rights norms. So long as *any* norms remained which were peculiar to aliens and not applicable to persons in general, the question of a privileged status for aliens could still arise. Another problem concerned the venerable doctrine of diplomatic protection. While that hotly disputed institution remained available to aliens they would enjoy at least a procedural protection unavailable to nationals. There was also the more technical, but still serious, problem that the rapporteur had not done the job which a good many members of the Commission thought they had assigned to him: his mandate had been to draft principles on State responsibility generally, whereas he had concentrated instead on the narrower subject of State responsibility for injuries to aliens.

The debates which the ILC had on Garcia-Amador's drafts were some of the most highly political ones which ever have occurred in that normally scholarly body.[39] Finally, after Garcia-Amador left the Commission in 1961, no action having been taken on his draft convention, an entirely fresh start was made on the subject of State responsibility under a new rapporteur, then Professor (now Judge) Roberto Ago from Italy. Ago's approach, which the ILC still pursues, has been to treat the subject of State responsibility as a whole. The consequence of this decision has been that the draft articles which he and his successor, Judge Riphagen, have produced (and continue to produce) are so abstract as to border on the ethereal.[40]

The approach the ILC has chosen to follow since Garcia-Amador's efforts makes a sharp separation between the wrongful act committed by a State, i.e. a violation of some substantive rule of international law, on the one hand, and the legal consequences of that act, i.e. the responsibility of the State, on the other hand. The law of State responsibility is concerned only with this latter category ('secondary rules', as one scholar has termed them)[41] and not with the substantive (or 'primary') rules of law which determine what acts by States are lawful and what acts are not.[42] The details of this ongoing initiative on State responsibility, then, are of no real concern to this study. The only relevant point that needs underscoring is that the ILC, through Ago's work, has made a decisive demarcation between the law of State responsibility in general and the law of State responsibility for injuries to aliens, a large part of the law governing the treatment of aliens. The former remains on the ILC's current agenda; the latter has been jettisoned entirely, at least for the present.

One cannot deny that it makes some sense for the ILC to distinguish sharply between State responsibility and the treatment of aliens, as Lauterpacht recommended and the Commission initially determined over thirty years ago. On the other hand, it is unfortunate that the Commission has not followed through its original decision to codify the law governing the treatment of aliens. Happily, though, the subject of the rights of aliens has not been ignored entirely in UN circles. It reappeared in the 1970s in fortuitous but most appropriate fora: in those UN bodies concerned with the development and enforcement of international human rights law. The activities therein, of great and perhaps lasting importance, are the next item to be considered.

E. UN Draft Declaration on the Human Rights of Non-Citizens

1. General background

The UN finally became involved with the law governing the treatment of aliens in 1972, following Uganda's expulsion of its Asian population.[43] When the expulsion was called to the attention of the Sub-commission on Prevention of Discrimination and Protection of Minorities, that body did nothing more than discuss whether to send a deferentially worded telegram of remonstrance to President Amin.[44] Looking to the future, however, the Sub-commission did adopt a resolution recommending that the Commission on Human Rights, its parent body, consider the problem of the applicability of the provisions of the international human rights instruments to aliens, as well as the question of what further measures might be desirable.[45]

At its 1973 session the Commission on Human Rights in turn requested its parent body, the Economic and Social Council, to return the matter to the Sub-commission to study what steps should be undertaken.[46] One possibility expressly mentioned by the Commission was the preparation of a declaration concerning the rights of aliens. Such a declaration would be simply a resolution of the UN General Assembly and therefore (as noted above)[47] would not automatically constitute binding international law. In UN practice, however, the term 'declaration' is usually reserved for resolutions concerning legal and political norms of the most fundamental character and on which the degree of international consensus is of the highest order. Frequently, as in the case of the Universal Declaration of Human Rights, they ripen, at least partially, into customary international law.[48] Other prominent declarations with such status are on the Granting of Independence to Colonial Countries and Peoples (1960),[49] Permanent Sovereignty over Natural Resources (1962),[50] and Torture (1975).[51]

By 1973, then, there was in place for the first time UN machinery for full consideration of the subject of the treatment of aliens. There is every reason to suppose, however, that matters would not have proceeded very far had it not been for one member of the Sub-commission, Baroness Elles of Great Britain. Taking the initiative, she produced for the 1974 session of the Sub-commission a draft Declaration on the Human Rights of Individuals who are not Citizens of the Country in which they Live,[52] the clumsiness of the title reflecting the fact that the very word 'alien' had become taboo in UN circles. The draft Declaration consisted basically of a list of rights, borrowed from the principal international human rights instruments, to which *certain* aliens were to be entitled. It did not purport to be a general charter of rights for all aliens, since it applied only to persons lawfully residing in States of which they were not nationals. Illegal and transient aliens, therefore, were not covered by its terms.

Apparently the Sub-commission as a whole was slightly taken aback by this flurry of activity on Elles's part. Some members expressed doubt whether her basic approach to the problem was sound, contending that any listing of specific rights carried with it the danger that other important rights might be omitted. An alternative strategy would be to adopt a much simpler yet more comprehensive declaration which would simply affirm once and for all that the general international human rights law norms apply to aliens as well as to nationals[53] (presumably also listing expressly those rights which do not, such as certain political and economic rights). In the event, the Sub-commission's first substantive step, if it can be called that, was the adoption at its 1974 session of a resolution which shed precisely no light at all on the subject: it states that 'restrictions [on human rights] on the grounds of a person's nationality or citizenship, can be admissible only when they are not contrary to the relevant provisions of international law'.[54] In other words, restrictions on the rights of aliens are unlawful except when they are lawful!

Fortunately, the Sub-commission's contribution to the procedural aspects of this subject was more fruitful. That same 1974 resolution appointed Elles as special rapporteur, with the task of preparing a report on the applicability of existing international human rights instruments to non-citizens, which would supplement a report the UN Secretariat had prepared the previous year. Elles also was to prepare 'a critical enumeration of measures which might be desirable, including the possibility of a declaration ...'.[55]

Elles presented a preliminary report the following year, in 1975,[56] submitted a final report in 1976,[57] and updated it in 1977.[58] A detailed analysis of these reports is not possible here. It is sufficient to note the general conclusion which Elles reached from her studies — that existing international human rights instruments do not adequately protect the rights of aliens. Accordingly, she favoured having the Sub-commission press ahead with the adoption of her draft Declaration (which had undergone some changes since 1974).[59] A brief consideration of the contents of this draft Declaration is now in order.[60]

2. Comparison with other international human rights instruments

The first noteworthy point about the draft Declaration has been mentioned already — it does not cover all aliens, but only those aliens who reside lawfully in the territory of the host State. Earlier drafts had contained the qualification that residence must be permanent or semi-permanent.[61] That restriction has been deleted, however, so it appears that lawful residence of any duration, however short, will suffice to bring an alien within the ambit of the draft Declaration. Illegal aliens, however, are still not covered. Nor are such persons as tourists, traders, athletes, journalists, or visiting scholars — all of whose visits, presumably, are too brief to qualify as residence.

Of the specific rights listed in the Elles draft Declaration, a substantial number replicate provisions contained in the International Bill of Rights.[62] These rights are the following:

1 The right to security of person and protection by the State against violence or bodily harm (Article 4[i]).
2 The right not to be subjected to torture or to cruel, inhuman or degrading treatment or punishment (Article 6).
3 The right to equal access to and equal treatment before the tribunals and other organs of justice (Article 4[ii]).
4 The right to be free from arbitrary arrest or detention (Article 5).
5 The right to freedom of movement and residence within the territory of the host country, subject, however, to 'such restrictions as are absolutely necessary for compelling reasons of public policy, public order, national security, or public health or morals' (Article 4[iii]).
6 The right to marriage and choice of spouse (Article 4[v]).
7 The right not to be subjected to arbitrary confiscation of lawfully acquired assets, including the right to 'just compensation' for any expropriated assets (Article 9).
8 The right to freedom of thought, conscience, and religion (Article 4[vii]).
9 The right to freedom of opinion and expression (Article 4[viii]).
10 The right of peaceful assembly and association (Article 4[ix]).
11 The right to just and favourable conditions of work, to equal pay for equal work, and to just and fair remuneration (Article 8[i]).
12 The right to join trade unions and to participate in their activities (Article 8[iii]); and
13 The right to public health, medical care, social security, social services, and education, provided that the alien meets the normal requirements for participation in national schemes, and provided also that 'undue strain' is not placed on the resources of the State (Article 8[iv]).

Before proceeding to consider those clauses of the Elles draft Declaration which go beyond the general provisions found in the principal international human rights instruments, it is well to note some interesting omissions. Most conspicuously absent, perhaps, is any set of guarantees for the protection of the rights of aliens in criminal proceedings. The provision of Article 4(ii) for equal treatment before tribunals is a step in that direction, but only a step. The draft Declaration would be improved if it were more specific on this subject and included expressly such matters as the right to be informed of any criminal charges in a language which the alien understands; the right to a public trial, with adequate time for the preparation of a defence; the right to legal representation; and the right of freedom from self-incrimination. The fact that guarantees of this nature already appear in the Covenant on Civil and Political Rights indicates that expressly extending them to aliens would not be too radical a step.

Another omission — though hardly a surprising one — is the right to work. It is true that aliens are entitled to certain rights when working (such as the right to equal pay for equal work, and so forth). The right to enter into employment in the first place, however, is not present.

3. Innovations in the UN draft Declaration

The number of rights conferred by the draft Declaration which do not merely replicate rights found in the International Bill of Rights is considerably shorter than the list of specific rights set forth above. Their importance for aliens, however, is very great. At least three rights fall into this category:

1 The right to repatriate earnings and savings 'in accordance with national laws in force' (Article 8[ii]).
2 The right to communicate with one's consulate or diplomatic mission (Article 10); and
3 The right to retain one's own language, culture, and traditions (Article 4[x]).

Each of these rights merits a brief comment.

a. Repatriation of earnings Article 8(ii) of the draft Declaration, on the repatriation of earnings, has the ring of tautology about it: allowing such repatriation only 'in accordance with national laws in force' appears to be tantamount to saying that States must allow the repatriation of earnings provided that their laws allow it.

The key issue is the extent to which Article 8(ii) restricts the host State's freedom of action, if indeed it does so at all. Some clues in this regard can be gleaned from United States case law, where at least on two occasions courts have had occasion to consider the meaning of similar language. One court reached the conclusion that the expression 'national laws' could not refer to laws imposing restrictions only on aliens.[63] Otherwise, in the context of Article 8(ii), the expression would be nothing more than a national treatment provision. In a second case, however, the holding was more cautious: the court concluded, basically, that the expression 'national laws' could include laws restricting aliens, but only to the extent that such laws were an integral part of an historical policy.[64] Even this more cautious approach, however, when applied to Article 8(ii), would not allow the expression to be used as a *carte blanche* licence automatically allowing discrimination against aliens.

The extent to which either of these two approaches from US case law might be applicable to the drafting of a declaration on the rights of aliens generally remains to be resolved. Certainly a straight national treatment norm would not be appropriate in this context, since most aliens — migrant workers in particular — obviously have a far greater interest than do nationals in the free movement of capital. The better approach would be the flexible one of the second case cited above: restrictions by host States on the repatriation of earnings by aliens ought to be allowed, but only if they are non-discriminatory in nature and reasonably consonant with the real economic interests of the host

State. This formulation, admittedly, is none too precise, albeit it does provide slightly more guidance than the present wording of Article 8(ii).

Finally, Article 8(ii) should provide expressly that no restrictions may be imposed on aliens regarding the removal from the host State of savings or other assets which they brought with them into the host State. Restrictions should be permitted, to the extent just outlined, only in the case of assets acquired during the alien's sojourn.

b. Communication with diplomatic and consular missions   Article 10, concerning the alien's right to communicate with his consular or diplomatic mission, is an innovative and useful provision which requires little comment. An obvious improvement which merits incorporation is to grant the mission a clear right of access to the alien, a matter that is commonly provided for in bilateral treaties regulating consular or diplomatic activities.[65]

c. Right to retain language, culture and traditions   Article 4(x) on the right of aliens to retain their own language, culture and traditions is in a category of its own.[66] Admittedly, it bears a distinct resemblance to Article 27 of the Covenant on Civil and Political Rights, which gives similar rights to member of ethnic, religious, and linguistic minorities. In their impact upon the State party, however, the two provisions are very different. What the above provision of the Elles draft Declaration appears to guarantee is the right of aliens to form cultural — though not juridical — enclaves within the host country, somewhat like the old privileged merchant communities operating under the capitulation systems of the past.[67] More broadly, one might characterise Article 4(x) as conferring upon aliens the legal right to resist integration into the life of the host country (although one should note that, under Article 2(2) of the draft Declaration, aliens are required to 'respect' the customs and traditions of the people of the host State).

The implications of this provision are vast and cannot be explored in detail here. It is sufficient for present purposes to note that any provision extending cultural rights to aliens raises sensitive issues generally not present when similar rights are granted only to nationals. This kind of problem illustrates particularly vividly that in many areas of life the legal problems of aliens are *sui generis*, i.e. they cannot be reduced simply to ensuring that aliens receive the same treatment as nationals.

4. *Present status of the UN draft Declaration*
At its 1978 session the Sub-commission completed its consideration of the Elles draft Declaration by adopting a resolution requesting the special rapporteur to present her study and draft Declaration to the full Commission on Human Rights at its session the following year.[68] This resolution also recommended that the Commission and the Economic and Social Council take steps

to ensure wide distribution of the Elles report. The Sub-commission, however, did not actually adopt the draft Declaration or, indeed, even recommend that it be adopted by higher UN bodies.

In the event, the Commission on Human Rights kept the question of the Elles report and draft Declaration on its agenda for two sessions. In 1979 it recommended that the Economic and Social Council consider the declaration with a view to submitting it to the General Assembly 'for its consideration'.[69] The following year the Commission resolved that the Economic and Social Council should recommend to the General Assembly that it 'consider the adoption of a declaration on the human rights of individuals who are not citizens of the country in which they live ...'.[70] The Economic and Social Council duly followed this recommendation at its 1980 session,[71] with the result that the question of the Elles draft Declaration — still not actually adopted by any UN body — came before the General Assembly at its 1980 session.

The General Assembly proceeded to set up an open-ended working group to elaborate a final version of the draft Declaration for submission to the full Assembly. That group has laboured during the 1980, 1981, 1982 and 1983 sessions of the General Assembly and has provisionally agreed — after a fashion — upon eleven articles of a draft Declaration.[72] Many of these articles, however, contain alternative language in parentheses or brackets, leaving difficult decisions for later resolution, e.g. whether the declaration will apply only to aliens lawfully within a State, and the quantum of compensation to be paid aliens if their assets are expropriated. The General Assembly in 1982 instructed the working group to conclude its drafting efforts during the Assembly's 1983 session, and expressed the hope that the draft Declaration would be adopted by the Assembly at that session.[73] The hope has not materialised.

Since work on the Elles draft Declaration is not yet complete, it is impossible to make a final assessment of this particular UN initiative. Assuming that the draft Declaration is eventually adopted in some form by the General Assembly, the next interesting question will be whether the UN decides to proceed to the drafting of a legally binding convention on the subject, in which case the international law norms governing the treatment of aliens — at long last — may be embodied in conventional, as well as in customary, international law. Thus, after several false starts and in somewhat indirect fashion, the aspirations of Garcia-Amador from the 1950s may yet be realised.[74]

Notes

1 The human rights provisions of the UN Charter are reprinted in R. Lillich, *International Human Rights Instruments*, 10.1–10.10 (1983).
2 See, e.g., E. Schwelb, 'The International Court of Justice and the human rights

clauses of the Charter', 66 *A.J.I.L.* (1972), 337; L. Sohn, 'The human rights law of the Charter', 12 *Tex. Int'l L.J.* (1977), 129.

3 *See* text at notes 5–15 *infra.*

4 As the author did some years ago, when he concluded that the four characteristics mentioned in the Charter 'surely are intended to be illustrative rather than exhaustive'. R. Lillich, 'Duties of States regarding the civil rights of aliens', 161 *Recueil des Cours* (Hague Academy of International Law) (1978–III), 333, at 395. For the 'teleological approach' to the issue under discussion, see M. McDougal, H. Lasswell and J. Miller, *The Interpretation of Agreements and World Public Order*, 457–8 (1967).

5 GA Res. 217A, 3(1) UN GAOR 71, UN doc. A/810 (1948), reprinted in R. Lillich, *supra* note 1, at 440.1–440.7.

6 See D. Elles, 'Aliens and activities of the United Nations in the field of human rights', 7 *Rev. des Droits de l'Homme (Human Rights J.)* (1974), 291, at 307–8.

7 Vienna Convention on the Law of Treaties, adopted 22 May 1969, opened for signature, 23 May 1969, entered into force 27 January 1980, art. 31, UN doc. A/Conf. 39/27, reprinted in 63 *A.J.I.L.* (1969), 679. See generally R. Kearney and R. Dalton, 'The treaty on treaties', 64 *A.J.I.L.* (1970), 495.

8 That the language used in preambles of treaties (and, by extension, in norm-setting resolutions such as the Universal Declaration) can have an important legal effect is evident from the *Golder* case, [1975] *Y.B. Eur. Conv. on Human Rights*, 290, at 292; 57 *I.L.R.* 201, at 216–17.

9 Note, however, that Article 13(2) technically applies to an alien, in that it gives him the right to return to 'his' country. A stateless person, however, would be excluded from any benefit under this article, as (by definition) there would be no State to which the adjective 'his' could refer.

10 See text accompanying notes 21–30 *infra.*

11 See generally R. Higgins, *The Development of International Law through the Political Organs of the United Nations* (1963); D. Johnson, 'The effect of resolutions of the General Assembly', 32 *B.Y.I.L.* (1955–56), 97; M. Virally, 'The sources of international law', in *Manual of Public International Law*, 116, at 160–2 (M. Sorensen, ed., 1968).

12 Professor Humphrey, who was one of the Universal Declaration's drafters, now believes that it is 'part of the customary law of nations and therefore is binding on all states'. J. Humphrey, 'The International Bill of Rights: scope and implementation', 17 *Wm. & Mary L. Rev.* (1976), 527, at 529. See also M. McDougal, H. Lasswell and L. Chen, *Human Rights and World Public Order*, 274, 325, 338 (1980); L. Sohn, *supra*, note 2, at 133.

13 For domestic and international law court cases invoking the Universal Declaration, see R. Lillich, *supra*, note 1, at 440.6–440.7 and, e.g., the *Namibia* case, I.C.J. *Rep.*, 1971, 16, at 46, 76. Perhaps the best example of a State's utilisation of the Declaration may be found in the United States Memorial to the International Court of Justice in the *Hostages* case, which cited no fewer than six articles of the Declaration to establish that certain minimum standards governing the treatment of aliens exist as a matter of customary international law. Memorial of the Government of the United States of America at 71–72, Case Concerning United States Diplomatic and Consular Staff in Tehran, I.C.J. *Rep.* 1980, 3. The Declaration has also had great effect on the drafting of the constitutions of various new States. See 1 T. Franck, *Human Rights in Third World Perspective*, 1–90 (1982).

14 See R. Lillich, 'Civil rights', in *Human Rights in International Law. Legal and Policy Issues*, 115, at 116 (T. Meron, ed., 1983).

15 See R. Lillich, 'The role of domestic courts in enforcing international human

rights law', in *Guide to International Human Rights Practice*, 223, at 232–6 (H. Hannum, ed., 1984).

16 For the historical background to the International Bill of Rights, see L. Sohn, 'A short history of United Nations documents on human rights', in Commission to Study the Organization of the Peace, *The United Nations and Human Rights*, 37 (1968).

17 GA Res. 2200, 21 UN GAOR Supp. (No. 16) 52, UN doc. A/6316 (1966), reprinted in R. Lillich, *supra*, note 1, at 170.1–170.15.

18 GA Res. 2200, 21 UN GAOR Supp. (No. 16) 49, UN doc. A/6316 (1966), reprinted in R. Lillich, *supra*, note 1, at 180.1–180.16.

19 GA Res. 2200, 21 UN GAOR Supp. (No. 16) 59, UN doc. A/6316 (1966), reprinted in R. Lillich, *supra*, note 1, at 370.1–370.3.

20 In the case of the two Covenants, one may argue that some, if not all, of the norms contained therein are now part of customary international law and hence binding even on States (such as the United States) which are not parties thereto. See R. Lillich, *supra*, note 4, at 397–9.

21 See Covenant on Civil and Political Rights, *supra*, note 17, at arts. 4, 8(3), 12(3), 14(1), 18(3), 19(3), 21, 22(2) (limitations on rights). For background on such restrictions, see A. Kiss, 'Permissible limitations on rights', in *The International Bill of Rights. The Covenant on Civil and Political Rights*, 290 (L. Henkin, ed., 1981); O. Garibaldi, 'General limitations on human rights: the principle of legality', 17 *Harv. Int'l L.J.* (1976), 503. On the related question of when States may derogate from their obligation to respect the rights set out in the Covenant, see T. Buergenthal, 'To respect and to ensure: State obligations and permissible derogations', in *The International Bill of Rights. The Covenant on Civil and Political Rights, supra*, at 72; J. Hartman, 'Derogation from human rights treaties in public emergencies', 22 *Harv. Int'l L.J.* (1981), 1; R. Higgins, 'Derogations under human rights treaties', 48 *B.Y.I.L.* (1976–77), 281.

22 See text at notes 5–15 *supra*.

23 On the applicability of the two Covenants to aliens, see, e.g., D. Elles, *supra*, note 6, at 308–9; G. Goodwin-Gill, *International Law and the Movement of Persons between States*, 66–71 (1978); R. Lillich, *supra*, note 4, at 394–7.

24 See R. Lillich, *supra*, note 4, at 395; M. McDougal, H. Lasswell and L. Chen, *supra*, note 12, at 768.

25 See *The International Bill of Rights, supra*, note 21 (various authors argue for expansive interpretation of the Covenant).

26 Since 1976 aliens have been able to take part in local elections in Sweden if they have been resident for at least three years. Similar legislation has been introduced in Denmark and Norway. See Council of Europe, *Human Rights Information Sheet No. 12* (October 1982–March 1983), 87, at 88 (paragraph 7 of Resolution 790 of the Parliamentary Assembly). See also G. van den Berghe, *Political Rights for European Citizens* (1982), chapters 8 and 9.

27 See text at and accompanying Introduction, note 6.

28 '[W]hile special reservations were made for nationals in Article 2(3) for the benefit of developing countries with regard to economic rights, there is no express restriction on social and cultural rights.' D. Ellis, *supra*, note 6, at 309.

It should be stressed, as the present writer already has, that Article 2(3) 'certainly does not reflect a norm that States may discriminate against aliens either in general or under this covenant in particular. Indeed, as McDougal has pointed out, the provisions "would be totally unnecessary if States may generally discriminate against aliens".' R. Lillich, *supra*, note 4, at 395–6, citing an article now incorporated in M. McDougal, H. Lasswell and L. Chen, *supra*, note 12, at 769, n. 113.

29 See text following note 24 *supra*.

30 See also R. Lillich, *supra*, note 4, at 396.

31 See text at Chapter II, notes 16–18.

32 On the activity of the ILC generally, see R. Dhokalia, *The Codification of Public International Law*, 147–332 (1970).

33 These twenty-five topics were chosen after the ILC's consideration of H. Lauterpacht, *Survey of International Law in Relation to the Work of Codification of the International Law Commission*, UN doc. A/CN. 4/1/Rev. 1 (1949). Of the proposed topics, the ILC provisionally selected fourteen for possible treatment. State responsibility and the treatment of aliens were both among them. *See ILC YB* (1949), 280–1, UN doc. A/CN. 4/SER. A/1949 (1949).

34 See text at Chapter I, note 35.

35 See H. Lauterpacht, *supra*, note 33, at 47.

36 GA Res. 799, 8 U.N. GAOR Supp. (No. 17) 52, UN doc. A/2630 (1953).

37 See F. Garcia-Amador, 'International Responsibility', *ILC YB* (1956–II), 173, UN doc. A/CN. 4/Ser. A/1956/Add. 1 (1956) [hereinafter cited as Garcia-Amador, *First Report*]; F. Garcia-Amador, 'International Responsibility: Second Report', *ILC YB* (1957–II), 104, UN doc. A/CN. 4/Ser. A/1957/Add. 1 (1957); F. Garcia-Amador, 'International Responsibility: Third Report', *ILC YB* (1958–II), 47, UN doc. A/CN. 4/Ser. A/1958/Add. 1 (1958); F. Garcia-Amador, 'International Responsibility: Fourth Report', *ILC YB* (1959–II), 1, UN doc. A/CN. 4/Ser. A/1959/Add. 1 (1959); F. Garcia-Amador, 'International Responsibility: Fifth Report', *ILC YB* (1960–II), 41, UN doc. A/CN. 4/Ser. A/1960/Add. 1 (1960); and F. Garcia-Amador, 'International Responsibility: Sixth Report', *ILC YB* (1961–II), 1, UN doc. A/CN. 4/Ser. A/1961/Add. 1 (1961). They are conveniently collected in F. Garcia-Amador, L. Sohn and R. Baxter, *Recent Codification of the Law of State Responsibility for Injuries to Aliens*, 1–132 (1974).

38 Garcia-Amador, *First Report, supra*, note 37, at 202–3. See also F. Garcia-Amador, 'State responsibility in the light of the new trends of international law', 49 *A.J.I.L.* (1955), 339, at 343–4; F. Garcia-Amador, 'State responsibility: some new problems', 94 *Recueil des Cours* (Hague Academy of International Law) (1958–II), 365, at 426–44.

39 See, e.g., the remarks of Padilla Nervo at the ILC's 413th meeting. *ILC YB* (1957–I), 155–56, UN doc. A/CN. 4/Ser. A/1957 (1957). See also the remarks of Fitzmaurice at the 415th meeting. *Id*. at 163–5.

40 Ago's work has been characterised as being 'at such a high level of abstraction as to shed but a dim light upon specific controversies'. M. McDougal, H. Lasswell and L. Chen, *supra*, note 12, at 762 n. 92.

41 Arnold Tammes from the Netherlands, at the ILC's 1075th meeting. The distinction between the two types of rule was expressed to be that 'primary rules ... had a direct bearing on the conduct of subjects of international law', whereas 'secondary rules ... were of a functional nature and were intended to ensure the observance of the primary rules'. *ILC YB* (1970–I), 184–85, UN doc. A/CN. 4/Ser. A/1970 (1970).

42 '[I]t is one thing to define a rule and the content of the obligation it imposes and another to determine whether that obligation has been violated and what should be the consequences of the violation. Only the second aspect comes within the sphere of [State] responsibility proper ....' R. Ago, 'Second Report on State Responsibility: the origin of international responsibility', *ILC YB* (1970–II), 177–8, UN doc. A/CN.4/Ser. A/1970/Add. 1 (1970).

43 On the legal issues raised by these expulsions, see J. Bonee, 'Caesar Augustus and the flight of the Asians — the international legal implications of the Asian expulsions from Uganda during 1972', 8 *Int'l Law.* (1974), 136.

44 For the text of the telegram, which was never despatched, see Report of the Sub-commission on Prevention of Discrimination and Protection of Minorities on its Twenty-fifth Session, at 22, UN doc. E/CN. 4/1101, E/CN. 4/Sub. 2/332 (1972).

45 *Id.* at 60.

46 Res. 6, Commission on Human Rights, Report on the Twenty-ninth Session, 54 UN ESCOR Supp. (No. 6) 98, UN doc. E/5265, E/CN. 4/1127 (1973).

47 See text at note 11 *supra*.

48 See text at notes 12–14 *supra*.

49 Declaration on the Granting of Independence to Colonial Countries and Peoples, GA Res. 1514, 15 UN GAOR Supp. (No. 16) 66, UN doc. A/4684 (1960), reprinted in R. Lillich, *supra*, note 1, at 460.1–460.2.

50 Permanent Sovereignty over Natural Resources, GA Res. 1803, 17 UN GAOR Supp. (No. 17) 15–16, UN doc. A/5217 (1962), reprinted in *Human Rights. A Compilation of International Instruments*, UN doc. ST/HR/1/Rev. 1 (1978).

51 Declaration on the Protection of all Persons from being Subjected to Torture and other Cruel, Inhuman or Degrading Treatment or Punishment, GA Res. 3452, 30 UN GAOR Supp. (No. 34) 91–2, UN doc. A/1034 (1975), reprinted in R. Lillich, *supra*, note 1, at 480.1–480.3.

52 UN doc. E/CN. 4/Sub. 2/L. 598 (1974).

53 For a summary of this discussion, see Report of the Sub-commission on Prevention of Discrimination and Protection of Minorities on its Twenty-seventh Session, at 22–6, UN doc. E/CN. 4/1160, E/CN. 4/Sub. 2/354 (1974).

54 *Id.* at 56.

55 *Id.*

56 D. Elles, 'The Problem of the Applicability of Existing International Provisions for the Protection of Human Rights to Individuals who are not Citizens of the Country in which they Live', UN doc. E/CN. 4/Sub. 2/L. 628 and Add. 1–4 (1975). On the early phases of the Elles draft declaration, see R. Lillich, 'The problem of the applicability of existing international provisions for the protection of human rights to individuals who are not citizens of the country in which they live', 70 *A.J.I.L.* (1976), 507.

57 D. Elles, 'The Problem of the Applicability of Existing International Provisions for the Protection of Human Rights to Individuals who are not Citizens of the Country in which they Live', UN doc. E/CN. 4/Sub. 2/369 and Add. 1–3 (1976).

58 D. Elles, 'The Problem of the Applicability of Existing International Provisions for the Protection of Human Rights to Individuals who are not Citizens of the Country in which they Live', UN doc. E/CN. 4/Sub. 2/392 (1977). It is substantially this version of the report which was later released for circulation to the general public as D. Elles, 'International Provisions Protecting the Human Rights of Non-citizens', UN doc. E/CN. 4/Sub. 2/392/Rev. 1 (1980).

59 The latest version of which is UN doc. E/CN. 4/1336 (1978), reprinted in D. Elles, 'International Provisions Protecting the Human Rights of Non-citizens', *supra*, note 58, at 53-4, also appearing in this volume as Appendix A.

60 On the Elles draft declaration generally, see R. Lillich and S. Neff, 'The treatment of aliens and international human rights norms: overlooked developments at the UN', 21 *Ger. Y.B. Int'l L.* (1978), 97, from which the following discussion draws heavily.

61 See, e.g., the 1974 draft, *supra*, note 52.

62 The phraseology, however, is not always identical.
63 *United States and Cuban Allied Works Eng'g Corp.* v. *Lloyds*, 291 F. 889 (2nd Cir. 1923), remanded for lack of jurisdiction, 265 U.S. 454 (1924).
64 *Pearl Assur. Co.* v. *Harrington*, 38 F. Supp. 411 (D. Mass.), aff'd per curiam, 313 U.S. 549, petition for rehearing denied, 314 U.S. 707 (1941).
65 See generally D. Williams, 'Consular access to detained persons', 29 *I.C.L.Q.* (1980), 238. It is worth noting that Article 38(1) of the UN's *Standard Minimum Rules for the Treatment of Prisoners* guarantees that alien prisoners be allowed 'reasonable facilities' for communication with the diplomatic and consular representatives of their home States. See UN Standard Minimum Rules for the Treatment of Prisoners, E.S.C. Res. 663(c), 24 UN ESCOR Supp. (No. 1) 11, UN doc. E/3048 (1957), reprinted in R. Lillich, *supra*, note 1, at 450.1–450.13.
66 See generally J. Claydon, 'Internationally uprooted people and the transnational protection of minority culture', 24 *N.Y.L. Sch. L. Rev.* (1978), 125.
67 See text at Chapter I, notes 13–15 and 66–70.
68 Res. 9, Report of the Sub-commission on Prevention of Discrimination and Protection of Minorities on its Thirty-first Session, at 69–70, UN doc. E/CN. 4/1296, E/CN. 4/Sub. 2/417 (1978).
69 Res. 16, Commission on Human Rights, Report on the Thirty-first Session, [1979] ESCOR UN Supp. (No. 6) 123, UN doc. E/1979/36, E/CN. 4/1347 (1979).
70 Res. 19, Commission on Human Rights, Report on the Thirty-sixth Session, [1980] UN ESCOR Supp. (No. 3) 179–80, UN doc. E/1980/13, E/CN. 4/1408 (1980).
71 Res. 1980/29, Resolutions and Declarations of the Economic and Social Council, [1980] UN ESCOR Supp. (No. 1) 20, UN doc. E/1980/80 (1980).
72 See Appendix B.
73 GA Res. 165, 36 UN GAOR (101st plen. mtg.) 2, UN doc. A/Res/36/165 (1982).
74 Baroness Elles has acknowledged the connection between her efforts at promoting a declaration and Garcia-Amador's earlier work. Indeed, she states in her final report that the adoption of her draft declaration on the rights of aliens would be in line with suggestions which Garcia-Amador has made. D. Elles, 'International Provisions Protecting the Human Rights of Non-citizens', *supra*, note 58, at 52.

CHAPTER FOUR

Other multilateral developments: refugees, stateless persons and migrant workers

A. Conventions on refugees and stateless persons

1. General background

As the discussion in Chapter II noted, a refugee is a person who is unable or unwilling to invoke the protection of his State of nationality because of a well founded fear of persecution.[1] During World War II and the years immediately following, however, there appeared several other categories of persons whose plight was subsumed under other, more ominous-sounding juridical labels. Terms such as 'displaced persons' and 'expellees' came to haunt both the readers of daily newspapers and the negotiators of international agreements. The former term referred to persons who had been removed forcibly from their homes for such purposes as forced labour in Nazi Germany (World War II generated a staggering total of some 40 million such persons).[2] 'Expellees', on the other hand, referred to persons of German extraction who had been uprooted from the various eastern European States after the war and sent to live in defeated and occupied Germany proper. There were some 12 million persons in this category.[3]

In contrast to these numbing figures, the number of refugees, technically speaking, which emerged from the war was surprisingly small — some 800,000 are recorded as having been expatriated from areas occupied or dominated by Nazi Germany.[4] The two most important organisations which dealt with this post-World War II refugee problem were the International Refugee Organisation[5] (a UN body, which existed from 1946 to 1952), and the Intergovernmental Committee for European Migration.[6]

Since the late 1940s and early 1950s, however, there have been massive changes in the refugee picture. The problems of displaced persons and expellees have largely faded into history. The refugee phenomenon, in striking contrast, far from fading away or even diminishing, has grown enormously. For some three decades now, the seemingly endless stream of conflicts within and between Third World countries (sometimes, as in Vietnam and Afghanistan, involving the great powers as well) have made the refugee an all too familiar sight on all continents: from south-east Asia, to Bangladesh, to Afghanistan and Pakistan, to Palestine, Somalia, Sudan, and to Cuba, Haiti and El Salvador in the New World, to name only a few of the most obvious examples. A United States government commission reporting on the refugee phenomenon several years ago highlighted the alarming scale of the phenomenon when it noted that there are approximately 17 million to 20 million refugees throughout the world.[7] The presence of floating groups of oppressed and miserable persons presents the international community today with one of its greatest challenges.

To date, the response of the international community has not come close to coping with the refugee problem. The present state of international law is such that little can be done beyond attempting to ensure that persons who become refugees receive reasonably humane treatment at the hands of whatever State acts as their (often reluctant) host. Since dealing with the root problems which cause persons to become refugees is more a matter of politics than of law, progress, unhappily, has been discouragingly slight in the refugee area.

2. The basic UN mechanisms for the protection of refugees

Two mechanisms for the protection of the rights of refugees exist within the framework of the UN: first, the activities of the UN High Commissioner for Refugees;[8] second, the Convention Relating to the Status of Refugees, concluded in 1951[9] and amended by a Protocol in 1967.[10] This section will give a brief outline of both of these aspects of refugee protection.

The office of the UN High Commissioner for Refugees is the successor of two earlier UN bodies: the UN Relief and Rehabilitation Administration (UNRRA), established in 1943, and its immediate successor body, the International Refugee Organisation (IRO), which functioned until 1952.[11] These two bodies were designed to handle the enormous refugee problems which followed World War II. The intention — or, rather, one should say the hope — was that this post-war European problem could be solved and that then these bodies could be disbanded. Although the post-World War II problems were eventually resolved, solving the host of new refugee problems around the world proved to be impossible. Thus it became necessary to establish the Office of the High Commissioner for Refugees.

The High Commissioner is a kind of international ombudsman, performing for refugees some of the tasks which States ordinarily provide for their nationals under the system of diplomatic protection of nationals abroad. More specifically, he acts in two capacities: first, under a mandate of the UN General Assembly (which is embodied in the Statute of the High Commissioner); and, second, under the 1951 Refugees Convention. A brief word may be in order about each of these roles.

Article 1 of the High Commissioner's Statute entrusts him with two tasks: first, providing international protection to refugees; and, second, 'seeking permanent solutions for the problems of the refugees'.[12] This latter mandate includes such tasks as facilitating voluntary repatriation of refugees, and assisting with their assimilation into new national communities. The Office of the High Commissioner has never been made a permanent part of the UN structure — a fact which is more indicative of hope than of realism. The original mandate was for three years beginning on 1 January 1951.[13] Since the expiry of that deadline, however, the Office has been continued for successive five-year intervals, the present one expiring at the end of 1988.[14]

Apart from his mandate from the General Assembly, the High Commissioner has important functions under the 1951 Refugees Convention, the second major mechanism within the UN for the protection of refugees. This Convention, as originally drafted, was narrower in scope than the mandate of the Statute of the High Commissioner, applying only to persons who had become refugees as a result of events occurring prior to 1 January 1951 — a temporal restriction removed by the 1967 Protocol.[15]

3. A Note on the problem of statelessness

Before considering the 1951 Refugees Convention, it is appropriate to draw attention briefly to the phenomenon of statelessness. In quantitative terms, statelessness is not the problem now that it was during the years before, during and immediately following World War II.[16] Nevertheless, the legal problems posed by the phenomenon continue to be serious. The justification for dealing with it here is that the legal measures which have been devised to cope with the problem parallel very closely those measures pertaining to refugees.

A stateless person differs from an 'ordinary' alien in that he is an alien everywhere and a national nowhere, whereas ordinary aliens are typically nationals of one State and aliens everywhere else. This apparently minor distinction should not lull one into thinking that the problems of stateless persons differ only in minor ways from the problems of other aliens. One important difference is that stateless persons are unable to benefit from the law of diplomatic protection of nationals abroad, since the right of protection, with certain minor exceptions, is available only when the link of nationality is present.[17] Still more serious is the fact that a stateless person may find himself effectively unable to travel internationally, since he usually lacks a passport, which functions not simply as an identification document but also — and sometimes more importantly — as a guarantee on the part of the issuing State to other States that it will accept the passport holder back into its territory in the event of the holder being expelled or deported.[18] In the absence of such a guarantee, countries are very reluctant to accept an alien into their territory. A person without a passport or nationality, then, faces the horrifying prospect of spending literally his entire life being shunted from one frontier to another in the desperate hope that some State for some reason may be induced to accept him.[19]

There are two international conventions which deal with the problem of statelessness: the Convention on the Status of Stateless Persons[20] (concluded in 1954, in force since 1960), and the Convention on the Reduction of State-lessness[21] (concluded in 1961, in force since 1975). The latter convention, as its title indicates, is concerned with reducing the problem of statelessness itself.[22] It does so, basically, by obligating States parties to grant nationality, in various specified circumstances, to persons who would otherwise be state-less. Similarly, it also restricts the right of States to deprive persons of their nationality if doing so would render the individuals concerned stateless. Since the convention does not really deal with the ongoing problems of persons who are stateless (for whatever reason), it is not of direct relevance to this discussion.

More important for present purposes is the 1954 Convention on the status of stateless persons.[23] Its provisions dovetail very closely the provisions of the Refugees Convention,[24] so the two will be taken up together here. The few areas in which the two conventions differ will be pointed out in the course of the discussion.

4. The Refugees and Stateless Persons Conventions — *general approaches*

While these two instruments represent a major step forward in the concern of the international community with the rights of aliens, they nevertheless have their shortcomings. For example, they do not grant refugees (or stateless persons) an affirmative right to enter the territory of States parties, although (as the discussion below will point out) there are restrictions, in the case of refugees, on sending persons back to their home States to face persecution.[25] In this regard, the UN's approach is more cautious than that of the League of Nations, whose 1933 convention on refugees provided for such a right.[26] Also of interest is the fact that Article 3(1) of the UN General Assembly's Declaration on Territorial Asylum of 1967 provides that '[n]o person seeking asylum from persecution shall be subject to measures such as rejection at the frontier ...'.[27] The Organisation of African Unity's 1969 Convention on Refugee Problems in Africa[28] contains wording similar to that of the 1967 Declaration, allowing one to argue that that convention accepts in principle this limited right of refugees to enter the territory of host countries.[29]

A point worth noting in the case of the Refugees Convention is that it does not resolve the fundamental problems which refugees pose for the international community. For instance, it does not require States hosting refugees to integrate them completely into their social, economic, political, and legal fabric. Instead, it contains a laundry list of particular rights to which refugees are entitled. The nearest the Refugees Convention comes to a general commit-ment is Article 34, which requires that States parties 'as far as possible facilitate the assimilation and naturalisation of refugees. They shall in particular make every effort to expedite naturalisation proceedings. ...' States are allowed to make reservations to this article, however, and some have done so.[30] In short, the Refugees Convention is clearly not a 'Convention on the Reduction of Refugeehood'.

Basically, the Convention simply acknowledges the refugees' presence and attempts to better their lot by ensuring them certain minimal rights. 'Permanent solutions' are left, as noted above, to the High Commissioner for Refugees. In light of the serious refugee crises which arose in several parts of the world in the late 1970s and early 1980s — such as South-east Asia, Afghanistan, Somalia and Central America — it is apparent that a more systematic approach to the problem is needed. What is required is some kind of quasi-comprehensive multinational arrangement for sharing the refugee burden, which at present falls unfairly on a few States, such as Thailand, Malaysia, Hong Kong, Pakistan, and the Sudan. As the 'system' now functions the politics of refugee assistance and resettlement are rather a diplomatic prisoner's dilemma. Any State unilaterally deciding to be generous thereby eases pressure on the non-co-operating States and reduces the incentive of the international community to develop the type of strong machinery for co-operation which is needed. Clearly, there is a great deal which remains to be achieved in this field.

5. The Refugees and Stateless Persons Conventions — specific provisions

A brief analysis of the contents of the two conventions is now in order. The specific rights and freedoms which they articulate fall, for present purposes, into two broad categories: first, those rights (referred to here as 'basic rights') which are laid down in absolute terms and which bear no expressed relation to rights enjoyed by other groups (such as nationals of the host country, other categories of aliens, and so forth); and, second, those rights (referred to here as 'equated rights') whose precise content is not specified in absolute terms but, rather, is expressed as being equal to rights possessed by other groups of persons. The basic rights, therefore, are common to refugees and stateless persons in all States parties to the two conventions. The equated rights, on the other hand, will vary between one host country and another, since those rights are based on whatever rights — many or few in number — that host countries have chosen to grant the other groups in question. This discussion will outline in brief fashion these two categories of rights.

a. The basic rights   One of the most important of the basic rights is non-discrimination, set forth in Article 3 of both conventions. It must be noted, however, that this non-discrimination norm does not refer to non-discrimination between refugees (or stateless persons) and some other group, such as nationals of the host country. Rather, it refers to non-discrimination *within* the class of refugees (or stateless persons) on the basis of race, religion, or country of origin. In other words, a host State, under Article 3, may not treat black and white refugees differently. However, it may treat refugees as a class differently from, say, other classes of aliens.

Another important basic rights is the right of access to courts of the host country (Article 16 of each convention). Also, refugees and stateless persons are to be exempt, after three years' residence in the host country, from conditions of legislative reciprocity (Article 7 of each convention). What these last provisions refer to is the practice of many States, particularly civil law ones, of making the rights granted aliens by statute conditional upon the aliens' home State granting reciprocal rights to host State nationals.

In the field of labour law, refugees and stateless persons have the basic right, again after three years' residence in the host State, to be free from measures designed to protect the nationals of the host country. In addition, host States may not apply such restrictive measures to refugees who have either a spouse or a child who is a national of the host State (Article 17 of both conventions).

Refugees also have the basic rights to be issued with valid identity papers and travel documents by the host State (Articles 27 and 28). Upon resettlement outside the host State, they have the basic right to take with them any assets which they brought into the host country (Article 30).

The most important of the basic rights protects refugees from expulsion from the host State. Article 32 of the Refugees Convention[31] (Article 31 of the Stateless Persons Convention) concerns expulsion in general: the host State may not expel a refugee or stateless person except on grounds of national security or public order, in which case the person concerned is entitled to certain minimal procedural guarantees. Article 33 of the Refugees Convention treats a special type of expulsion — *refoulement*, the returning of the refugee to the frontier of a country where his life or freedom would be threatened on the ground of his race, religion, nationality, or membership of a particular social or political group. Exceptions to this *non-refoulement* rule are permitted only in the case of refugees who are a security risk to the host State or who, having been convicted of a 'particularly serious crime', represent a danger to the community. The Stateless Persons Convention, it should be noted, does not contain a provision analogous to Article 33.

The provisions regarding the basic rights of refugees who enter the host State illegally merit special attention. (Again, no corresponding provisions exist for stateless persons.) Whether entry into the territory of the host State is lawful or not has no bearing on an individual's status as a refugee. It does have some bearing, however, on the treatment to which he is entitled at the hands of the host State. Unfortunately, the Refugees Convention is neither notably humane nor clear on this question. The basic provision on unlawful entry (Article 31) provides that, if the unlawful entrant presents himself without delay to the host State authorities and shows good cause for his illegal entry or presence, then the host State shall not 'impose penalties'.

This last provision is much less liberal than one might suppose. In the first place, it is not clear whether it prohibits the prosecution and conviction of the refugee for unlawful entry. It may mean only that, *after* convicting the refugee, the State may not impose penalties such as imprisonment upon him or her. Private employers, however, may be free to discriminate against the refugee on the ground that he possesses a criminal record. A second noteworthy point is that Article 31 does not require the host State to recognise the person in question as being lawfully in the territory after he presents himself. It thereby remains free to withhold from the individual in question the benefits of a number of provisions of the convention which are expressly guaranteed only to refugees lawfully in the territory, such as the rights relating to association (Article 15), wage-earning employment (Article 17), housing (Article 21), public relief (Article 23),[32] and — most important of all — protection from ordinary expulsion (i.e. to States other than ones which will persecute the refugee), together with the related procedural guarantees. In short, one might say that if refugees are second-class citizens of their host State, then refugees entering unlawfully — even if they duly present and explain themselves — are doubly handicapped by being, in effect, second-class refugees. In this area, as in many others, there is a need on the part of the international community to develop a coherent — and humane — body of law relating to illegal aliens.

b. The equated rights   As noted above, the so-called equated rights in the two conventions are those rights which are not uniform for all refugees and stateless persons but, rather, are expressed in terms of rights which each host State grants to various other categories of persons. There are four such categories to which the rights of refugees are equated: (1) nationals of the State from which the refugees (or stateless persons) have come; (2) nationals of the host country; (3) aliens of the most favoured category; and (4) aliens generally, under the law of the host State. In the case of stateless persons, there are no rights in category 3. Only a brief summary of each of these categories is possible here.

The most important respect in which the rights of a refugee (or stateless person) are equated to the rights of persons from his or her home State is in the area of personal status: Article 12 of the Refugee Convention (also Article 12 of the Stateless Persons Convention) provides that the personal status of a refugee (or stateless person), which would determine such matters as the capacity of the person to enter into contracts or the validity of a marriage, is determined by the law of the country of his domicile.

The rights of refugees and stateless persons are equated to the rights of nationals of the host country in the following instances: freedom of religion and religious education of children (Article 4 of both conventions); protection of artistic and industrial property rights (Article 14 of both conventions); eligibility for legal assistance (Article 16 of both conventions); participation in rationing systems if such exist in the host State (Article 20 of both conventions); the right to elementary education (Article 22 of both conventions); the right to public relief (Article 23 of both conventions); and, generally, rights under labour and social security legislation (Article 24 of both conventions).

With respect to the following matters, refugees — but not stateless persons — are to receive equal treatment with whatever category of aliens is accorded the most favourable treatment by the host State: the formation of non-political and non-profit-making associations and trade unions (Article 15 of the Refugees Convention), and the engaging in wage-earning employment (Article 17 of the Refugees Convention). In both these respects, stateless persons receive treatment not less favourable than that accorded to aliens generally (Articles 15 and 17 of the Stateless Persons Convention).

In the following respects, both refugees and stateless persons are granted the same rights that the host State grants to aliens generally: rights relating to property (Article 13 of both conventions); the right to engage in self-employment or to practise a liberal profession (Articles 18 and 19 respectively of both conventions); housing (Article 21 of both conventions); public education above the elementary level (Article 22 of both conventions); and freedom of movement within the host State (Article 26 of both conventions).[33]

B. International Labour Organisation Migrant Workers Conventions

1. General background

During the nineteenth century the phenomenon of migrant labour was perceived as a blessing rather than as a problem. In the high days of *laissez-faire*, with its ethos of free enterprise and ready movement of labour and capital, even the system of requiring travellers to carry passports with them fell into disuse.[84] The problems of migrant labour were simply the problems of labour generally. This century, however, has witnessed a dramatic change, spurred in large part by World War I, with its welter of restrictions and controls. It was then that the phenomenon of international migration for employment began to command attention as a problem in its own right.

To the credit of the international community, concern for the well-being of migrant workers has manifested itself more or less continuously since World War I. In the Versailles Treaty, for instance, which laid down the general principles for the new International Labour Organisation (ILO), Article 427 stated that 'the standard set by law in each country with respect to the conditions of labour should have due regard to the equitable economic treatment of all workers lawfully resident therein'. At its very first session in 1919 the International Labour Conference (which is the general assembly of the ILO) adopted as one of its aims the promotion of equality of treatment for migrant workers *vis-à-vis* nationals, and the bilateral and tripartite co-ordination of migration policies.[35]

The ILO's position is and has been that its conventions and recommendations generally protect nationals and aliens equally.[36] The present concern, however, is with those instruments which by their very nature deal with problems affecting alien workers. In this regard, some of the Organisation's earliest work was in the field of accident compensation: the Equality of Treatment (Accident Compensation) Convention, 1925 (No. 19),[37] and the accompanying Equality of Treatment (Accident Compensation) Recommendation, 1925 (No. 25).[38] The next year witnessed the adoption of the Inspection of Emigrants Convention, 1926 (No. 21).[39] In the following decade there was activity in the area of social security: the Maintenance of Migrants' Pension Rights Convention, 1935 (No. 48).[40] Then, at last, came two general instruments for the protection of migrant workers: the Migration for Employment Convention, 1939 (No. 66),[41] and the Migration for Employment Recommendation, 1939 (No. 61).[42] This last convention, which never came into force,[43] was superseded by the adoption of the Migration for Employment Convention (Revised), 1949 (No. 97),[44] together with the Migration for Employment Recommendation (Revised), 1949 (No. 86).[45] In the following years the Protection of Migrant Workers (Underdeveloped Countries) Recommendation, 1955 (No. 100)[46] and the Equality of Treatment (Social Security) Convention, 1962 (No. 118) were adopted.[47] The most recent developments, both in 1975, are the Migrant Workers (Supplementary Provisions) Convention, 1975 (No. 143)[48] and the Migrant Workers Recommendation, 1975 (No. 151).[49]

The most basic of these various instruments protecting migrant workers is the Migration for Employment Convention (Revised), 1949 (No. 97), which came into force in 1952.[50] This discussion will therefore focus first on this convention and its accompanying recommendation, and will then consider briefly the 1975 convention and recommendation.[51]

2. The 1949 Convention and Recommendation

The structure of the 1949 Convention is somewhat complicated. On the one hand, it consists of certain core or basic provisions, together with, on the other hand, three annexes which contain more elaborate provisions. While States parties are obligated to implement the core provisions, they are free to exclude any or all of the annexes if they so declare.[52] In general, the core provisions relate to furnishing migrants with accurate information and also guaranteeing equality with nationals in a number of employment-related areas. Annex I is a more detailed code for the recruitment, placement, and conditions of those migrant workers recruited by private groups (such as special recruitment agencies or employers hiring on their own account). Annex II is a similarly oriented code covering recruitment taking place under government sponsorship. Annex III concerns the importation into the host country of the personal effects of migrant workers. Only a brief discussion of the more salient parts of the core provisions and of the first two annexes is possible here.

As noted above, one of the major concerns of the core provisions is to ensure that potential migrants have access to accurate information about their prospects before departing from their State. States parties are accordingly to maintain a free service to assist migrants with employment, provide them with information, and take steps against misleading propaganda relating to emigration and immigration.

Article 6 sets out the basic right of migrants to equality of treatment with nationals in the following areas:

1 Remuneration (including family allowances if they form part of remuneration).
2 Hours of work, overtime arrangements, and holidays with pay.
3 Restrictions on home work.
4 Minimum age for employment.
5 Apprenticeship and training.
6 Provisions relating to work by women and young persons.
7 Membership of trade unions and enjoyment of the benefits of collective bargaining.
8 Accommodation.
9 Social security.
10 Employment taxes, dues, or contributions; and
11 Legal proceedings relating to matters covered by the convention.

Article 9 of the convention (also part of the core provisions) concerns the transfer of earnings and savings by migrants. States parties undertake to permit such transfers as the migrants may desire, 'taking into account the limits allowed by national laws and regulations concerning export and import of currency'. The requirement 'taking into account' the national laws appears to mean that the right to transfer savings and earnings is not unlimited. Exactly what the limits are, however, is very difficult to say. As will be recalled, phraseology of this kind appears in the Elles draft Declaration;[53] it is also found in bilateral treaties relating to migrant labour, which will be discussed in Chapter VI.[54]

Annex I to the convention (adherence to which is optional for States parties) concerns recruitment and placement of workers other than under government-sponsored arrangements for group transfer. Its basic thrust is to ensure at least a measure of supervision by the State where the recruiting takes place, even if the public authorities there have no direct interest in the employment. Particularly important is Article 5, which provides that the migrant be furnished with a copy of his contract of employment before his departure for the host country (or, if the governments concerned agree, the contract can be furnished at a reception centre in the host State). The contract must indicate the conditions of work and the remuneration involved. Also, the migrant must receive in writing before his departure information concerning the general conditions of life and work which he can expect in the host country. Anyone who promotes clandestine or illegal immigration is to be subjected to 'appropriate penalties' according to Article 8.

Annex II, relating to the recruitment, conditions and placing of migrant labour under government-sponsored arrangements for group transfer, is broadly similar to Annex I but contains several extra protective measures. For instance, Article 8 requires that the competent authority in the host State take '[a]ppropriate measures' to assist migrants during their initial period in matters relating to the conditions of their employment. There also is a provision in Article 10 that the host State, in the case of a migrant worker who is found to be unsuitable for the employment for which he was engaged, must assist the worker in finding 'suitable employment which does not prejudice national workers'. It is obliged to see to his maintenance pending such new placement or to his resettlement elsewhere.

Recommendation 86, which accompanied the 1949 Convention, contains more detailed provisions than does the convention concerning recruitment procedures. In terms of substantive rights, however, two points are noteworthy. The first is the priviso that any restrictions on the employment of migrant workers should be removed in the case of migrants who have resided regularly in the country for a period the length of which should not, as a rule, exceed five years. The other substantive point is that States are urged not to remove persons from their territory on the ground of lack of means or the softness of the employment market, unless an agreement between the sending and the receiving States so permits. Even if such an agreement exists, the recommendation sets forth certain minimal provisions concerning such matters as the exhaustion of the migrant's right to unemployment insurance benefits, transport arrangements, and so forth. In addition, the recommendation provides in Article 18 that any treaty allowing for expulsion in cases of this kind should state that 'in principle no migrant shall be removed who has been [in the host State] for more than five years'.

The final point about this 1949 initiative is that the recommendation contains, as an annex, a model bilateral agreement on temporary and permanent migration for employment.[55] This model agreement, however, appears to have had relatively little impact upon State treaty practice.

3. The 1975 Convention and Recommendation

In 1970s interest in migrant labour once again came to the fore in the ILO. At the 1974 International Labour Conference work commenced on the drafting of new instruments covering some of the gaps left by the 1949 ones. The result was the adoption in 1975 of the Migrant Workers (Supplementary Provisions) Convention, 1975 (No. 143), together with the Migrant Workers Recommendation, 1975 (No. 151).

The 1975 ILO Convention[56] is really two separate conventions welded into one. Part I is concerned with migration in abusive conditions, while Part II provides for equality of opportunity and treatment of migrant workers. States parties are free to exclude either one of these parts at the time of ratification.

Part I of the 1975 Convention, on migration in abusive conditions, contains in Article 1 the general obligation of each State party to respect the 'basic human rights of all migrant workers' (this undertaking is not confined, one should note, to legal migrants alone). States are to adopt 'all necessary and appropriate measures' to suppress both the clandestine movement of workers and the illegal employment of migrants, with a view to prosecuting traffickers in manpower regardless of the country from where they exercise their activities. States must provide for the application of administrative, civil and penal sanctions — the latter must include the ability to imprison — against employers of illegal immigrants (something for which federal law in the United States, for example, does not yet provide).[57]

Part I does contain some provisions which relate to the general welfare of migrants. Article 8, for instance, provides that, where a legal migrant is made redundant, his loss of employment shall not lead to the withdrawal of either a residence or a work permit. A legal migrant in such a position shall enjoy equality with nationals regarding security of employment, the provision of alternative employment, relief work, and the right to retraining. Significantly, Article 9 provides that even illegal migrants and their families shall enjoy equal treatment with nationals regarding rights arising out of past employment, such as remuneration and social security. In other words, a migrant worker can sue a former employer for, say, unpaid wages even if his employment was illegal. This provision does not, however, preclude the host State from taking appropriate civil or criminal action against an alien's possible illegal activities.

Part II of the 1975 Convention, concerning equality of opportunity and treatment, is confined to legal migrants. The basic obligation of States parties is set out in Article 10: to declare and pursue a national policy to promote equality of treatment between migrant workers and nationals in the areas of employment and occupation, social security, trade union and cultural rights and individual and collective freedoms generally. This provision is fairly far-reaching in principle, although in detail Part II is actually rather modest. The specific steps which States parties must take are the following:

1 The formulation of a social policy to enable migrants and their families to 'share in advantages enjoyed by nationals' while at the same time taking account of the 'special needs' of migrants during their period of adaptation to their new environment.

2 The encouragement of efforts of migrants and their families to 'preserve their national and ethnic identity and their cultural ties with their country of origin, including the possibility for children to be given some knowledge of their mother tongue'; and

3 The guaranteeing of equality of treatment regarding working conditions (curiously, the provision seems to refer to migrants' having the right to be treated equally with other migrants performing the same activity, rather than with nationals).

In addition, the convention provides that States parties:

1 *May* facilitate the reunification of families of migrant workers (this measure is particularly important — even though it could be more strongly worded — since the 1949 Convention did not have analogous provisions on family reunification); and

2 *Must* allow a migrant free choice of employment at the end of his first working contract or of two years, whichever is earlier.

The Migrant Workers Recommendation, 1975 (No. 151), contains a wealth of measures designed to promote the human rights and improve the general well-being of migrant workers. It is possible in this context to give only a few examples of the liberality of this instrument. In the area of equal treatment with nationals, for example, there is express mention of access to vocational guidance and placement services; to advancement in accordance with individual character, experience, ability, and diligence; and to the right of eligibility for office in trade unions. The provisions on family reunification are couched in much stronger language than in the 1975 Convention: under Article 13 States should take '[a]ll possible measures' to facilitate family reunification. There also are fairly extensive provisions relating to the protection of the health of migrants, to the provision of social services, and to the protection from expulsion of migrants upon loss of employment.

With these ILO provisions in mind, the discussion now may proceed to treat briefly the latest measure for the protection of the rights of migrant workers, still in the pre-natal stage: the draft UN Convention on the Protection of the Rights of all Migrant Workers and their Families.

C. Draft UN Migrant Workers Convention

Simultaneously — and to some extent in competition with — the ongoing activities of the ILO, the UN has been showing great interest in migrant workers.[58] The first aspect of this problem claiming the UN's attention was illicit and clandestine trafficking in labour, a subject which the General Assembly, at its 1972 session, asked the Commission on Human Rights to consider.[59] The Commission in turn entrusted the Sub-commission on Prevention of Discrimination and Protection of Minorities with the question.[60]

At its 1973 session the Sub-commission requested one of its members, Mrs Warzazi of Morocco, to prepare a preliminary study on illicit and clandestine labour trafficking.[61] Her report, submitted the following year, contained a number of recommendations.[62] In particular, it suggested that host States should control immigration by establishing or strengthening public agencies with a monopoly on the recruitment, admission, and placement of foreign workers. She recommended the application of severe penalties, including imprisonment, for employers who knowingly recruit illicit workers, traffickers, carriers and other persons who contribute to the illicit traffic. The report also concluded that host States should publicise the risks of exploitation in legal, economic, and social matters to which the clandestine workers are exposed.

Meanwhile another UN body, the United Nations Institute for Training and Research (UNITAR), was studying the problems involved with the migration of highly skilled manpower from developing countries, popularly known as the 'brain drain'.[63] These studies took more of an economic and sociological than a legal approach. Nevertheless, they have provided important background information which lawyers will have to consider when they come to deal with the legal issues raised by the exodus of skills from Third World countries, with all the negative implications which this phenomenon has for the economic growth of developing States.[64]

By the late 1970s, however, the UN was beginning to take an interest in broader aspects of the problems relating to migrant labour and to the question of the human rights of aliens generally. The discussion above revealed the interest which the UN is now taking in the Elles draft Declaration.[65] For present purposes, it need be noted only that in 1979 the UN also decided to draft a general convention (not merely a declaration, note) on the human rights of migrant workers and their families. That year the General Assembly resolved to establish a working group at its 1980 session, open to all member States, to elaborate such a convention.[66] Simultaneously it called for comments from States and from other UN bodies on the best approach to take towards the issue.[67]

The Assembly formally established the working group, chaired by Mr Gonzalez de Leon of Mexico, in 1980. It met for the first time that autumn and has established a pattern of semi-annual sessions. Taking the lead from its chairman,[68] the working group decided to draft an all-inclusive convention covering the whole gamut of human rights to which *all* (not just 'legal') migrant workers are entitled, rather than just those rights which pertain to the employment relationship.[69] In this respect the draft convention goes well beyond the ILO's 1975 Convention,[70] and indeed beyond the new European Convention on the Legal Status of Migrant Workers, to be considered in Chapter V.[71]

Since the working group has adopted an *ad hoc* rather than a systematic approach to elaborating the articles of the draft convention, its progress to date can be assessed only after piecing together the sixty-four articles which, after six sessions, it has tentatively approved. These articles, found in five separate reports, have been collated and are included as Appendix C to this volume. It is therefore unnecessary to paraphrase them here, as well as impracticable, since they read like a laundry list of all the basic human rights spelled out in the Universal Declaration and the two UN Covenants, as well as in numerous other international human rights instruments, including the Elles draft Declaration (e.g. Article 10 of the draft convention provides that '[m]igrant workers and members of their families shall not be subjected to torture or to cruel, inhuman or degrading treatment or punishment'). Suffice to say that not only does the draft convention guarantee migrant workers almost all previously articulated civil rights, but also most economic, social and cultural rights, plus additional rights in these last three categories of especial interest to persons in their status. Even political rights are guaranteed to migrant workers in their country of origin (Article 41) and recommended in their State of employment (Article 42).

It is far too early, of course, to judge whether this all-inclusive approach will be successful, or whether it will produce an unnecessarily lengthy and repetitious document that, even if approved by the Third Committee and adopted by the General Assembly, will fail for want of sufficient ratifications. The very fact that the basic human rights set out in Part II are deemed to cover all migrant workers — including 'illegal' migrants — will give many States pause, as it already has in the case of the Elles draft Declaration.[72] Moreover the extension of the draft convention to 'members of their families' (Article 1), broadly defined (Article 3), may further complicate matters. Thus, while the overall objectives of the exercise are laudable, the more limited, functional approach of the ILO and the Council of Europe seems preferable, given the present state of the world economy.[73] One can only hope that the controversies surrounding the UN Migrant Workers Convention do not prove so divisive as to prevent this potentially worthy effort from ever bearing fruit.

Notes

1 See text at and accompanying Chapter II, notes 43–4. On the definition of 'refugee' and on problems of eligibility for refugee status, see P. Weis, 'Concept of the refugee in international law', 87 *J. Droit Int'l* (1960), 928.

2 M. Proudfoot, *European Refugees 1939–52. A Study in Forced Population Movement*, 34 (1955). See also J. Schachtman, *European Population Transfers 1939–1945* (1946).

3 J. Vernant, *The Refugee in the Post-war World*, 95 (1953). The transfers of Germans from Poland, Czechoslovakia and Hungary were provided for by Article XIII of the Potsdam Agreements. Although that article stipulated that the transfers were to take place 'in an orderly and humane manner', such was hardly the case. Bulgaria, Rumania and Yugoslavie expelled Germans on their own initiative. *Id.* at 95–6. See generally A. de Zayas, *Nemesis at Potsdam. The Anglo-Americans and the Expulsion of the Germans* (rev. ed., 1979).

4 M. Proudfoot, *supra*, note 2, at 76–7.

5 See generally L. Holborn, *The International Refugee Organization. A Specialized Agency of the United Nations. Its History and Work 1946–1952* (1956).

6 On the activities of the Intergovernmental Committee for Migration (known as the Intergovernmental Committee for European Migration until 1980), see the *Review of Achievements* which the organisation publishes annually. The ICM, which began work in 1952, is not a UN body, although it works closely with the Office of the UN High Commissioner for Refugees. In the period 1952–80 the ICM assisted in the moving of some 2·9 million persons (nearly 1·9 million of whom were in the 'Refugees and Special Programmes' category) to new places of settlement. Intergovernmental Committee for Migration, *Review of Achievements*, 34 (1980).

7 J. Thomas, 'Undocumented aliens: some international aspects', 73 *Am. Soc. Int'l L. Proc.* (1979), 131. This figure, it might be noted, predates the Soviet military involvement in Afghanistan and the worsening conflicts in Central America.

8 On the activities of the UN High Commissioner generally, see S. Aga Khan, 'Legal problems relating to refugees and displaced persons', 149 *Recueil des Cours* (Hague Academy of International Law) (1976–I), 287, at 334–50. See generally A. Grahl-Madsen, *The Status of Refugees in International Law* (1972) (2 vols.).

9 Convention Relating to the Status of Refugees, 1951, 189 UNTS 137, reprinted in R. Lillich, *International Human Rights Instruments*, 280.1–280.30 (1983). The Office of the UN High Commissioner for Refugees reported in November 1983 that ninety-three States were parties to the Convention.

10 Protocol Relating to the Status of Refugees, 1967, 606 UNTS 267, reprinted in R. Lillich, *supra*, note 9, at 110.1–110.7. The Office of the UN High Commissioner for Refugees reported in November 1983 that ninety-three States were parties to the Protocol. Ninety-one States are parties to both instruments.

11 See *supra*, note 5.

12 For the text of the Statute, see GA Res. 428, 5 UN GAOR Supp. (No. 20) 46, UN doc. A/1775 (1950) reprinted in *Human Rights. A Compilation of International Instruments*, UN doc. ST/HR/1/Rev. 1 (1978), at 95–7.

13 GA Res. 319A, 4 UN GAOR 36, UN doc. A/1251 (1949).

14 GA Res. 32/68, 32 UN GAOR Supp. (No. 45) 140, UN doc. A/32/45 (1977).

15 *Vis-à-vis* States which are parties to the 1967 Protocol, that is. In the case of the few States which are parties to the 1951 Convention but not to the Protocol, the restriction still applies.

16 On the magnitude of the problem of statelessness during this period, see J. Carey, 'Some aspects of statelessness since World War I', 40 *Am. Pol. Sci. Rev.* (1946), 113; Department of Social Affairs, A Study of Statelessness, UN doc. E/1112 and Add. 1 (1949).

17 See, e.g., I. Brownlie, *Principles of Public International Law*, 401 (3rd ed. 1979).

18 G. Goodwin-Gill, *International Law and the Movement of Persons between States*, 26, 44–50 (1978).

19 See generally P. Weis, *Nationality and Statelessness in International Law*, 219–36 (1956).

20 Convention Relating to the Status of Stateless Persons, 1954, 360 UNTS 130, reprinted in R. Lillich, *supra*, note 9, at 300.1–300.10.

21 Convention on the Reduction of Statelessness, 1961, reprinted in R. Lillich, *supra*, note 9, at 350.1–350.6.

22 See generally P. Weis, 'United Nations Convention on the Reduction of Statelessness', 11 *I.C.L.Q.* (1962), 1073; P. van Krieken, 'The High Commissioner for Refugees and Stateless Persons', 26 *Neth. Int'l L. Rev.* (1979), 24.

23 See generally N. Robinson, *Convention Relating to the Status of Stateless Persons. Its History and Interpretation* (1955); P. Weis, 'Convention Relating to the Status of Stateless Persons', 10 *I.C.L.Q.* (1961), 255.

24 See generally N. Robinson, *Convention Relating to the Status of Refugees. Its History, Contents and Interpretation* (1953); P. Weis, 'International protection of refugees', 48 *A.J.I.L.* (1954), 193.

25 This restriction on *refoulement* of refugees (discussed below) operates indirectly to grant a right of entry to a refugee: if it happens that the only choices which a State party has before it are admitting the refugee or sending him back to his home State to face possible persecution, then the Refugees Convention requires that the State admit the person. It remains the case, however, that there is no *general* requirement to admit refugees under the Convention.

The policy of the United Kingdom in this regard follows the Convention approach closely. See para. 64 of the *Statement of Changes in Immigration Rules* (1980), which states that '[s]pecial considerations arise' in cases where the only country to which a person could be removed (on being refused leave to enter the United Kingdom) is one that would persecute him. 'Leave to enter will not be refused if removal would be contrary to the provisions of the Convention and Protocol relating to the Status of Refugees.' Under this policy, it would still be open to the United Kingdom to deny a refugee leave to enter if a third State (i.e. one other than his home State or the United Kingdom) could be induced to accept him.

United States law, at long last, has incorporated the 1951 definition of refugee into its domestic legislation (even though the United States is still technically not a party to the Convention). Refugee Act of 1980, Pub. L. No. 96–212, 94 Stat. 102 (1980). See Martin, 'The Refugee Act of 1980: its past and future', *Transnational Legal Problems of Refugees*, 1982 *Mich. Y. Int'l L. Stud.*, 91, at 101. The new statute provides that an alien will not be deported to a country if the Attorney General determines that his life or freedom would be threatened there. 8 U.S.C. § 1253(h)(l) (1982).

26 See text at Chapter II, notes 59–60.

27 GA Res. 2312, 22 UN GAOR Supp. (No.16) 81, UN doc. A/6716 (1967), reprinted in *Human Rights. A Compilation of International Instruments, supra*, note 12, at 97. Attempts to conclude a convention on territorial asylum, however, have not proved fruitful. See P. Weis, 'The draft United Nations Convention on Territorial Asylum', 50 *B.Y.I.L.* (1979), 151; and A. Grahl-Madsen, *Territorial Asylum* (1980), *passim*.

28 Organisation of African Unity, Convention Governing the Specific Aspects of Refugee Problems in Africa, reprinted in 8 *I.L.M.* (1969), 1288.

29 Article 2(3) of the OAU Convention states that '[n]o person shall be subjected by a Member State to such measures as rejection at the frontier, return or expulsion, which would compel him to return to or remain in a territory where his life, physical integrity or liberty would be threatened ...'. The language would appear to allow States to refuse entry to refugees absent the above conditions. Essentially, this provision amounts to one of *non-refoulement*, which the discussion below will cover. On the other hand, the OAU Convention is more positive than the UN's in that it at least mentions the question of admission of refugees in a separate provision from the one on *refoulement*.

30 See, e.g., R. Lillich, supra, note 9, at 280.19 (Malta).

31 On Article 32, see A. Grahl-Madsen, 'Expulsion of refugees', 33 *Nordisk Tidsskrift for International Ret* (1963), 41.

32 In the Stateless Persons Convention these rights also are expressly reserved to persons legally in the country.

33 In the case of stateless persons, as noted in the previous paragraph of the text, this list should be extended to include the rights relating to the formation of non-political

and non-profit-making associations and trade unions, and the right to engage in wage-earning employment.

34 C. Hays, *A Generation of Materialism 1871–1900*, at 76 (1941).

35 International Labour Organisation, *Conventions and Recommendations Adopted by the International Labour Conference 1919–1966*, at 11 (1966).

36 Report of the Committee of Experts on the Application of Conventions and Recommendations (Articles 19, 22 and 35 of the Constitution), General Survey of the Reports Relating to Conventions Nos. 97 and 143 and Recommendations Nos. 86 and 151 Concerning Migrant Workers, 33 (1980). There are two ILO conventions (not otherwise concerned with the problems of aliens) which expressly prohibit discrimination on the ground of nationality in their implementation: the Maternity Protection Convention (Revised), 1952 (No. 103), 214 UNTS 321; and the Plantations Convention, 1958 (No. 110), 348 UNTS 275.

37 International Labour Organisation, *supra*, note 35, at 92–3.

38 *Id.* at 94.

39 *Id.* at 99–101.

40 *Id.* at 285–91.

41 *Id.* at 438–42.

42 *Id.* at 443–6.

43 Report of the Committee of Experts on the Application of Conventions and Recommendations (Articles 19, 22 and 35 of the Constitution), *supra*, note 36, at 3.

44 International Labour Organisation, *supra*, note 35, at 743–55; 120 UNTS 71.

45 International Labour Organisation, *supra*, note 35, at 756–69.

46 *Id.* at 865–74.

47 *Id.* at 1022–7; 494 UNTS 271, reprinted in R. Lillich, *supra*, note 9, at 340.1–340.6.

48 Report of the Committee of Experts on the Application of Conventions and Recommendations (Articles 19, 22 and 35 of the Constitution), *supra*, note 36, at 171–6. The United Kingdom is a party.

49 *Id.* at 176–83.

50 *Id.* at 184. The United Kingdom has ratified the Convention. But see text at and accompanying note 52 *infra.*

51 It will not cover the question of social security. On that subject, see International Labour Office, *Social Security for Migrant Workers* (1977).

52 The United Kingdom, for instance, excluded Annexes I and II from its ratification. Report of the Committee of Experts on the Application of Conventions and Recommendations (Articles 19, 22 and 35 of the Constitution), *supra*, note 36, at 184.

53 See text at Chapter III, notes 63–4.

54 See text at Chapter VI, note 9.

55 For the text of which, see International Labour Organisation, *supra*, note 35, at 760–9.

56 On the Convention generally, see F. Russo, 'Migrant workers: existing and proposed international action on their rights', 15 *Rev. Int'l Comm'n Jur.* (1975), 51, at 55–7.

57 For pending United States legislation which would impose sanctions on employers who hire illegal immigrants, see the so-called Simpson-Mazzoli Bill, S. 529, 98th Cong., 1st Sess. (1983). See generally *Systems to Verify Authorization to Work in the United States: Hearings Before the Subcomm. on Immigration and Refugee Policy of the Senate Comm. on the Judiciary*, 97th Cong., 1st Sess. (1981); Notre Dame University Law School, Employer Sanctions Research Study, Appendix E to the Staff Report of the Select Commission on Immigration and Refugee Policy, 568 (1981). See text at and accompanying Chapter VI, notes 22–3.

58 For a useful summary of measures taken in the field of migrant labour by various UN bodies through 1978, see Report of the Secretary-General Prepared Pursuant to Paragraph 1 of Commission Resolution 21B, 'Measures to Improve the Situation and Enhance the Human Rights and Dignity of all Migrant Workers', UN doc. E/CN. 4/1325 (1978).

59 GA Res. 2920, 27 UN GAOR Supp. (No. 30) 62, UN doc. A/8730 (1972).

60 Via the Economic and Social Council. See Res. 3, Commission on Human Rights, Report on the Twenty-ninth Session, 54 UN ESCOR Supp. (No. 6) 68, UN doc. E/5265, E/CN. 4/1127 (1973), which recommended that the Economic and Social Council request the Sub-commission to consider the question. The Council duly did so. Res. 1789, 54 UN ESCOR Supp. (No. 1), 25, UN doc. E/5367 (1973).

61 Res. 6, Report of the Sub-commission on Prevention of Discrimination and Protection of Minorities on its Twenty-sixth Session, at 43, UN doc. E/CN. 4/Sub. 2/343, E/CN. 4/1128 (1973).

62 H. Warzazi, 'Exploitation of Labour through Illicit and Clandestine Trafficking', UN doc. E/CN. 4/Sub. 2/351 (1974).

63 See W. Glaser and G. Habers, *Brain Drain, Emigration and Return. Findings of a UNITAR Multinational Comparative Survey of Professional Personnel of Developing Countries who Study Abroad* (1978). See also UNCTAD, 'The Reverse Transfer of Technology: A Survey of its Main Features, Causes and Policy Implications', UN doc. TD/B/C./6/47 (1979). For a useful summary of action by various UN bodies in this area, see Report of the Secretary-General, 'The "Brain Drain" Problem: Outflow of Trained Personnel from Developing to Developed Countries', UN doc. E/1978/92 (1978).

64 See generally R. Pomp and O. Oldman, 'Tax measures in response to the brain drain', 20 *Harv. Int'l L.J.* (1979), 1.

65 See text at Chapter III, notes 43–74.

66 GA Res. 34/172, 34 UN GAOR Supp. (No. 46) 188–9, UN doc. A/34/46 (1979).

67 For the views of six States and one UN body on the subject, see Report of the Secretary-General, 'Measures to Improve the Situation and Ensure the Human Rights and Dignity of all Migrant Workers: Addendum', UN doc. A/34/535/Add. 1 (1979).

68 Working Paper Presented by the Chairman of the Working Group: Outline for an International Convention on the Protection of the Rights of all Migrant Workers and their Families, UN doc. A/C. 3/35/WG. 1/CRP. 5 (1980).

69 See Article 1 of the Draft International Convention on the Protection of the Rights of all Migrant Workers and their Families, collated at Appendix C.

70 See text following note 56 *supra*.

71 See generally text at Chapter V, notes 42–52.

72 See text at Chapter III following note 72.

73 On the effect of the 1973–1983 economic slump on attitudes towards aliens and their legal rights, see generally Chapter VII.

CHAPTER FIVE

Regional arrangements

The contemporary developments described in the last two chapters all involve attempts, primarily under UN auspices, to create or clarify norms governing the treatment of aliens on a global basis. In addition to such universal efforts, however, there have also been numerous attempts to handle the various problems of aliens through regional arrangements. The present chapter illustrates the importance of such regional approaches by examining in survey fashion a number of European initiatives, which may serve as models elsewhere and ultimately contribute to the development of norms of universal applicability.

A. Free movement of workers provisions of the European Economic Community

Ensuring free movement of workers within the ten States of the European Economic Community (EEC) is one of the express aims of the Treaty of Rome,[1] the constitutional instrument of the Community. Actually, the EEC's ambition in this area extends further. It attempts to encompass the eventual elimination of all kinds of discrimination on grounds of nationality relating to matters within the scope of the treaty (which essentially is concerned with matters of an economic nature). This norm in its most general form is set forth in Article 7 of the Treaty of Rome, which states that '[w]ithin the scope of this Treaty ... any discrimination on grounds of nationality shall be prohibited'.[2]

The more detailed formulations of this principle, however, appear in Title III of the Treaty,[3] the most important provision for present purposes being Article 48, which stipulates the realisation of free movement by the end of the transition period (i.e. by the end of 1969 for the original six States parties). Article 48(2) specifies that such freedom of movement 'shall entail the abolition of any discrimination based on nationality ... as regards employment, remuneration and other conditions of work and employment'. An exception to these rules exists in Article 48(4), however, for employment in the public service.[4]

Another important exception, found in Article 48(3), permits considerations of 'public policy, public security or public health' to justify infringements by member States of the free movement norms.[5] The European Court of Justice (ECJ) case law concerning this exception will be discussed briefly below.[6]

Since the fundamental rules concerning free movement of workers are enshrined within the Treaty of Rome itself, they do not derive their legal force from the subsidiary legislation of the EEC Commission and Council.[7] Nevertheless, these two bodies have promulgated legislation spelling out in greater detail the nature of the member States' obligations, defining and clarifying the broad language appearing in the treaty itself, and so forth. For example, Council Directive 64/221[8] defines the above-quoted phrase 'public policy, public security or public health' and is therefore of great importance for workers migrating within the EEC. The detailed rules relating to the free movement of workers are set out in Council Regulation 1612/68 'On Freedom of Movement for Workers within the Community',[9] while the mechanical and procedural aspects are the subject of the accompanying Council Directive 68/360 on 'Removal of Restrictions on Travel and Residence for Workers of the Member States and their Family Members within the Community'.[10] There is also legislation relating specifically to social security arrangements for migrating workers.[11]

An apt illustration of the relationship between the 'constitutional' norms of the Treaty of Rome, on the one hand, and the subsidiary nature of the Commission's and Council's legislation, on the other hand, may be found in *Procureur du Roi* v. *Royer*.[12] This case involved a worker from another EEC State who resided in Belgium without having complied with various administrative formalities of that country. Specifically, he had not applied for a residence permit, which Belgium was entitled to require him to do under Directive 68/360. Belgium attempted to expel Royer for this failure, but the ECJ, when the case came before it, held that it could not. The worker's right to live and work in Belgium, it decided, was guaranteed by the Treaty of Rome itself, and no subsidiary legislation could permit derogation from that basic right. It was true that member States could require workers from other EEC States to apply for permits in certain circumstances and could invoke 'appropriate sanctions' when workers failed to comply.[13] The permits, however, were mere administrative devices — i.e. they related only to the mechanics of free movement. They did not confer the substantive right itself, which came from the Treaty of Rome. Any State wishing to punish workers for failing to comply with the formalities of free movement must do so in such a way as not to infringe this substantive right. Expulsion from its territory of a national of another EEC State for offences of this nature, therefore, was not permitted.

As mentioned above, both the Treaty of Rome and subsidiary legislation allow exceptions to be made to the general freedom of movement norms in cases involving 'public policy, public security or public health'. One finds such exceptions scattered throughout almost all international human rights instruments, from the European and American Conventions on Human Rights to the International Bill of Rights to the Refugees and Stateless Persons Conventions. What is unique about the EEC's public policy exception is the extent to which it has been the subject both of detailed definition and of norm-clarifying litigation. It is surprising, therefore, that only recently has it received much attention from legal commentators.[14]

The basic subsidiary legislation in this area is Directive 64/221,[15] which articulates a number of restrictions on the potentially wide ambit of the expression 'public policy, public security or public health'. For example, the exception may not be invoked merely to serve a State's economic ends. Also, any action by a State on public policy grounds must be based exclusively on the personal conduct of the individual concerned. The directive additionally guarantees that a person whose right of free movement is being interfered with on such grounds will have the opportunity to present his case to the authorities. These and other restrictions found in Directive 64/221 have helped the ECJ to determine the scope of the public policy exception, although some commentators have suggested that additional legislative guidance is required.[16]

The ECJ's general approach to the exception, rhetorically if not always in its actual holdings, has been to interpret it strictly. Thus reasons of a 'general preventive nature' cannot justify a State's interference with the right of free movement: a State, it has been held, may not expel a worker from another EEC State simply to make an example of him to other aliens.[17] In *van Duyn* v. *Home Office*,[18] however, the first ECJ case to interpret the public policy exception, the more difficult question arose of whether membership of an officially disapproved (but not illegal) organisation constituted 'personal conduct', permitting the exclusion of a Dutch national who wished to accept employment in Great Britain with the Church of Scientology. The ECJ ruled that it did, thus establishing the principle that 'a Member State can exclude Community nationals for engaging in legal activities if it has clearly indicated that it considers these activities to be socially harmful'.[19] The ruling has been criticised for allowing governments 'to infringe on the civil liberties of non-nationals by excluding members of groups espousing disfavoured beliefs or ideologies as long as their activities have been declared to be harmful'.[20]

The weight to be given previous criminal convictions, which Directive 64/221 states shall not in themselves constitute grounds for expulsion, has also raised difficult questions. In *R.* v. *Bouchereau*[21] an EEC national had been convicted twice within six months of drug-related offences under English law. The question which the English court referred to the ECJ was whether, even if the fact of a criminal conviction could not justify expulsion in and of itself, British authorities could consider the conduct which resulted in that conviction in making their decision to invoke the public policy exception. The ECJ approached the issue cautiously, holding that the underlying conduct could be considered, but subject to certain protective criteria. Specifically, it held that a previous criminal conviction could be considered by the host State 'only ... in so far as the circumstances which gave rise to that conviction are evidence of personal conduct constituting a *present* threat to the requirements of public policy'.[22] The ECJ added, however, that 'past conduct alone may constitute such a threat to the requirements of public policy',[23] leaving it to the courts of the member States to work out individual cases on their merits.

The litigation which Article 48(3) and Directive 64/221 have spawned, which shows no signs of slackening, is an excellent example of how international law, here on a regional basis, can be used to limit the sovereign prerogatives of States and enhance the rights of aliens in one area of ever-increasing international importance. In so far as the free movement of workers within the EEC is concerned, as Goodwin-Gill has observed, '[i]nternational standards as hitherto applied are still relevant, but they have been overtaken by a substantive law which is supra-national. Within the sphere of application of the Treaties, the legality of action taken in the name of "ordre public" stands to be determined by impartial decision.'[24] It is to be hoped that in making such decisions the ECJ and the domestic courts of the EEC States will increasingly give less weight to the 'margin of appreciation' concept favouring State action,[25] and more closely confine what in many areas of the world today, in the absence of treaty regimes, still remains the unfettered freedom of decision of States as to the admission and expulsion of alien workers.

B. European Convention on Establishment, European Social Charter, and European Migrant Workers Convention

Although the EEC is the best known and most tightly integrated of the regional organisations of Europe, it has no monopoly of progressive legal measures for improving the status of aliens. In particular, several important measures have emerged from the Council of Europe, a regional organisation comprised of the democratic States of western Europe.[26] The Council of Europe differs in several respects from the EEC. One such difference is that, unlike the EEC, it is oriented towards general co-operation between the member States rather than towards more or less full integration in the economic sphere alone. Many of the Council of Europe's initiatives are of a technical nature — such as the supervision of television broadcasting, the exchange of medical reagents, and even the transfer of corpses — but some are of a more distinctly political cast than the EEC's normal concerns. This last category includes conventions on such matters as extradition or the prevention of terrorism.[27]

Since its establishment in 1949 the Council of Europe has sponsored over 100 conventions, the most important of which in the human rights area is the European Convention for the Preservation of Human Rights and Fundamental

Freedoms (concluded in 1950, in force since 1953),[28] which will be the subject of discussion in the next section. The present section will focus on three less well known Council of Europe Conventions: the European Convention on Establishment (concluded in 1955, in force since 1965);[29] the European Social Charter (concluded in 1961, in force since 1965);[30] and the European Convention on the Legal Status of Migrant Workers (concluded in 1977, in force since 1983).[31]

1. European Convention on Establishment

Although the basic purpose of the European Convention on Establishment, as expounded in Articles 1 and 2, is stated to be the facilitating of temporary visits and of long-term residence by nationals of the various States parties in each others' territories, the Convention actually appears to function more as a charter of rights for persons already settled in other countries. In a number of respects, of which the most obvious is the granting of permission to aliens to enter the territory, the Convention makes only modest inroads into the traditional international law doctrine that States have an unfettered discretion in admitting aliens.[32] It is true that, while the general goal of facilitating visits and residence by nationals of other States parties must be interpreted in good faith, according to the general law relating to treaties,[33] the fact remains that the Convention on Establishment contains a number of loopholes whereby States could follow restrictive policies without breaching their obligations.

Consider, for instance, the question of admission into the territory. Even in principle, the Convention goes no further, as just noted, than to commit States to 'facilitate' movement by nationals of other States parties. Even this obligation, however, is qualified by the *caveat* in Article 1 that the duty is not applicable when the activities of the aliens concerned 'would be contrary to *ordre public*, national security, public health or morality'. There certainly is nothing new in international law about tempering obligations by limitation provisions such as this one. The discussion above, for instance, noted the presence of such exceptions to the EEC's rules on the free movement of workers.[34] What is distinctive about the European Convention on Establishment is the latitude which the States parties are given to interpret these provisions. Section I of the Protocol to the Convention states that each party has the right to judge by 'national criteria' what these phrases mean. Furthermore, Section III(a) of the Protocol on the meaning of the term '*ordre public*' states that the expression 'is to be understood in the wide sense generally accepted in continental countries. A Contracting Party may, for instance, exclude a national of another Party for political reasons ...'.[35]

Similar considerations appear regarding the facilitating of prolonged or permanent residence. By the terms of Article 2, States parties are required to facilitate such settlement only 'to the extent permitted by ... economic and social conditions ...'. Once again, the Protocol effectively allows States to be as restrictive as they wish in this area, since the meaning of the expression 'economic and social conditions' — like that of *ordre public* — is determined by 'national criteria'.

It is perhaps understandable that the Convention should allow States to be restrictive in the admission of aliens. By refusing to admit an alien into its territory in the first place, a State does not thereby interfere with what might be termed vested rights or interests, as it might when deciding to expel an alien already in the country. One would therefore expect to see more liberal treatment of aliens in the area of expulsion than of admission. In a sense the Convention bears out this expectation. It states in Article 3(1) that host countries can expel the nationals of other States parties 'only if they endanger national security or offend against *ordre public* or morality'. In addition to this basic protection, aliens who have lawfully been in the host country for a period of at least two years receive some additional protection. Under Article 3(2) they may not be expelled, except in cases involving 'imperative considerations of national security', unless they are first allowed to submit reasons against their expulsion and to appeal to, and be represented before, a competent authority of the host State. Aliens who have lawfully resided in the host State for over ten years are even better off (at least in principle): under Article 3(3) they may be expelled only for reasons of national security or for the commission of offences 'of a particularly serious nature' against *ordre public* or morality.

The catch, however, is that once again the ambit of these various exceptions is judged by national, rather than supranational, criteria. Section I(a) of the Protocol gives each State the right to decide for itself what constitutes a threat to national security or an offence against *ordre public* or morality. Similarly, Section I(b) allows each State to decide what the expression 'particularly serious nature' in Article 3(3) means.

In sum, one might say that in the areas of admission and expulsion of aliens the European Convention on Establishment adds little, if anything, to the restraints on States found in customary international law.[36]

The position is otherwise, however, regarding aliens who are lawfully settled within the host State. The Convention accords such aliens a number of important rights worth noting, even though an extensive analysis of them here is not feasible. Most notably, aliens are entitled under the Convention to equal treatment with nationals in the following respects:

1 The 'possession and exercise of private rights' generally, whether of person or property (Article 4). This right, however, is subject to two exceptions: first, it can be restricted by the host government for 'reasons of national security or national defence' (Article 5), the meaning of 'national security' again being judged by national criteria; and, second, in cases where State laws in force at the date of signature of the Convention restricted alien

ownership of certain types of property, those types were excluded from the ambit of Article 4. States are forbidden to add further such restrictions, however, and are also obligated to endeavour to reduce the number of them (Article 6).

2 The 'full legal and judicial protection of ... persons and property and of ... rights and interests', with especial reference to the right of access to competent judicial and administrative authorities and the right to representation before these authorities (Article 7).

3 Access to legal aid (Article 8).

4 The right to engage in gainful occupation, including industrial, commercial, financial, and agricultural occupations, skilled crafts, the professions, and activities involving self-employment generally (Article 10). This right, however, is subject to a number of exceptions. In the case of short-term aliens (though not of long-term ones),[37] for instance, the host country can restrict this right for 'cogent economic or social reasons' (Article 10), judged by national criteria. Host countries are also allowed to reserve for their own nationals public functions relating to national security or defence (Article 13). In addition, there is a provision, analogous to that concerning property, which excludes from the scope of the basic Article 10 obligation any jobs in which, at the date of the Convention's signing, a State restricted alien employment. As in the case of the property restrictions, States parties cannot extend their lists of such jobs; also they are under a general obligation to reduce the number of restricted jobs and to allow individual exemptions in favour of aliens from other States parties to the extent that their laws permit (Article 14).

5 The right to benefit from any statutory regulation by public authorities concerning wages and working conditions generally (Article 17).

6 Access to public education at the primary and secondary levels and to institutions of vocational and technical training (Article 20). The application of this principle to the granting of scholarships, however, expressly remains within the discretion of the State.

7 National treatment with regard to taxes, duties, charges, social contributions, and the like (Article 21).

8 The obligation to perform civilian services (Article 22); and

9 The right to compensation upon the expropriation or nationalisation of property (Article 23).

It also is worth noting that the Convention prohibits host States from preventing aliens who have been lawfully employed for at least five years from taking part on an equal footing with nationals in elections held by such bodies as chambers of commerce or trade unions (Article 18). The prohibition falls short, however, of granting full national treatment to such aliens, because apparently the bodies *themselves* remain free to impose restrictions of their own in these matters.[38]

The European Convention on Establishment, then, is clearly a less than revolutionary document, more in the nature of a codification than of a progressive development of the law governing the treatment of aliens. Nevertheless, it is of some value with respect to the human rights of aliens, in that it does insist — at least in principle — on national treatment in a fairly wide range of activities for those aliens admitted by States parties. That even this obviously cautious convention comes out so firmly for non-discriminatory treatment of aliens is a very strong sign that a general norm of non-discrimination against aliens in most walks of life is emerging.[39]

2. European Social Charter

The European Social Charter is a companion document, of a sort, to the European Convention on Human Rights. The former is concerned chiefly with economic and social rights and the latter with civil rights. In contrast to the European Convention, however, the European Social Charter does not have a custom-made system to adjudicate issues which arise under it. Instead, it requires the States parties to submit regular reports to a Committee of Experts, together with any comments on those reports which may have been made by employers' organisations or trade unions. The Committee of Experts communicates any conclusion it may have concerning the reports to the Secretary-General of the Council of Europe, to the Consultative Assembly (which is the parliamentary arm of the organisation), and ultimately to the Council of Ministers, the highest-ranking body in the Council of Europe, for 'any necessary recommendations' (Article 29). Although this procedure can be of some value in ensuring that States parties live up to their obligations under the Charter, it does not permit an individual to trigger an adversarial proceeding, as may be done by the filing of a petition before the European Commission on Human Rights.[40]

The general approach of the Charter is to set forth a number of rights in the economic and social fields — such as the right to fair remuneration, to safe and healthy working conditions, to trade union organisation and collective bargaining, to vocational guidance and training, to social security, and so forth — rather like the International Covenant on Economic, Social and Cultural Rights.[41] It differs from the later UN-sponsored instrument, however, by clarifying the extent to which these rights apply to aliens. The Appendix to the Charter states, essentially, that aliens who are either lawfully resident or working regularly in the territory of a State party are entitled to the enumerated rights.

In addition to this general provision bringing aliens within the scope of the Charter's coverage, there are two provisions which by their very terms apply especially to non-nationals. The first is Article 18, which guarantees 'the effective exercise of the right to engage in a gainful occupation in the territory of any other Contracting Party' by requiring host States to apply existing regulations 'in a spirit of liberality', to simplify formalities and reduce administrative expenses, and to liberalise (either individually or collectively) regulations governing the employment of foreign workers. There is, however, an important *caveat* to this article: the Appendix states expressly that these measures are not concerned with the question of entry into the territories of the member States, meaning apparently that the States parties are not obliged to liberalise their general substantive law on the admission of aliens.

The other Charter provision which is explicitly concerned with aliens is Article 19, on the right of migrant workers and their families to protection and assistance. In this regard, host States are required to secure for migrant workers lawfully within their territories equal treatment with nationals in the following matters:

1 Working conditions generally, with remuneration being expressly mentioned.
2 Membership of trade unions and the enjoyment of collective bargaining benefits.
3 Accommodation.
4 Taxes, dues, and contributions connected with employment; and
5 Legal proceedings relating to matters concerning employment.

In addition to these national treatment provisions, Article 19 contains several other measures to promote the welfare of migrant workers and their families. The more important of these are facilitating family reunions, securing freedom from expulsion for migrant workers lawfully residing within host States ('unless they endanger national security or offend against public interest or morality'), and permitting, 'within legal limits', the transfer of savings and earnings.

3. European Convention on the Legal Status of Migrant Workers
This convention,[42] along with the 1975 ILO convention on migrant workers discussed in Chapter IV,[43] is the chief product of the increased concern in international bodies during the 1970s with the problems of migrant workers. Currently it represents the furthest progression of international human rights law with respect to migrant workers. The reason for so stating is that the European Convention, to a greater extent than any of the other bilateral or multilateral instruments considered so far, concerns itself with the life of migrant workers *in toto* and not just with respect to the employment relationship. To be sure, it is certainly not a perfect document, even if it were universal in coverage; further international instruments in this field, such as the pending UN convention on the subject which may emerge in the not too distant future,[44] can be anticipated. For the moment, however, this European initiative is the high-water mark in the migrant labour field.

This section will consider, albeit only briefly, the two types of provisions found in the European Convention. First, the national treatment provisions, of which this instrument has its full share, will be considered. The discussion will then turn to other matters relating to specialised concerns of migrant workers. It is in the latter area, rather than the former, that the Convention stands out from previous legal measures.

Regarding the Convention's national treatment provisions, the present discussion can do little more than identify briefly the principal ones, which concern the following subjects:

1   Access to housing and rents, in so far as those matters are covered by domestic laws and regulations (Article 13). An interesting extension of this principle is the obligation of the host State to protect migrant workers against exploitation in respect of rents, in accordance with its laws and regulations on the matter. In effect, this provision appears to be an obligation on States parties diligently to enforce whatever domestic laws they may have on this subject, but not an obligation to enact any new legislation.

2   Education and training (Article 14). It is noteworthy that this article covers not only primary and secondary education, but higher education as well. Regarding the granting of scholarships to children of migrant workers, the host State must 'make efforts' towards equality of treatment with nationals, although the actual attainment of such equality is not strictly required. Article 14 also mandates the recognition of the previous qualifications and diplomas of migrant workers, although, curiously, only 'in accordance with arrangements laid down in bilateral and multilateral agreements'. This last qualification would appear to render that provision of Article 14 devoid of any real meaning.

3   Conditions of work generally (Article 16).

4   Social security (Article 18).

5   Social and medical assistance (Article 19).

6   Industrial accidents and occupational diseases (Article 20).

7   Taxes, duties, charges, and social contributions relating to earnings (Article 23).

8   Treatment upon expiry or cancellation of contracts of employment (Article 24).

9   Re-employment after the loss of a job for reasons beyond the migrant's control (Article 25), and access to employment services in the host State (Article 27).

10   The right to organise (Article 28).

11   Participation in the affairs of the undertaking (such as acting as an employee representative on a board of directors) (Article 29); and

12   Rights in respect of legal proceedings. This right is significant in that it extends to all areas of life, not simply to those areas pertaining to employment. Migrant workers are entitled, under the same conditions as nationals, to 'full legal and judicial protection of their persons and property and of

their rights and interests', with the right of access to competent courts and administrative authorities receiving express mention. The rights to representation before such bodies and to legal aid are also mentioned. Host States are to provide migrant workers with 'the possibility of obtaining the assistance of an interpreter' where they cannot understand or speak the language used in the court. Apparently, however, the State itself need not provide the interpreter, nor is it stated that the services of an interpreter be free. In civil litigation, one could perhaps justify leaving the migrant worker to his own devices in this respect; but in criminal cases it is unfortunate that the convention does not require the State to guarantee free access to an interpreter.[45]

The more innovative portions of the Convention, as mentioned above, occur in the provisions relating to matters not directly connected with employer–employee relations. One of the most notable of these innovations is the use in Article 4 of the expression 'the right to admission to the territory of a Contracting Party ...'. The right referred to, of course, is one which is conferred by the treaty itself, not one which is supposed to exist under customary international law. Nevertheless, the fact that such an expression appears in a binding international legal instrument is one indication that international law is inching ever further from the blackletter rule of traditional international law that no right of entry into foreign territories exists. The question of the extent to which this blackletter rule still holds sway in the contemporary world is the subject of more detailed treatment below.

Article 10(3) contains an interesting, if somewhat obscure, provision: it guarantees freedom of worship for migrant workers, a subject which none of the other treaties on this subject covers. The ambiguity lies in the fact that the focus of Article 10 is not on religion exclusively or even on matters relating to civil rights generally. Rather, it is concerned with the reception of the migrants upon their arrival in the host country. It is somewhat puzzling that the right to freedom of religion, assuming that it needed explication in the first place,[46] is treated in so narrow a context, since presumably it extends well beyond the reception process.

Family reunion is the subject of Article 12, which prescribes as a general rule that spouses and dependent children of migrant workers are authorised to join the worker in the host State, subject to the availability of family housing considered normal for national workers in the region where the migrant is employed. States are allowed to impose a requirement that a period of up to twelve months elapse before the families are allowed to exercise this right. Moreover, they may derogate from this general requirement. When doing so, however, they must keep the Secretary-General of the Council of Europe fully informed of measures taken in derogation.

Article 15 is one of the most significant advances contained in the Convention.

It requires that States parties take action 'by common accord' to arrange special courses for the teaching of the migrant workers' mother tongue to their children. One should note carefully, however, that the innovation lies not so much in the breadth of language rights actually granted as in the recognition of language problems as a central concern of migrant workers. For instance, Article 15 refers to the teaching *of* the mother tongue and not to the teaching of ordinary courses *in* the mother tongue. Furthermore, the purpose of teaching the mother tongue to the children of migrants is stated to be 'to facilitate, *inter alia*, their return to their State of origin'. Finally, it may be noted, as remarked above, that Article 15 is concerned with action by common accord among the States parties in this field. It does not expressly require individual, unco-ordinated action on the part of individual States.

Article 17, concerning the transfer of savings, constitutes a progressive development of traditional international law along the lines recommended by the Elles draft Declaration.[47] Specifically, it contains two positive departures from existing practice. First, it permits the transfer of savings and earnings 'according to the arrangements laid down by [the host State's] legislation ...'. The innovation here lies in the use of the term 'arrangements' in contrast to the typical phrase 'laws and regulations in force'. The term suggests that the restrictions on the right of transfer are of a procedural and mechanical, rather than of a substantive, nature.[48] For example, migrants must comply with rules relating to declarations of funds transferred; they must arrange their currency exchanges through the officially approved channels; and so forth. Assuming they comply with such technical requirements, migrant workers arguably have an absolute right to transfer their earnings and savings.

The second positive step taken by Article 17 is to permit the transfer not only of earnings and savings, but also of sums due by migrant workers for the maintenance of dependants in the home country. Article 17 states that '[t]he transfer of sums due by migrant workers in respect of maintenance shall on no account be hindered or prevented'. The scope of this provision seems unnecessarily narrow, however, applying as it does only to the transfer of sums *due* in respect of maintenance, with the implication that there must be some kind of official obligation based upon the law of the worker's home State to pay the sums involved (say, a decree ancillary to divorce or separation). A preferable approach would be to make clear that such transfers are allowed so long as their purpose is the maintenance of dependants in the home State. Of course, it would be hard to ensure that money sent was indeed for maintenance, but the difficulties should not in fact be terribly great. Even now, many of the bilateral treaties on migrant labour require that workers officially certify before their departure the number of family dependants they have (this information frequently being relevant for host States which grant family allowances on the basis of the number of family members). Also, it should not be difficult, if the host State wished to be especially meticulous in checking on such transfers, to have the money for maintenance paid into a special account so that its distribution to dependants could be supervised, either by the home State authorities (if the special account were in the home State) or by consular officials from the home State (if the special account were in the host country).

The Convention's provisions relating to the migrant worker's loss of employment are also of some interest. If a worker becomes unemployed through no fault of his own (such as redundancy or prolonged illness), then under Article 25 the host State may not send him back to his home State immediately: it must facilitate his re-employment, including the promotion of measures of vocational retraining and occupational rehabilitation. These measures, according to Article 9(4), must allow the worker to remain in the host State for a period of at least five months after the termination of the employment — subject to the proviso that, if the worker's entitlement to unemployment benefits comes to an end during this five-month period, the host State then may require the worker to leave. This approach to unemployment represents a welcome liberalisation of much current practice, which often allows States to send workers home upon the expiration of their employment for whatever reason.

One of the most striking innovations of the European Convention is the concern which it manifests for the reintegration of the worker into the society and economy of his home State after his return. The discussion of Article 15 touched upon one aspect of this concern.[49] In the present context it should be noted that Article 14, on vocational training and related matters, has a similar orientation. Article 14(5), specifically, states that contracting parties 'shall endeavour to ensure that the vocational training and retraining schemes ... cater as far as possible for the needs of migrant workers with a view to their return to their State of origin'.

More elaborate provisions for the return of migrant workers to their home countries appear in Article 30. Paragraph 2 of this article requires that the various States of origin supply information to the host State, which the latter will keep available for those workers who request it, on the following subjects:

1 Possibilities and conditions of employment in the home country.
2 Financial aid available for economic reintegration.
3 Maintenance of social security rights acquired abroad.
4 Steps to be taken to facilitate the finding of accommodation.
5 Rules relating to equivalence accorded to occupational qualifications obtained abroad; and
6 Rules relating to equivalence accorded to educational qualifications, so that children can be admitted to schools without downgrading.

The European Convention, therefore, contains a number of interesting innovations extending the present law and practice relating to the treatment of migrant workers. As the discussion above has noted, there still remains room for improvement. Nevertheless, the Convention is a most important instrument in so far as aliens coming under it are concerned. Its significance probably lies, however, more in its role as a signpost or direction pointer indicating how the international law governing the treatment of aliens may evolve in coming years. Its immediate, practical impact on the status of migrant workers may not be so very great. One reason is that, in so far as existing or future bilateral or multilateral treaties grant rights equal to or greater than the rights found in this Convention, those agreements, rather than the Convention, are to prevail (Article 32). More important is the fact that the definition of the term 'migrant worker' in Article 1 is limited to workers coming from one State party (i.e. one Council of Europe country) to another. Workers from Turkey, Greece, Spain, and Portugal fit within this definition. Yugoslavs, however, do not (Yugoslavia not belonging to the Council of Europe), nor, of course, do workers from such countries as Algeria, Morocco or Tunisia. Also, one should bear in mind that among nine of the European States (ten, after the expiration of transitional provisions relating to Greece), the stricter regime of EEC law applies.[50] Similarly, the Nordic Council States have their own free movement of labour regime which makes much of this Convention irrelevant in so far as those States are concerned.[51]

Nevertheless, the role of the European Convention as a major component in the international legal system should not be underestimated. It is the first major instrument to emerge which is concerned not exclusively with the employment-related aspects of the migrant labour phenomenon, but rather with the status of migrant workers generally. In that respect alone it represents a major advance in the consciousness of the international community. It is indeed high time the world came to realise — and to embody that realisation in legally binding instruments — that migrant workers are not just a labour problem, but a human problem as well. As such, it merits full and enthusiastic consideration, which it has not yet received, from the international human rights law community.[52]

C, Impact of the European Convention on Human Rights

The European Convention on Human Rights[53] provides a classic example of how, with a bit of imagination, principles relating to the human rights of aliens can be extracted from legal instruments which on their surface seemingly have little or nothing to do with the subject. Of course, there can be no serious doubt that this Convention protects aliens as well as nationals: this conclusion is compelled by Article 1, which states that the parties shall secure the rights provided for in the Convention to 'everyone within their jurisdiction ...'. The concern here will not be so much with the ordinary basic rights guaranteed by the European Convention as with matters of particular interest to aliens. In particular, this discussion will focus on how it is possible to make use of the Convention's provisions to secure for aliens a limited right of entry into foreign countries and to give them a measure of protection from expulsion from such countries — neither of which right expressly appears in the Convention.[54]

Before taking up this task, however, it should be noted for the record that there are certain provisions of the Convention which expressly concern aliens. These provisions are the following:

1 Article 5, which guarantees the right to liberty and security of person, lists a number of specific instances in which this right may be curtailed. One of these instances is 'the lawful arrest or detention of a person to prevent his effecting an unauthorised entry into the country or of a person against whom action is being taken with a view to deportation or extradition'.

2 Article 16 expressly authorises the imposition of certain restrictions on the political activities of aliens.[55]

3 Article 2 of the Fourth Protocol, concerning freedom of movement and residence, protects only persons lawfully within the territory of the State party, thereby excluding illegal aliens from its coverage; and

4 Article 4 of the Fourth Protocol, which prohibits the collective expulsion of aliens.[56]

The discussion may now proceed to consider some of the more subtle aspects of the European Convention, particularly the attempts by aliens to gain admission to foreign countries and also to protect themselves against deportation and expulsion by such States, neither of which appears as a specific right in the Convention.

1. Admission of aliens

Among the more remarkable cases to come before the European Commission on Human Rights were the *East African Asians* cases,[57] which in part concerned twenty-five persons who were citizens of the United Kingdom and its colonies, under then existing English domestic law, but who had been denied the right to settle in the mother country. Under the domestic law in force, the United Kingdom was perfectly entitled to deny entry to these persons.[58] The complainants contended, however, that this law was racially discriminatory and that a refusal of leave to enter the country on that basis constituted degrading treatment, contrary to Article 3 of the European Convention. Incredibly, the British government, while conceding that the law was racially discriminatory,[59] denied that the refusal of admission constituted a violation of Article 3. The European Commission disagreed, finding unanimously that the article had been violated in all twenty-five cases.

In its decision on the admissibility of the complainants' petition the Commission held that 'special importance should be attached to discrimination based on race', concluding that 'discrimination based on race could, in certain circumstances, of itself amount to degrading treatment within the meaning of Art. 3 of the Convention'.[60] The decision is an important indication of the fact that a State's absolute right under traditional international law to decide whether to admit aliens on to its territory[61] is becoming obsolete. Under contemporary international law the right should be deemed to be subject to the important proviso that a State cannot exercise its right of admission in a fashion which is racially discriminatory in effect.[62]

The *East African Asians* cases are important for the evolution of the law protecting aliens for another reason, quite apart from the Article 3 issue just discussed. These cases also generated a claim under Article 8 of the European Convention, which guarantees to everyone 'the right to respect for his private and family life, his home and his correspondence'. Two of the *East African Asians* cases involved husbands who were attempting to gain admission to Great Britain for the purpose of joining their wives, who already had settled there. The practice of the British government at the time was not to allow husbands automatically to enter the country to join wives, although wives were allowed to enter to join husbands. The complainants alleged that such treatment constituted an infringement of Article 8. The British government's position was grounded upon the assumption that the locus of family life for the purpose of Article 8 was the domicile of the husband. In its report the Commission held that there had been a violation of Article 8 (read in conjunction with Article 14, which prohibits certain types of discrimination in the enjoyment of rights provided for by the Convention). Great Britain later altered its immigration policy to conform to the decision. As in the case of the Article 3 claim, the complainants here had contrived to gain admission into Great Britain through the medium, as it were, of the Article 8 right to respect for family life, which on its face has nothing to do with rights of aliens.[63]

The *East African Asians* cases clearly represent a milestone in European Convention jurisprudence. One must certainly not gain the impression, however, that such triumphs are in any way easy or commonplace. The Commission is usually fairly strict when scrutinising claims of a right of entry into a State on the basis of Article 8. One example well illustrates this point. It concerns another case originating in Great Britain,[64] involving a man from Cyprus who was married to a British national. The government granted the husband only a limited period of stay in the country, during which he lived with his wife in the same household with her parents. At the end of his alloted stay, the husband was required to leave. He and his wife both petitioned the European Commission, alleging that this action violated Article 8 of the European Convention in two respects: first, it constituted a forcible separation of husband from wife; and, second, if alternatively the wife accompanied her husband back to Cyprus (thereby keeping their marital life intact), it would necessarily be at the expense of separation from her parents and thus destructive of another facet of family life.

The Commission disagreed with both claims and ruled the petition inadmissible.[65] On the first claim, it held that Great Britain was not requiring the husband and wife to separate, as they were free to live together in Cyprus. The Convention, in other words, does not provide that family life be allowed to continue in any particular location; it only prohibits States parties from directly causing such ruptures, so to speak. On the second claim, the Commission, after looking carefully at the specific circumstances of the wife's relationship with her parents, concluded that it was not close enough to merit protection under Article 8. In this respect, the Commission considered such matters as the age and employment status of the wife and the degree of financial dependence present in the parent–child relationship. The mere presence of the normal sentiments of family affection, the Commission stated, is not sufficient to bring Article 8 into play.

2. Expulsion of aliens

Turning to the area of the expulsion of aliens from host countries, there have been a number of attempts to make use both of Article 3 and Article 8 of the European Convention in ways broadly similar to the attempts just discussed in the context of admission to a State.

One important case which made use of each of these articles was *Amekrane* v. *United Kingdom*.[66] Amekrane, who was Moroccan, was allegedly involved in a *coup* attempt against the king of Morocco in 1971. When the attempt failed, Amekrane fled by helicopter to Gibraltar, for whose actions Great Britain is responsible under international law. The Gibraltar authorities finally decided to expel Amekrane on the ground that he was an 'undesirable emigrant'. In the event, the so-called expulsion bore a remarkable resemblance to an extradition.[67] Moreover, Amekrane was given no opportunity to find a State which would accept him, contrary to the normal practice in expulsion proceedings.[68] With no prior warning, he was delivered directly into the hands of Moroccan authorities. Several months later he was executed in Morocco.

Amekrane's widow subsequently petitioned the European Commission, alleging a violation by Great Britain of Article 8 (on the ground that the 'expulsion' prevented Amekrane from joining his family, who at the time of the *coup* were outside Morocco) and of Article 3 (on the ground that the delivery of Amekrane into the hands of the Moroccan authorities was an illegal extradition which was in fact tantamount to sending him to his death without so much as a warning, to say nothing of a hearing). After the European Commission had held her application to be admissible under both counts, the British government reached a settlement with Mrs Amekrane,[69] so the precise legal verdict on these claims remains technically in doubt.

While there have thus been some legal victories by aliens seeking to curtail the right of States to expel them, as in the cases involving admission into States, the number of triumphs for claimants has not been high. There is no doubt, however, about the general principle involved. The Commission has stated on a number of occasions that, even though the right of an alien not to be expelled from a State is not, as such, protected by the European Convention, the State's right of expulsion is restricted to the extent necessary to ensure that the rights which are set forth in the Convention are not violated under-handedly.[70] On the subject of expulsion, one may sum up the present state of European Convention jurisprudence by noting the paradox that, while aliens may have won the war (by the Commission's recognition of the principle just set forth),[71] it is still notoriously difficult for them to win individual battles. In this respect the *Amekrane* outcome is definitely an exception rather than the rule.

The following case illustrates briefly the type of problem in store for potential claimants in the expulsion area. The West German government ordered the expulsion of an Egyptian applicant, who alleged that he was a pacifist and that if he returned to Egypt he would be compelled either to perform military service or to face imprisonment.[72] His expulsion, he argued, therefore violated Article 3. The Commission invoked the general principle just discussed — that expulsion, even though not provided for as such by the European Convention, nevertheless could be unlawful if it involved the infringement of rights which the Convention did protect — but then ruled that this particular expulsion would not infringe Article 3, since an obligation to perform military service does not violate basic human rights.

The cases considered above should serve to give a flavour of the kinds of argument which aliens can advance before tribunals in order to secure rights which the law does not expressly accord them. The basic lesson is that the progressive development of the law governing the treatment of aliens must proceed on a wide variety of fronts. Initiatives which concentrate expressly on aliens — such as the Elles draft Declaration[73] or the various conventions on migrant workers[74] — should be undertaken hand in hand with the creative use of 'ordinary' international human rights law, such as that of the European Convention. The construction of a comprehensive international human rights regime protecting aliens, in other words, is an art as well as a science, one in which the skills of imaginative advocates are as important as the work of enlightened draftsmen.

Notes

1 Treaty Establishing the European Economic Community (with Annexes and Protocols), 1957, 298 UNTS 3, commonly called the 'Treaty of Rome'.
2 Note that Article 7 does not state, even as an ideal, that *all* discrimination on grounds of nationality is to be prohibited: it addresses only discrimination falling within the general ambit of the Treaty of Rome, which means basically that its impact is

confined to matters of an economic nature. See 36/74 *Walrave* v. *Association Union Cycliste Int'l*, [1974] E.C.R. 1405, [1975] 1 C.M.L.R. 320; 13/76 *Dona* v. *Mantero*, [1976] E.C.R. 1333, [1976] 2 C.M.L.R. 578.

3 In addition to covering the free movement of workers, Title III concerns itself with norms relating to the right of establishment, the provision of services and the free movement of professionals, none of which will be discussed herein. On the right of freedom of movement for workers generally, see P. Mathijsen, *A Guide to European Community Law*, 130-5 (3rd ed., 1980); B. Sundberg-Weitman, *Discrimination on the Grounds of Nationality*, 127-36 (1977); Bowyer, 'Social services', in 3 *Common Market Law*, 529, at 532-67 (A. Campbell, ed., 1973); Foster, 'The free movement of workers', in *The Law of the Common Market*, 170 (B. Wortley, ed., 1974); Jacobs, 'The free movement of persons within the EEC', in 30 *Current Legal Problems* (1977), 123; J.-C. Seche, 'Free movement of workers under Community law', 14 *C.M.L. Rev.* (1977), 385.

Note that the free movement provisions under discussion speak only to workers travelling from one EEC country to another. Regarding the Community's concern for migrant workers from non-EEC countries, see Duyssens, 'Migrant workers from third countries in the European Community', 14 *C.M.L. Rev.* (1977), 501. See also text at notes 42-52 *infra*.

4 Note that this provision permits discrimination against aliens only in regard to *entry* into public service; it does not justify discriminatory treatment *after* they have entered it. See 152/73 *Sotgiu* v. *Deutsche Bundespost*, [1974] E.C.R. 153, Comm. Mkt. Rep. (CCH) § 8257.

5 See generally 1 H. Smit and P. Herzog, *The Law of the European Economic Community*, § 48.08 (Supp. 1983).

6 See text at notes 12-23 *infra*.

7 See the case cited at note 12 *infra*.

8 J.O. 1964, 850; O.J. Spec. Ed. 1963–64, 117.

9 J.O. 1968, L 257/2; O.J. Spec. Ed. 1968, 475.

10 J.O. 1968, L 257/13; O.J. Spec. Ed. 1968, 485.

11 On the question of social security, not considered herein, see generally P. Watson, *Social Security Law of the European Communities* (1980). For recent EEC initiatives extending the application of regulations governing social security for migrant workers to self-employed persons and members of their families, see Coeffard, 'Regulations governing social security for persons moving within the European Community', 121 *Int'l Lab. Rev.* (1982), 243.

12 48/75 [1976] E.C.R. 497, [1976] 2 C.M.L.R. 619.

13 *Id.* at 514, [1976] 2 C.M.L.R. at 640.

14 See the bibliography in 1 H. Smit and P. Herzog, *supra*, note 5, at § 48.02.

15 See note 8 *supra*.

16 See, e.g., O'Keeffe, 'Practical difficulties in the application of Article 48 of the EEC Treaty', 19 *C.M.L. Rev.* (1982), 1, at 1-2.

17 67/74, *Bonsignore* v. *Oberstadtdirektor of Cologne*, [1975] E.C.R. 297, [1975] C.M.L.R. 472.

18 41/74, [1974] E.C.R. 1337, [1975] 1 C.M.L.R. 1. For commentary on this case, see G. Goodwin-Gill, *International Law and the Movement of Persons between States*, 302-4 (1978); P. Allott, 'Exclusion of aliens and E.E.C. law', 35 *Camb. L.J.* (1976), 3, at 3-6; A. Evans, '*Ordre public*, public policy and United Kingdom immigration law', 3 *Eur. L. Rev.* (1978), 370, at 375-6; F. Wooldridge, 'Free movement of EEC nationals: the limitation based on public policy and public security', 2 *Eur. L. Rev.* (1977), 190, at 193-6; Note, 'Free movement of workers in the

European Economic Community: the public policy exception', 29 *Stan. L. Rev.* (1977), 1283, at 1288-90.

19 Note, *supra*, note 18, at 1288.

20 *Id.* at 1289.

21 30/77, [1977] E.C.R. 1999, [1977] 2 C.M.L.R. 800.

22 *Id.* at 2012-13, [1977] 2 C.M.L.R. at 823 (emphasis added).

23 *Id.* at 2013, [1977] 2 C.M.L.R. at 823.

24 G. Goodwin-Gill, *supra*, note 18, at 304-5. For a general comment on the impact of EEC law on UK immigration law and practice, see J. Evans, *Immigration Law*, 220-32 (1983).

25 The European Court of Human Rights invoked this concept in the *Handyside* case, [1976] *Y.B. Eur. Conv. on Human Rights*, 506, at 508-9, 58 *I.L.R.* 150, at 173-4, where in a close case it upheld the United Kingdom's seizure of an allegedly obscene book, holding that the author's freedom of expression guaranteed by Article 10 of the European Convention had not been violated, since 'States have a margin of appreciation in deciding what is "necessary" to protect morals'. The concept has been criticised extensively and its 'tilt', which favours State action, should be watched carefully by the European Court and the ECJ as well. Cf. G. Goodwin-Gill, *supra*, note 18, at 305-6.

26 On the Council of Europe, see generally D. Bowett, *The Law of International Institutions*, 168-80 (4th ed., 1982).

27 See European Convention on Extradition, 1957, 359 UNTS 273; European Convention on the Suppression of Terrorism, 1977, Europ. T.S. No. 90, reprinted in R. Lillich, *Transnational Terrorism. Conventions and Commentary* 120-9 (1982).

28 European Convention for the Preservation of Human Rights and Fundamental Freedoms, 1950, 213 UNTS 222, reprinted in R. Lillich, *International Human Rights Instruments*, 500.1-510.7 (1983).

29 European Convention on Establishment (with Protocol), 1955, 529 UNTS 141.

30 European Social Charter (with Appendix), 1961, 529 UNTS 89, reprinted in R. Lillich, *supra*, note 28, at 520.1-520.18.

31 European Convention on the Legal Status of Migrant Workers, 1977, Europ. T.S. No. 93, reprinted in 16 *I.L.M.* (1977), 1381-90.

32 For a classic exposition of this doctrine, see 1 L. Oppenheim, *International Law*, 675-6 (8th ed., H. Lauterpacht, ed., 1955). Compare text accompanying note 61 *infra*.

33 See, e.g., Article 31 (1) of the Vienna Convention on the Law of Treaties, adopted 22 May 1969, opened for signature, 23 May 1969, entered into force, 27 January 1980, UN Doc. A/Conf. 39/27, reprinted in R. Lillich, *supra*, note 28, at 540.5, which states that treaties are to be interpreted 'in good faith in accordance with the ordinary meaning to be given to the terms of the treaty in their context *and in the light of its object and purpose*' (emphasis added).

34 See text at notes 15-25 *supra*.

35 The French text is phrased even more strongly, using the word 'notamment' instead of the English phrase 'for instance'.

36 For a less pessimistic assessment, see G. Goodwin-Gill, *supra*, note 18, at 168-9 and 229-31.

37 Long-term aliens, under Article 12(1), are persons who have been lawfully engaged in gainful employment for a continuous period of at least five years; persons who have lawfully resided in the host country's territory for an uninterrupted period of at least ten years; or persons who have been admitted to the host State for permanent residence. Article 12(2) permits the host government to increase the

requisite period of continuous lawful employment to a maximum of ten years, provided that after the first five-year period the renewal of authorisation to work is automatic.

38 The prohibition found in Article 18 expressly is made 'subject to the decisions which such bodies or organizations may take in this respect within the limits of their competence'. Thus it appears directed only at host States, not private bodies therein.

As mentioned in the text accompanying note 3 *supra*, the right of establishment under the Treaty of Rome is not taken up in this chapter. It is worth noting in passing, however, that its Article 52, coupled with legislation promulgated thereunder, has been read to place upon host States 'an obligation not only to abolish discrimination laid down by law but also to ensure that beneficiaries are not discriminated against by these [private] organizations themselves'. B. Sundberg-Weitman, *supra*, note 3, at 201.

The above commentator concludes approvingly that 'discrimination performed by such organizations comes within the scope of restrictions on freedom of establishment. This standpoint is of fundamental importance, since it involves the conclusion that ... the definition of freedom of establishment provided for in Article 52 is incomplete and should not be interpreted as meaning that the right to equal treatment in the field of establishment is limited to restrictions applied by public authorities.... Obviously, discrimination performed by professional or trade organizations could obstruct the aim pursued by Article 52 just as much as could discriminatory restrictions laid down by law'. *Id.* at 203. Cf. 2 H. Smith and P. Herzog, *supra*, note 5, at § 52.04.

39 On the international law norm of non-discrimination generally, see M. McDougal, H. Lasswell and L. Chen, *Human Rights and World Public Order* (1980); W. McKean, *Equality and Discrimination under International Law* (1983); B. Ramcharan, 'Equality and nondiscrimination', in *The International Bill of Rights. The Covenant on Civil and Political Rights*, 246 (L. Henkin, ed., 1981).

40 On the filing of such individual petitions, see K. Boyle, 'Practice and procedure on individual applications under the European Convention on Human Rights', in *Guide to International Human Rights Practice*, 133 (H. Hannum, ed., 1984).

41 See text at Chapter III, notes 28-30. For the first comprehensive treatment of the Charter in English, see D. Hania, *The European Social Charter* (1984).

42 See note 31 *supra*.

43 See text at Chapter IV, notes 56-7.

44 See text at Chapter IV, notes 58-72.

45 The major international human rights instruments all contain such a guarantee. See R. Lillich, 'Civil rights', in *Human Rights in International Law. Legal and Policy Issues*, 115, at 142 (T. Meron, ed., 1983).

46 'Although the undertaking set out in paragraph 3 [of Article 10] is already covered by the provisions of Article 9 of the Convention for the Protection of Human Rights and Fundamental Freedoms, it was decided to mention it specifically in the Convention in view of the latter's humanitarian purpose.' Council of Europe, *Explanatory Report on the European Convention on the Legal Status of Migrant Workers*, 17 (1978).

47 See text at Chaper III, notes 63-4.

48 'It was made clear that Article 17, paragraph 1, refers to arrangements for implementing the principle and that such arrangements must not have the effect of offending against the principle itself.' Council of Europe, *supra*, note 46, at 22.

49 See the discussion of Article 15 in the paragraph preceding note 47 *supra*.

50 See text at notes 1-25 *supra*.

51 See Agreement (with Protocol) Concerning a Common Labour Market, 1954, 199 UNTS 3.

52 But see Note, 13 *Texas Int'l L.J.* (1978), 353.
53 See note 28 *supra*. For commentary on the European Convention, see F. Castberg, *The European Convention on Human Rights* (1974); J. Fawcett, *The Application of the European Convention on Human Rights* (1969); F. Jacobs, *The European Convention on Human Rights* (1975); L. Mikaelsen, *European Protection of Human Rights* (1980); C. Morrisson, Jr., *The Dynamics of Development in the European Human Rights Convention System* (1981); Z. Nedjati, *Human Rights under the European Convention* (1978).
54 See G. Goodwin-Gill, *supra*, note 18, at 161-2, 284-6.
55 Article 16 allows such restrictions in three specific areas: (1) freedom of expression (Article 10); (2) freedom of assembly and association (Article 11); and (3) the general right of non-discrimination in the enjoyment of the rights and freedoms guaranteed by the Convention. See generally A. Evans, 'The political status of aliens in international law', 30 *I.C.L.Q.* (1981), 20, at 22.
56 To this list might be added the guarantee, found in Article 1 of the First Protocol, of the 'peaceful enjoyment of ... possessions'. On its face, this provision makes no distinction between nationals and aliens. The article proceeds to state, however, that this right is guaranteed in accordance with 'general principles of international law', which the European Commission on Human Rights had decided have a different impact upon aliens than upon nationals: such principles entitle aliens, but *not* nationals, to receive compensation if a State takes their property. App. No. 511/59, [1960] *Y.B. Eur. Conv. on Human Rights*, 394, at 422-4 (Eur. Comm'n on Human Rights). See E. Schwelb, 'The protection of the right of property of nationals under the First Protocol to the European Convention on Human Rights', 13 *Am. J. Comp. L.* (1964), 518.
57 These cases involved thirty-one applications, which were considered in two groups: *Twenty-five Applications* v. *United Kingdom*, App. No. 4403 and Others, [1970] *Y.B. Eur. Conv. on Human Rights*, 928 (Eur. Comm'n on Human Rights); and *Harilal G. Patel (4501/70) and Others (Six Applications)* v. *United Kingdom, id.* at 1014.
58 Under the Immigration Act, 1971, 19 and 20 Eliz. II, c. 77, possession of citizenship of the United Kingdom or its colonies does not automatically confer on the holder the right of abode within the United Kingdom. In order to acquire such a right, a person must meet the requirements for 'patriality' set out in Section 2 of the Act. See G. Goodwin-Gill, *supra*, note 18, at 103.
59 *Twenty-five Applications* v. *United Kingdom, supra*, note 57, at 992.
60 *Id.* at 994.
61 See, e.g., L. Oppenheim, *supra*, note 32, at 675-6. But see a recently published reassessment of traditional international law in this area which provocatively concludes that '[t]he proposition that states have an absolute right to deny territorial access to all aliens has unusual resilience and resonance, but little historical or jurisprudential foundation'. J. Nafziger, 'The general admission of aliens under international law', 77 *A.J.I.L.* (1983), 804, at 845.
62 Cf. G. Goodwin-Gill, *supra*, note 18, at 164-5.
63 *Id.* at 165-6.
64 *X and Y* v. *United Kingdom*, App. No. 5269/71, [1972] *Y.B. Eur. Conv. on Human Rights*, 564 (Eur. Comm'n on Human Rights).
65 *Id.* at 572, 574.
66 App. No. 5961/72, [1973] *Y.B. Eur. Conv. on Human Rights*, 356 (Eur. Comm'n on Human Rights).
67 With respect to 'disguised extradition', the leading British case is *R.* v. *Governor*

of Brixton Prison (ex parte *Soblen*), [1963] 2 Q.B. 243, [1962] 3 All E.R. 641. On the subject generally, see G. Goodwin-Gill, *supra*, note 18, at 223-8; I. Shearer, *Extradition in International Law*, 76-91 (1971); P. O'Higgins, 'Unlawful seizure and irregular extradition', 34 *B.Y.I.L.* (1960), 279. See also A. Evans, 'Extradition and rendition: problems of choice', in *International Aspects of Criminal Law. Enforcing United States Law in the World Community* [Fourth Sokol Colloquium], 1 (R. Lillich, ed., 1981).

68 Report of the Commission of 19 July 1974.

69 Council of Europe Press Communiqué C(73) 28 (1974). The British government made an *ex gratia* payment of £37,500 to Mrs Amekrane. See C. Morrison, Jr., *supra*, note 54, at 62.

70 See, e.g., *X* v. *Federal Republic of Germany*, App. No. 6513/73, [1974] *Y.B. Eur. Conv. on Human Rights*, 480, at 488 (Eur. Comm'n on Human Rights).

71 Goodwin-Gill has offered the following summation of European Convention law in the area of expulsion: 'The guarantees which the Convention does provide reflect closely [the] standards of general international law .... There can be no doubt that an expulsion would also be in breach of the Convention if it resulted in personal injury or damage to the property of an alien, if it was executed in breach of the local law, or without due consideration being given to the alien's family, or if it led to the alien's removal to a State in which he faced political or other persecution. Although States alone may be competent to decide upon the adequacy of the reasons for expulsion, the Convention clearly requires that the alien be permitted to challenge the legality of his arrest and detention. The fundamental assumption throughout the Convention is that discretionary powers are subject to control, and that State actions which are arbitrary, in that they are inspired by bad faith or otherwise reveal a "détournement de pouvoir", may be challenged .' G. Goodwin-Gill, *supra*, note 18, at 292.

72 *X* v. *Federal Republic of Germany*, App. No. 4314/69, [1970] *Y.B. Eur. Conv. on Human Rights*, 900 (Eur. Comm'n on Human Rights).

73 See text at Chapter III, notes 43-74.

74 See text at Chapter IV, notes 34-72, and notes 42-52 *supra*.

CHAPTER SIX

Bilateral treaties

Over the past few centuries, bilateral treaties not only have established legal regimes between various States parties, but they also have contributed to the development of customary international law norms in many areas. This chapter will examine bilateral FCN, migrant worker, and migration and assisted passage treaties of the post-World War II period to see whether this process may be at work once again with respect to the norms governing the treatment of aliens.

A. Friendship, Commerce and Navigation treaties

As was explained in Chapter I, the practice of concluding bilateral treaties of friendship, commerce and navigation is not new. With antecedents going back to the Middle Ages, a substantial body of law governing the rights of aliens had emerged from bilateral treaty practice by the nineteenth century.[1] The purpose of the present discussion is not to reveal anything strikingly new about this technique, but rather to look briefly at one of these treaties — more or less randomly selected — in order to convey in concrete fashion one of the major methods by which the international legal process works to protect the rights of aliens. The agreement selected for this purpose is a Treaty of Friendship, Establishment and Navigation concluded in 1962 between Great Britain and Japan.[2]

This agreement does not accord the nationals of each State the right to enter the other State's territory; it is concerned only with the treatment they are to receive once they have gained entry. In general, each State party promises to accord the other's nationals 'treatment not less favourable than that accorded to the nationals of any other foreign country' (Article 3[1]) — i.e. treatment on a most-favoured-nation basis. That standard is actually a minimum or residual one, however, since in a number of areas the treaty guarantees aliens either equal treatment with nationals or certain rights absolutely. In the latter category, for instance, is the right of aliens to 'constant and complete protection and security for their persons and property' (Article 7[1]). More specifically, if an alien has any of his property requisitioned or expropriated, then he is entitled at a minimum to the traditional international lawyer's dream: 'prompt, adequate and effective compensation' (Article 14). Aliens are also to be exempt from military conscription, from compulsory labour (excepting jury duty), and from any fees assessed in lieu thereof (Article 4).

Another guarantee which is of an absolute nature is liberty of conscience and freedom of worship, although religious services will not be allowed if 'contrary to public morals or public order' (Article 5[1]). Aliens may bury and cremate their dead according to their own religious customs, subject to 'any non-discriminatory sanitary or medical requirements laid down by the authorities' of the host State (Article 5[2]). The erection and maintenance of buildings for religious worship are permitted, with a guarantee that these buildings will not be searched except by due process of law (Article 5[1]).

The list of areas in which aliens covered by the treaty are to be accorded national treatment by the host State is impressive.[3] For example, once they have been admitted by the host State, aliens are guaranteed liberty to travel throughout its territory without the need to carry travel documents or permits. This right can be restricted only for reasons of national security, and even then only on the condition that any restrictions imposed apply equally to nationals as well (Article 3[2]). The treaty also provides national treatment for aliens respecting taxes (Article 8). Aliens' dwellings or offices are to be subject to search by host State authorities only to the extent that premises of nationals are so subject (Article 9). In the ownership and disposal of property — though not its acquisition — aliens and nationals are to have equal rights. The same is true regarding the removal of property and transferral of proceeds (Article 10).

It is interesting to note that the treaty contains fairly elaborate provisions concerning criminal proceedings against aliens. Article 7 grants them a number of rights in absolute terms: if an alien is taken into custody, he has the right to be informed without delay of the grounds for such action; he is entitled to reasonable and humane treatment; the authorities may not dispose of his property except by due process of law; he is entitled to be tried in public without undue delay; he is free to make use of advisers and representatives of his own choice during the proceedings; and he has the right to be provided with an interpreter if necessary. In general, the alien is to be entitled to national treatment regarding 'all rights and privileges in connection with [the] trial permissible under the law' of the host State. Also, the alien is entitled to similar treatment with respect to eligibility for legal aid and liability for court fees.

In the civil area, aliens and nationals are to be on an equal footing regarding access to courts, tribunals and administrative authorities (Article 7[4]).

In other areas of life, aliens are entitled to treatment on a most-favoured-nation basis, which as noted above is the basic standard set forth in Article

3(1). Two particularly important applications of this general, or residual, principle are expressly stated in the treaty. Article 3(4) provides that aliens covered by the treaty will be allowed to engage in employment only on a most-favoured-nation basis. Also, Article 10(1) stipulates that regarding the acquisition — as opposed to the ownership or disposition — of property, aliens will be entitled only to most-favoured-nation treatment.

The treaty contains several other provisions in the nature of procedural guarantees. For example, Article 3(3) states that any conditions imposed on aliens covered by the agreement regarding length of stay allowed, or any restrictions relating to employment or to the exercise of a profession or business, must be made known to the alien at the time that they are imposed (which normally would be the time of entry into the host State). Once imposed, these conditions or restrictions may not be made more severe. Also, national treatment or most-favoured-nation treatment to which an alien might be entitled under the treaty 'shall be accorded immediately and unconditionally, without request or compensation' (Article 28).

Article 29 of the treaty is in the nature of a saving clause, stipulating that the agreement does not apply to any customs union or free-trade area to which either State party might belong. Thus Great Britain is not obligated under the treaty to grant Japanese nationals free movement comparable to that which it must allow to nationals of its fellow EEC States under the Treaty of Rome.[4]

B. Migrant worker treaties

1. The European Experience

The discussion in Chapter II mentioned the early bilateral treaties concerning migrant workers which France concluded with Czechoslovakia and Poland immediately after World War I.[5] These early initiatives, however, pale into relative insignificance when compared with the developments which have occurred since World War II.

The post-World War II migrant worker treaties fall into two quite distinct historical phases, with a third phase possibly just beginning, a matter which the discussion below will treat briefly. The two major phases occurred, first, in the period immediately following the war (i.e. the late 1940s and early 1950s), when the emphasis was upon the relief of short-term labour shortages in the war-torn economies of the allied powers (chiefly through the employment of Italian labour);[6] and, second, in the period beginning around the mid-1950s and extending into the 1970s, with an emphasis upon the long-term, systematic channelling of labour from developing countries (and also the poorer countries of western Europe, such as Spain and Portugal) to the industrialised States.

The legal arrangements adopted during these two periods also were quite distinct. In the earlier period the treaties tended to be very short. Since they were oriented towards the solution of very specific and temporary problems (such as manpower shortages in a particular industry), there was no general format common to them all. The later treaties, in contrast, are very general in scope. Since their intention is to set up long-term mechanisms to channel labour from developing countries into the economies of industrialised States, procedural and administrative details bulk very large. Also, as imported labour is generally of a different ethnic stock from the majority of the host States' populations, more concern is shown for spelling out the standard of treatment to which the migrant workers are to be entitled.

There is no need to dwell at any length on treaties from the first period; their interest is primarily historical. The only point worth noting here is that most of these agreements did contain provisions for the equality of treatment between migrants and nationals in matters relating to the employment relationship.

Of more concern to the present discussion is the second category of treaties — those agreements concluded between the western European industrialised States and various Third World and poorer European countries. It is difficult to state with any certainty how many such treaties exist, because not all of them have been registered with the UN Secretariat. The following discussion is based upon an analysis of sixteen treaties which have been so registered.[7] The Netherlands has been the most active of these treaty-making States (it is a party to eight of these sixteen treaties). Austria, Belgium, France and West Germany have also figured prominently as importers of labour. Among the labour-exporting countries, no single one stands out conspicuously. The list includes Algeria, Greece, Italy, Morocco, Portugal, Spain, Tunisia, Turkey and Yugoslavia.

First, a brief word is needed about the mechanics of the labour-transfer processes established by these treaties. The basic policy is to ensure that labour recruiting takes place under the supervision of the governments of the two States, rather than through direct recruiting by employers. The typical procedure is for the employers in the importing State to inform their government of their requirements for labour from an exporting State. The importing State then relays that information to an exporting State, which itself publicises the requests to workers. The exporting State generally pre-selects workers to go to the importing State, although the latter has the final say over who is selected. (Most of the treaties contain provisions allowing the importing State to delegate its duty of selection to an agent, which in practice might be a representative of an employers' federation or a similar body.)

The provisions of the employment contracts also are subject to the supervision of the two governments. Some treaties contain annexes with model contracts, to which the actual contracts must conform. Other treaties simply stipulate in the texts certain provisions which the contracts must contain, e.g. an express statement of what the worker's wage is to be, of the duration of the contract (usually no more than twelve months, with a possibility of renewal), and of the respective rights of the employer and the employee. The treaties usually require that the contract be signed both by the employer and by the employee before the latter's departure to the host State.

The treaties also provide for the mechanics and payment of the expenses of the worker's journey to his country of sojourn. They also typically create, or at least provide for the establishment of, mixed commissions to oversee the operation of the agreements. These commissions are charged with such matters as resolving any difficulties which might arise between the two governments and proposing amendments to the treaties.

The main focus in this study is on the human rights aspects of these bilateral treaties, the significance of which has so far largely escaped the attention of the international legal community. This state of affairs is unfortunate, because the degree of consistency among the various treaties on these human rights matters is so great that it arguably constitutes them a major source of international legal norms in the treatment of aliens area. The concern of the balance of the present discussion, therefore, is with identifying the main patterns which emerge from these treaties.

The most outstanding point about the treaties is the extent to which they articulate a general policy of equality of treatment between migrant workers and nationals in matters relating to the employment relationship. For example, the migrants are guaranteed equal wages with nationals for equal work (although the value of this guarantee is often of only limited practical use, since frequently migrant workers do not perform the same kind of work as nationals). The treaties frequently specify that migrants and nationals are to receive equal treatment regarding conditions of employment, social benefits, occupational health and safety matters, the right to form or participate in trade unions, and the right to have access to relevant tribunals for the redress of grievances.

Concerning one of the most important human rights concerns of migrant workers, the right of family reunification, there is less consistency. Some treaties ignore the question altogether. Other agreements, such as the ones concluded by Belgium, allow the immediate family of the migrant to join him once he has completed a certain period of work (three months in the case of the Belgian treaties), subject, however, to the availability of suitable accommodation.

Several of the treaties — not, however, the majority — have specific provisions for equal access of migrants and nationals to vocational training schemes. Even for those treaties which do not mention the subject explicitly, however, one could advance the argument that vocational training falls under the heading of social benefits.

The question of cultural rights is covered in some of the treaties, although only in a very limited way. For example, three of the Belgian and two of the

Dutch treaties contain provisions allowing migrant workers to have unpaid time from work on their national holidays.[8]

With respect to the repatriation of earnings, the usual provision is similar to the one found in the Elles draft Declaration: that repatriation will be allowed in accordance with the laws of the host State. There is no need to repeat here the analysis of this type of provision made earlier on.[9]

One of the most interesting aspects of the treaties is their provision for the right of migrants to remain in the host country after the expiration of their contract of employment. The reason that this provision is so significant is that it constitutes a slight but important inroad into the sovereign right of States to exclude or expel aliens from their territory at will. To be sure, the host governments in all cases continue to supervise the activities of migrants very closely. Most of the treaties allowing the migrant to stay on, for instance, require that he conclude a new contract of employment. In the case of the Dutch agreements, this new contract must be approved by the government. The Austrian policy is slightly less stringent — the new contract must be concluded in accordance with the country's general law on the employment of aliens. Belgium is the most liberal of the labour-importing States in this respect, as it allows the migrant worker at the end of three years of employment under temporary permits (two years, if his family is present) to obtain a permit valid for any type of employment.

Provisions of the sort under consideration are admittedly very far from establishing a general right on the part of the migrant worker to remain in the host country. It is important to note, though, that none of the treaties states an absolute time limit for the migrant's stay. Most important yet is the fact that the duration of the migrant's stay, at least to an extent, is determined partly by him and therefore is not wholly within the discretion of the host State. In practice, of course, the position of the worker is likely to be very circumscribed: his ability to conclude a new contract of employment, for example, may be very restricted in times of economic recession. Nevertheless, these treaties do modify the unfettered freedom of countries to expel aliens and hence represent a progressive development in the law governing the treatment of aliens.

Having briefly surveyed some of the human rights provisions contained in these migrant worker treaties, it is now appropriate to mention some of the features which they omit. Basically, they do not contain any guarantees relating to matters outside the employment context. They do not provide, therefore, for any of the traditional civil rights, such as the right of freedom of expression or freedom of religion. Nor do they contain provisions for the integration of the migrants into the society of the host State. Most important, they do not make any special provision for naturalisation. If a migrant wishes to become a national of the host State, then his only option is to go through the normal naturalisation process. Finally, on the cultural side there are no provisions for the education of the children of migrant workers.

These treaties, thus, can hardly be considered broad charters of the rights of migrant workers and their families. Basically they are functional in character: their purpose is to secure an orderly flow of labour to the industrialised States of western Europe. They contain little more in the way of human rights guarantees than is necessary to implement this goal in a humane fashion.

In a sense, however, this last point makes these treaties all the more valuable as a potential source of international human rights law. The outstanding point about them is the fact that they contain so many provisions of a human rights character when their orientation is so obviously in another direction. It has always been something of an embarrassment to the human rights community how many of its supposed norms are based upon resolutions or declarations of international organisations, which are often discouragingly remote from the cut and thrust of day-to-day international life. No such criticism, however, can be levelled against the human rights norms which emerge from these treaties. Although they are modest in scope, they are an important indication that human rights considerations do have a role to play even in the harsh world of the international labour market.

One final point mentioned above needs further elaboration: that there may now be dawning a third phase in bilateral treaty law relating to migrant labour. What may be the first straw in the wind heralding this phase is an agreement concluded in 1980 between France and Algeria for the orderly return to Algeria of migrant workers whom France was no longer able to employ.[10] Basically, the agreement provides for the co-operation of the two countries in an organised campaign to entice migrant workers back to their home country, instead of leaving the matter to the vagaries of the employment outlook, on the one hand, or the general law relating to aliens, on the other.

The French-Algerian agreement envisages action on three fronts: first, a programme of professional training for the migrant workers; second, an aid programme to help finance returning migrants who wish to set up small businesses of their own in Algeria; and, third, a flat cash grant for repatriatees (available only to those migrants who do not benefit from the first two measures). This cash grant, in the nature of a 'golden handshake', is to consist of a payment of four times the net monthly wage which the worker was earning in the six months before his application for it.

It is too early to tell whether this humane approach to the problem of returning unwanted migrant workers to their home State will become a common technique. Given the outlook of the industrialised countries for the immediate future in so far as unemployment and economic growth are concerned, however, it is a reasonable assumption that the labour-importing States of western Europe at least will begin to consider this problem more seriously than they have in the past.

2. The American dilemma

In the Americas, three countries are consistent labour importers on a large scale: Argentina, Venezuela and the United States.[11] In all three cases the imported labour comes chiefly from adjacent countries — Bolivia, Chile and Paraguay in the case of Argentina;[12] Colombia in the case of Venezuela;[13] and Mexico in the case of the United States.

All three of these countries have serious problems with illegal immigration. In both Argentina and Venezuela the numbers of illegal migrants are estimated to be in the range of half a million.[14] In the United States the phenomenon is on a much larger scale, entailing a corresponding uncertainty as to the magnitude of the numbers involved — offical estimates fall in the three to five million range; unofficial estimates (such as that of the labour movement) place the figure as high as ten million.[15] One can glean an indication of the scale of the problem, however, by considering that even a conservative estimate of four million illegal workers would mean that twenty-five per cent of Mexico's entire economically active population was north of the Rio Grande.[16]

The United States once had a formal arrangement with Mexico concerning the employment of Mexican migrant workers. This arrangement, the so-called *bracero* programme,[17] began during World War II with the importation of Mexican labour for agricultural work. It continued until 1964, since which time the two States have had no formal treaty arrangements on migrant workers. In 1981, however, the Reagan administration sought to revive the *bracero* approach, not through bilateral United States – Mexican initiatives (nor through the multilateral Migrant Workers Convention now being drafted at the UN, for which the United States has displayed little enthusiasm in any event), but through the enactment of a United States law of the most retrogressive sort.

The proposed legislation, Title VI of the fortunately ill fated Omnibus Immigration Control Act, was named 'The Temporary Mexican Workers Act'.[18] In brief, it authorised the establishment of a two-year 'pilot' guest worker programme under which up to 50,000 Mexican workers would be admitted annually to perform jobs lasting nine to twelve months in states and occupations where there was a shortage of United States workers.[19] These numbers are so small as to be almost derisory in comparison with even the most conservative estimates of the size of the illegal migrant worker population in the United States. Size aside, however, the real difficulty with the proposed legislation lay in the onerous conditions it imposed on the migrant workers involved, conditions drafted either in blissful ignorance or utter disregard of the accumulated experience of western European countries since World War II.

To say that the United States under the Reagan proposals would not be nearly so generous to Mexican migrant workers as the west Europeans have been to their migrants in the treaties just discussed actually gives the proposals far more credit than is due. The Mexican migrants are guaranteed normal wages and working standards, true, but they are not allowed to bring their families with them and they are expressly denied any of the following welfare benefits: food stamps, unemployment compensation, assisted housing and various social security benefits, including medical care.[20] Given the present economic (not to mention political) climate in the United States, coupled with Mexico's own economic difficulties and resultant lack of political leverage, the Reagan proposals were hardly surprising. Nevertheless, from an internationalist's perspective, economic hard times are no justification for compromising the human rights norms governing migrant workers which have been evolving gradually over the past several decades from dozens of bilateral and multilateral treaties.

Happily, the proposed legislation now appears to be a dead letter, albeit more for selfish economic reasons than as a result of human rights concerns.[21] The Omnibus Immigration Control Act never received Congressional approval, being replaced by S. 529,[22] the so-called Simpson-Mazzoli Bill, which now has passed the United States Senate and is pending before the House of Representatives. This Bill squarely rejects the Reagan proposals, although it does establish a complex special procedure for the expeditious admission of temporary or seasonal workers, especially in agriculture.[23] Should it receive House assent and eventually become law, it will constitute no more than a stop-gap measure, however, merely postponing the day when the United States, Mexico and perhaps other States in the Americas will have to address, either bilaterally or regionally, the many problems generated by the phenomenon of legal as well as illegal migrant workers. When that day arrives, it is hoped that model regimes more closely approximating the European experience than the Reagan proposals will serve as the negotiators' guide.

C. Migration and assisted passage agreements

Similar in character to the European migrant worker treaties which were considered in the above section are those agreements which relate to permanent migration. The migration of peoples is clearly nothing new — it is a phenomenon older than history itself. From the legal standpoint, however, the process assumes a special significance when the government of either the sending or the receiving area (or both) becomes a more or less active party in the adventure. Such was notably the case in the colonial period which began in the sixteenth century. It was not until the nineteenth century, however, that international law came to have a significant impact in this area, especially when China and Japan began to send their people overseas to such countries as Australia and the United States, where they were more welcome as manual workers than as fellow human beings.[24]

The nineteenth century also witnessed the inauguration by Great Britain of a significant departure in the area of colonial settlement — the use of government financial resources to assist the working class in their quest for a new life in the sparsely settled lands overseas. The pioneer of this effort was the famous Gibbon Wakefield, whose plan called for the colonial governments of such areas as Australia and New Zealand to stop their policy of selling land to new settlers for a mere pittance. Instead, he recommended that they increase the price at which they sold off their public lands and use the resulting revenues to subsidise emigration of working-class persons from England. The Wakefield plan caught the imagination of at least part of the general public and of officaldom. Governments applied varying forms of his ideas in practice, with varying degrees of success.[25]

One serious drawback to these nineteenth-century experiments was that the governments concerned were either unable or unwilling to exercise effective control over the movements of the people involved. The assisted passage schemes had an unfortunate tendency to degenerate into systems whereby the governments simply paid bounties to shipping companies to deliver immigrants to the colonies. Naturally, under such arrangements, the profits of these companies were higher the less money they expended on the safety and comfort of their passengers. The conditions under which many migrants travelled were appalling — so much so that as early as the 1820s the British government adopted a number of Passenger Acts which set minimum conditions for food, medical care, the regulation of overcrowding, and so forth.[26]

Assisted passage schemes went out of fashion in the late nineteenth century, in part because they were opposed by the settled colonists, who disliked the competition for jobs, housing, and the like.[27] After World War I, however, the idea came back into vogue briefly, for the benefit of war veterans and their families; a similar phenomenon occurred after World War II.[28]

The present concern, however, is with assisted passage and migration plans which existed outside the colonial context. While such arrangements had not been entirely unknown even in the nineteenth century,[29] it is only in the twentieth, and particularly since World War II, that they have become at all common. The most important country in this new movement was Australia, which in the 1950s and 1960s concluded a series of bilateral treaties with such countries as Italy, Malta, the Netherlands, Turkey, West Germany, Yugoslavia, and of course Great Britain. Another area of the world where such schemes assumed a certain importance was Latin America, where Argentina, Brazil and Paraguay entered into immigration treaties with other States.[30]

The typical provisions in these treaties[31] are broadly similar to the provisions found in the migrant worker agreements. The basic idea is that the sending and the receiving States agree to co-operate with one another to ensure that the flow of migrants is orderly, subject to proper supervision, and in accord with the interests and needs of both States. Commonly, the States parties leave for later agreement the precise number of persons who will be involved in the plan. Typically, the sending State pre-selects the migrants, using criteria supplied by the receiving State, leaving the latter free to make the final selection.

The financial arrangements vary. Sometimes the two governments share the assistance expenses equally. Sometimes the migrants themselves are responsible for paying a certain fixed sum, with the governments then paying the remainder of the fare. In one treaty with Italy, for example, Australia agrees to pay the lesser of £25 or a quarter of the fare (provided that Italy contributes the same amount or proportion).[32] Sometimes the treaties leave the financial details for later decision.

Most of the treaties make it abundantly clear that certain obligations are incumbent on the recipients of the largesse of the two governments, although the arrangements are less strict than they were in the case of the migrant worker treaties. Instead of insisting that the migrants sign contracts of employment before their departure, as in the migrant worker treaties, Australia's assisted passage agreements typically provide that the migrant will enter into a written undertaking before his departure that he will stay in his allotted employment for two years, failing which he must refund to the Austalian government whatever sum it had contributed towards his passage. Only after his arrival in his new home will the migrant be allocated to a particular employer. Upon the completion of the obligatory two years, the migrant — in striking contrast to the migrant workers in western Europe — will be entitled to apply for permanent residence in Australia and to have his application approved.[33]

The Latin American treaties are rather different in that they are more oriented towards the promotion of rural settlement and development than towards industrial employment, as is the case with Australia. The requirements, however, are analogous: the migrants must remain in government-approved activity, failing which they forfeit their benefits under the agreement.[34]

As for the specifically human rights-related aspects of these agreements, the most notable point is that the Australian (and New Zealand) treaties consistently provide for equality of treatment in employment-related areas between migrants and nationals. While most of the treaties do not spell out specifically the civil rights to which the migrant is entitled, such silence is not an indication of any claim on the part of the host State or any recognition on the part of the sending State that discrimination in these areas is permitted. Rather, it reflects the fact that the host State's interest in the subject was basically more economic than humanitarian in origin.

The Australian treaties are illustrative, in that they provide for equality of treatment between migrants and nationals in the area of housing. In some treaties there is even an undertaking that, if the migrant's employer supplies him with accommodation, the Australian government will take steps to ensure that the standards and charges involved will be the same as for nationals of the same category in the same area.[35]

Regarding social security benefits, there is a trend once again towards equality of treatment between migrants and nationals. Most of the Australian treaties, for example, provide that the migrant is to be entitled to 'normal' social service benefits — i.e. unemployment benefits, sickness benefits, child allowances, maternity allowances, and hospital and pharmaceutical benefits. In addition to these provisions, the Australian treaties generally commit the host State to provide after-care services for the migrants, through advice on assimilation problems.

The area of cultural rights presents some interesting issues which do not arise in the migrant worker context. Since these assisted passage treaties contemplate that ultimately the migrants will be assimilated into the host community, there is seldom any provision for allowing the migrants an opportunity to retain their own language or traditions. In fact, the Australian treaties typically request the migrants to commence the study of English before their arrival.[36] Such a request, of course, is hardly an unreasonable one. What is more questionable is the usual failure of the host State, except in the case of Australia's treaty with Yugoslavia,[37] to make any provision assisting the migrants in retaining as much of their past tradition as they feasibly can, by such methods as allowing some teaching of, or even in, the mother tongue to the children of migrants.

On the subject of the transfer of funds, the Australian assisted passage agreements are less liberal than the European migrant worker treaties.[38] The Australian agreements, for instance, allow the transfer of reasonable funds only for the purpose of maintaining dependent relatives.[39] The difference is explicable, once again, in terms of the different nature of the underlying migration pattern: since the assisted passage agreements envisage permanent settlement in the host State, the migrants involved should have correspondingly less reason to wish to transfer funds out of the country. Granted that such is the case, migrants should still have a guaranteed right to transfer funds on the same basis as nationals. Ironically, one would naturally assume that such was the case had the agreements been wholly silent on the subject. The better approach, presumably, would be for the agreements to provide specifically for equal treatment with nationals with respect to the transfer of funds, adding a proviso that in any event the migrants should be entitled to send reasonable sums abroad for the maintenance of dependants.

The conclusion that one may draw from these various agreements closely parallels that which the migrant worker treaties revealed: there is a broad trend in treaty practice towards a norm of national treatment for migrants. The conclusion here rests on a less firm base, however, since so much of the evidence comes from the practice of one State alone — Australia. This discussion does not suggest that Australia has singlehandedly wrought a quantum change in the law governing the treatment of aliens. The point, rather, is that when the Australian experience is read in conjunction with the practice of the western European States in the migrant worker field, the high degree of consistency between the two is powerful evidence suggesting the emergence in contemporary international law of a general norm of equality of treatment between aliens and nationals.[40]

Notes

1 See text at Chapter I, notes 73-8.
2 Treaty of Commerce, Establishment and Navigation, 1962, 478 UNTS 86. This discussion will cover only the human rights-related aspects of the treaty and not its more technical economic provisions.
3 Actually, the phraseology is usually that the alien in question will receive either national treatment or most-favoured-nation treatment. On the reasonable assumption that national treatment is generally the more advantageous of these standards, such a provision amounts effectively to a national treatment guarantee. Compare text at and accompanying note 40 *infra*.
4 See text at Chapter V, note 1.
5 See text at Chapter II, notes 39-40.
6 See International Labour Office, 'Post-war manpower problems in Europe', 55 *Int'l Lab. Rev.* (1947), 485.
7 These sixteen treaties are the following:
   (1) Agreement [between France and Greece] Concerning Emigration, 1954, 222 UNTS 299.
   (2) Convention [between Belgium and Spain] Respecting Emigration, 1956, 308 UNTS 285.
   (3) Agreement [between the Netherlands and Italy] Concerning the Recruitment and Placement of Italian Workers in the Netherlands, 1960, 455 UNTS 259. For subsequent amendments (mostly for the purpose of co-ordinating the agreement with the requirements of EEC law), see Protocols of 1965, 551 UNTS 327; and 1970, 753 UNTS 381; and Procès-verbal, 1971, 834 UNTS 357.
   (4) Agreement [between the Netherlands and Spain] Concerning the Immigration, Recruitment and Placement of Spanish Workers in the Netherlands, 1961, 482 UNTS 193.
   (5) Agreement [between the Netherlands and Portugal] Concerning the Migration, Recruitment and Employment of Portuguese Workers in the Netherlands, 1963, 492 UNTS 31.
   (6) Agreement [between France and Portugal] Concerning the Migration, Recruitment and Employment of Portuguese Workers in France, 1963, 811 UNTS 253.
   (7) Agreement [between the Netherlands and Turkey] Concerning the Immigration, Recruitment and Placement of Turkish Workers in the Netherlands, 1964, 521 UNTS 197.
   (8) Agreement [between Austria and Turkey] Concerning the Recruitment and the Employment in Austria of Turkish Workers, 1964, 515 UNTS 109.
   (9) Agreement [between Austria and Yugoslavia] Concerning the Regulation of Employment of Yugoslav Workers in Austria, 1965, 587 UNTS 256.
   (10) Agreement [between Greece and the Netherlands] Concerning the Recruitment, Placement and Employment of Workers in the Netherlands, 1966, 688 UNTS 3.
   (11) Convention [between Morocco and the Netherlands] Concerning the Recruitment and Placement of Moroccan Workers in the Netherlands, 1969, 686 UNTS 139.

(12) Convention [between Belgium and Tunisia] Concerning the Employment and Residence in Belgium of Tunisian Workers, 1969, 696 UNTS 73.

(13) Convention [between Algeria and Belgium] Concerning the Employment and Residence in Belgium of Algerian Workers and their Families, 1970, 717 UNTS 321.

(14) Agreement [between the Netherlands and Yugoslavia] Concerning the Regulation of the Employment of Yugoslav Workers in the Netherlands, 1970, 753 UNTS 75.

(15) Agreement [between Belgium and Yugoslavia] Concerning the Employment and Residence in Belgium of Yugoslav Workers, 1970, 784 UNTS 223; and

(16) Convention [between the Netherlands and Tunisia] Concerning the Recruitment in Tunisia of Tunisian Workers and their Placement in the Netherlands, 1971, 795 UNTS 225.

8 The three Belgian treaties are with Algeria, Tunisia and Yugoslavia (Nos. 13, 12 and 15 respectively, listed in note 7 *supra*). The two Dutch treaties are with Morocco and Tunisia (Nos. 11 and 16 respectively, listed in note 7 *supra*).

9 See text at Chapter III, notes 63-4.

10 For the text of the agreement, see 'Décret No. 80-1150 du 30 décembre 1980 portant publication de l'échange de lettres franco-algérien du 18 septembre 1980 relatif au retour en Algérie de travailleurs algériens et de leurs familles', 113 *Journal Officiel de la République Française*, 4 January 1981, at 162.

France had previously taken several initiatives of a similar sort. In June 1977, for example, she unilaterally established a procedure for granting repatriation assistance to migrant workers who were receiving unemployment benefits. Secretary-General of the UN, 'Welfare of Migrant Workers and their Families', UN doc. E/CN. 5/568 (1978), at 15. Also in 1977, France concluded an agreement with Portugal relating to migrant labour matters which included a provision on the training of migrants to prepare them for returning to their home country. For the text of this agreement, see 'Décret No. 77-496 du 11 mai 1977 portant publication de l'accord entre le Gouvernement français et le Gouvernement portugais relatif à l'immigration, à la situation et à la promotion sociale des travailleurs portugais et de leurs familles en France' (ensemble quatre annexes), 109 *Journal Officiel de la République Française*, 17 May 1977, at 2787.

11 In both Argentina and Venezuela immigrants constitute approximately seven per cent of the total population and about twenty per cent of the labour force. F. Breton, 'Working and living conditions of migrant workers in South America', 114 *Int'l Lab. Rev.* (1976), 339, at 342.

12 Bolivia and Paraguay in particular are sources of migrant labour: in the case of Bolivia, approximately twelve per cent of its population or forty per cent of its working population is estimated to have migrated; for Paraguay the figure is approximately thirty per cent. *Id.*

13 See generally E. Guerrero Medino, 'Migration between Colombia and Venezuela', in *Migrant Workers Occupational Safety and Health* (International Labour Office, Occupational Safety and Health Series, No. 34, 1977), at 71.

14 F. Breton, *supra*, note 11, at 346. In Venezuela, though not in Argentina, there have been expulsions on a serious scale in the past.

15 'The ins and outs of immigration policy', *The Economist*, 8 August 1981, at 29, col. 1 (UK ed.).

16 Secretary-General of the UN, *supra*, note 10, at 6.

17 See generally R. Craig, *The Bracero Program. Interest Groups and Foreign Policy* (1971). On the problem of illegal Mexican labour in the United States, see *Illegal*

Mexican Immigrants to the United States (A. Porter, ed.), a special issue of 12 *Int'l Migration Rev.* (1978); W. Fogel, *Mexican Illegal Alien Workers in the United States* (1978); *Immigrants and Immigrants. Perspectives on Mexican Labor Migration to the United States* (A. Corwin, ed., 1978); G. Kiser and M. Kiser, *Mexican Workers in the United States. Historical and Political Perspectives* (1979); and P. Ehrlich, L. Bilderback and A. Ehrlich, *The Golden Door. International Migration, Mexico, and the United States* (1979).

18 S. 1765, 97th Cong., 1st Sess. § 601 (1981).

19 The guest worker proposals were only one part of the administration's proposed package. Other important elements were an amnesty for illegal migrants who had arrived in the United States before 1 January 1980, and the imposition of federal penalties on employers who knowingly employed illegal migrants. Sections 101, 201.

Although the latter provision, if eventually enacted into law, would be the first such sanction against employers to be imposed by the federal government, it should be noted that since 1971 the state of California has provided for both civil and criminal sanctions against employers hiring illegal migrant labour. Cal. Lab. Code § 2805 (West 1983), whose compatibility with the United States Constitution was confirmed by the Supreme Court in *De Canas* v. *Bica*, 424 U.S. 351 (1976). Other states have followed suit. See generally 2 P. Mutharika, *The Alien under American Law*, ch. IX, at 79 (1981).

20 Section 601(g), (h).

21 The Senate Judiciary Committee cited 'adverse impacts on U.S. workers' and fears that migrants would remain in the United States as reasons for rejecting the guest worker programme. S. Rep. No. 98-62, 98th Cong., 1st Sess. 18 (1983).

22 S. 529, 98th Cong., 1st Sess. (1983).

23 Section 214.

24 The United States unilaterally restricted immigration from China with the adoption of the Chinese Exclusion Act of 1882, which remained in force in one form or another until 1943. With Japan the case was slightly different, since an 1894 treaty between the two countries gave to the nationals of each country the right to enter and settle in the other State. In 1907, however, the United States enacted legislation allowing the President to exclude persons whose presence would adversely affect labour conditions in the United States. Under this provision the President declared Japanese to be inadmissible, a policy resulting in the so-called Gentlemen's Agreement of 1907 whereby Japan agreed to restrict the issue of travel documents to the United States. A. Schwartz, *The Open Society*, 100-1 (1968).

25 See R. Younger, *Australia and the Australians: A New Concise History*, 195-9 (1970).

26 G. Blainey, *The Tyranny of Distance. How Distance Shaped Australia's History*, 158-65 (1968).

27 *Id.* at 168.

28 For example, from 1946 to 1952 Australia had a policy of granting free passage to British ex-servicemen and their dependants. T. Millar, *Australia's Foreign Policy*, 226 (1968). See also Note, 'Assisted migration in the British Commonwealth', 52 *Int'l Lab. Rev.* (1946), 414. In the case of Commonwealth countries the British government possessed a blanket authority to enter into assisted passage agreements (i.e. it did not have to have each agreement approved individually), beginning with the Empire Settlement Act, 1922, 12 and 13 Geo. V, c. 13, as amended by the Empire Settlement Act, 1937, 1 Edw. VIII and 1 Geo. VI, c. 18, and by the Commonwealth Settlement Act, 1967, 15 and 16 Eliz. II, c. 31 (which Acts are known collectively as the Commonwealth Settlement Acts, 1922 to 1967). Under this legislation the blanket authority terminated in 1972.

29 For example, as early as 1847–51 nearly 4,000 Germans colonised South Australia with government assistance. R. Younger, *supra*, note 25, at 211.

30 See, e.g., Nos. 1, 3, 10, 11 and 12 listed in note 31 *infra*.

31 This discussion is based on a consideration of the following eighteen treaties:

(1) Convention [between the Netherlands and Argentina] Concerning Immigration, 1938, 194 LNTS 409.

(2) Migration Agreement [between the Netherlands and New Zealand], 1950, 83 UNTS 269.

(3) Agreement [between the Netherlands and Brazil] Concerning Emigration and Settlement, 1950, 123 UNTS 101.

(4) Agreement [between Australia and the Netherlands] for Assisted Migration, 1951, 128 UNTS 115.

(5) Agreement [between Australia and Italy] for Assisted Migration, 1951, 131 UNTS 187.

(6) Agreement [between Australia and West Germany] for Assisted Migration, 1952, 184 UNTS 147.

(7) Assisted Migration Agreement [between the Netherlands and Australia], 1956, 280 UNTS 3.

(8) Agreement [between Australia and Great Britain] Relating to an Assisted Passage Migration Scheme, 1957, 271 UNTS 235.

(9) Agreement [between Australia and West Germany] for Assisted Migration, 1958, 320 UNTS 303.

(10) Agreement [between Japan and Paraguay] Concerning Migration, 1959, 373 UNTS 85.

(11) Agreement [between Japan and Brazil] Concerning Migration and Settlement, 1960, 518 UNTS 29.

(12) Agreement [between Brazil and Spain] on Migration, 1960, 658 UNTS 39.

(13) Assisted Passage Agreement [between Australia and Great Britain], 1962, 434 UNTS 219.

(14) Agreement [between Australia and Malta] for Assisted Migration, 1965, 548 UNTS 203.

(15) Migration and Settlement Agreement [between Australia and the Netherlands], 1965, 560 UNTS 85.

(16) Agreement [between Australia and West Germany] on Assisted Migration, 1965, 542 UNTS 53.

(17) Agreement [between Australia and Turkey] Concerning the Residence and Employment of Turkish Citizens in Australia, 1967, 660 UNTS 55; and

(18) Agreement [between Australia and Yugoslavia] on the Residence and Employment of Yugoslav Citizens in Australia, 1970, 742 UNTS 299.

32 No. 5 listed in note 31 *supra*.

33 Note that the provision is commonly for permanent residence and not for nationality. The assisted migrants must qualify for nationality, if at all, under the normal rules.

34 See, e.g., Article 27 of the Agreement between Japan and Brazil, No. 11 listed in note 31 *supra*.

35 See, e.g., Article 15 of the Agreement between Australia and Turkey, No. 17 listed in note 31 *supra*.

36 See, e.g., Article 14(2) of the Agreement between Australia and West Germany, No. 6 listed in note 31 *supra*.

37 See Article 11(2) of the Agreement between Australia and Yugoslavia, No. 18 listed in note 31 *supra*.

38 See text at note 9 *supra*.

39 See, e.g., Article 19(1) of the Agreement between Australia and Turkey, No. 17 listed in note 31 *supra*.
40 Subject, of course, to the overriding effect of the international minimum standard, now infused with the norms of international human rights law. See generally text at Chapter II, notes 8-21, and Chapter III, notes 31-40. Compare text at and accompanying note 3 *supra*.

   For a recent, more comprehensive treatment of the Australian experience, going well beyond the brief survey contained in this chapter, see R. Lillich and S. Neff, 'The promotion of human rights through bilateral treaties: the Australian experience with migration and settlement agreements', 8 *A.Y.I.L.* (1983), 142.

CHAPTER SEVEN

The rights of aliens:
some general observations

Traditional international law, based upon the nation-State system, developed the doctrine of diplomatic protection to enable States to seek reclamation when their nationals were injured, physically or economically, by other States. Whether a compensable claim arose in a particular case was determined under what became known as the law of State responsibility for injuries to aliens, which contained an international mimimum standard by which a State's treatment of an alien was measured. Since, absent a treaty obligation, States were not required to admit aliens, this body of law focused primarily upon the rights of the alien and the duties of the State after the alien's admission, with secondary attention paid to the norms governing the expulsion process should the State exercise its acknowledged right (once again, absent a treaty obligation) to expel the alien. This relatively narrow focus, however, has not led to widespread agreement among States either about the jurisprudential underpinnings or the practical application of this body of law, witness the unsuccessful codification efforts of the League of Nations and, to date, the UN.[1] Codification of the treatment of aliens in a wider context, moreover, has not even been attempted by the international community.[2]

Of course, through the international agreement route — initially capitulations and then reciprocal FCN treaties — States established more comprehensive regimes governing the admission, stay and expulsion of aliens on an *ad hoc* basis. These bilateral treaties have in the past contributed to the development of customary international law norms.[3] There is no reason, moreover, why they may not make similar contributions in the future. The same can be said of regional arrangements, such as the ones discussed in Chapter V,[4] as well as the international agreements concluded under UN or other auspices, considered in Chapters III and IV, that are designed to create or clarify the norms governing various aspects of the treatment of aliens on a worldwide basis.[5] Many provisions in these treaties, admittedly binding only upon States parties thereto, will undoubtedly ripen over the years into norms of customary international law binding even States which have not ratified them. As the late Judge Baxter, in his fine treatment of this subject, concluded: 'Treaties that do not purport to be declaratory of customary international law at the time they enter into force may nevertheless with the passage of time pass into customary international law.'[6]

In the meantime, the law governing the treatment of aliens — in its broadest sense — resembles a giant unassembled juridical jigsaw puzzle, as mentioned in the Introduction. Actually, this figure of speech is not entirely apt, since it conveys the impression that there exists a certain number of pieces which, when assembled, will complete a predetermined design. With respect to the treatment of aliens, however, the number of pieces is uncertain and the grand design is still emerging, as is obvious from a perusal of the preceding chapters, which have attempted to bring some rough order out of what Dean Christenson has called 'the rich chaos' of existing international law.[7] Thus another figure of speech, taken from the fashion world, might be more appropriate: 'the layered look'. For, over the basic garment (the customary international law of State responsibility for injuries to aliens), nation-States have placed shirts, sweaters and jackets (bilateral treaties, regional arrangements and multilateral conventions), leaving the alien's body protected by a varying number of layers (legal regimes) depending upon the sartorial tastes of the State involved. While the trend has been towards greater protection of the alien from the chilling effect of the State's far-reaching sovereign powers over his or her admission, stay and expulsion, the extent of such protection varies greatly, leaving aliens in many States inadequately protected, both substantively and procedurally, at the present time.

Efforts to develop a comprehensive legal regime to govern the treatment of aliens on a global basis, as illustrated by the ILC's failure to follow through its initial decision to codify the topic,[8] have met with little success, although the UN's elaboration of the Elles draft Declaration and its Migrant Workers Convention may prove fruitful in so far as certain types of aliens are concerned.[9] Bilateral treaties and especially regional arrangements, as EEC and Council of Europe experience shows,[10] may prove to be more profitable codification ventures, serving as models for similar agreements between other States as well as contributing to the development of norms of general applicability, e.g. non-discrimination.[11] Backstopping all these initiatives, of course, is the gradual infusion of international human rights norms into the law of State responsibility for injuries to aliens and other areas of international law affecting aliens.[12] In addition, the progressive development of a more comprehensive yet specific customary international law governing the human rights of aliens may ultimately require the absorption, under the rubric of 'the general principles of law recognised by civilised nations' found in Article 38(1)(c) of the Statute of the International Court of Justice, of a good many constitutional or legislative norms contained in the domestic law of more enlightened countries.[13]

One recent development stands out, however, in any survey of the human rights of aliens in contemporary international law, such as this volume has essayed: not only is the word 'alien' no longer taboo in UN circles,[14] but what their rights are and should be has become one of the most pressing and debated issues in the international community. While there are many reasons for this development, by far the most significant was the Arab oil embargo and the recessionary impact it has had upon the economies of most States, especially the States of western Europe. Many of the fifteen million foreign workers and their families living in these countries[15] almost overnight became liabilities rather than assets. Headlines such as 'West German Distrust of Foreigners Grows'[16] and 'France and Aliens in its Midst: Fear on both Sides'[17] reveal how the migrant workers in western Europe's two largest labour-importing States suddenly came to be regarded as guests who had outstayed their welcome. Similar problems surfaced in other countries, including Sweden[18] and Switzerland.[19] The home States of the migrants soon felt the repercussions from the economic downturn too. The factors motivating the conclusion of the European Migrant Workers Convention, the support now given by numerous Third World States to the Elles draft Declaration, and the expressions of concern voiced by several unlikely States over the treatment of their nationals abroad,[20] all support the belief that at long last most States now view it as in their inclusive interest to help develop a body of law governing the treatment of aliens acceptable to all members of the international community.[21]

Admittedly, the present world economic situation may not make this decade the best time to reformulate or codify, must less extend, the human rights accorded to aliens. Viewing such prospects from the perspective of the Council of Europe, one commentator noted several years ago that '[s]ince the oil crisis of 1973, the countries concerned have been faced with economic recession and no longer seem willing to enter into obligations protecting migrant workers which would impose considerable restrictions on their freedom of action'.[22] Non-discriminatory treatment, he believed, was just about as far as States were willing to proceed with respect to aliens. Since both Council of Europe and many other international agreements are riddled with exceptions to the non-discrimination norm, its more widespread acceptance, in conventional or customary international law, would be an achievement not to be taken lightly. 'As a rule,' he concluded with a mixture of satisfaction and resignation, 'equality of treatment of nationals and aliens does mean an improvement in the position of aliens and, at the same time, it forms the limit of the lengths to which one can go in this respect.'[23] In view of its long-standing interest in the protection of human rights and the well-being of individuals, he urged the Council of Europe to pay great attention to the law governing the treatment of *all* aliens.

The Council of Europe later did just that, holding a three-day colloquy on the 'Human Rights of Aliens in Europe' in Funchal-Madeira, Portugal, in October 1983. Among the four papers presented,[24] one's attention is drawn to the brief introductory report by Dr Plender on the general subject-matter of the colloquy. Surveying the great progress that has been made in the promotion and protection of human rights since the adoption of the UN Charter, including the rights of aliens when seeking or after admission to other States, he nevertheless recognises 'the magnitude of the problem which west European States face in containing the mutual hostility of some groups of immigrants and members of the communities in which they live ...'.[25] Cautiously he concludes that 'it is possible that [the] problem may be best resolved by a form of international co-operation entailing the multilateral declaration of common minimum standards of treatment for alien minorities'.[26] What form the legal instrument might take — whether treaty, recommendation or arrangement concluded under the aegis of the Council of Europe — Dr Plender leaves the reader to speculate. From the general thrust of his comments, however, it would be surprising, to paraphrase another writer in an analogous context, if the instrument were not to demand equality of treatment for aliens within Council of Europe countries, at least when the alien was a national of a member State.[27] What legal procedures might be thought useful to guarantee the enforcement of the instrument's rights Dr Plender also leaves unsaid. Presumably the individual alien would be given the opportunity to protect his rights himself, without having to rely upon the intervention of his own or his host State, for Dr Plender evinces considerable scepticism — and rightly so — as to 'the practical efficacy of international arrangements [depending] upon the activities of national governments'.[28]

The above modest initiative by the Council of Europe, as was the case with the European Migrant Workers Convention, should add further impetus to the UN's efforts with respect to the Elles draft Declaration and its Migrant Workers Convention. Also, it should encourage the UN and other international and regional organisations to undertake broader and more comprehensive studies of the human rights of aliens in contemporary international law. The problems aliens face today, like all human problems, obviously cannot be solved by law alone. Economists, sociologists and members of the cloth, as Dr Plender rightly remarks, all have a crucial role to play.[29] Yet it is up to lawyers — especially international human rights lawyers, who until now have shown relatively little interest in the law governing the treatment of aliens — to assess, develop and establish the legal regimes under which the rights of aliens may be more effectively protected. It has been the purpose of this volume to assist them in that grand endeavour.

Notes

1 See text at Chapter II, notes 16-21, and Chapter III, notes 31-42.
2 Recall the ILC's failure to study the subject despite its inclusion in the Commission's original agenda. See text at Chapter III, notes 33-6.
3 See text at Chapter I, note 73.
4 For the impact of the Treaty of Rome upon customary international law, see generally G. White, 'The impact of European Community law on international law', in *International Law. Teaching and Practice*, 77 (B. Cheng, ed., 1982).
5 For the impact of multilateral human rights treaties upon the customary international law governing the treatment of aliens, see R. Lillich, 'Duties of States regarding the civil rights of aliens', 161 *Receuil des Cours* (Hague Academy of International Law) (1978–III), 329, at 391-9.
6 R. Baxter, 'Treaties and custom', 129 *Receuil des Cours* (Hague Academy of International Law) (1970–I), 25, at 57.
7 See R. Lillich, 'The valuation of nationalized property in international law: toward a consensus or more "rich chaos"?', in 3 *The Valuation of Nationalized Property in International Law*, 183, at 196 n. 64 (R. Lillich, ed. and contrib., 1975).
8 See text at and accompanying note 2 *supra*.
9 The former, as drafted by Baroness Elles, covers only those aliens who 'reside' in a State. See text at Chapter III, note 61. Compare Article 1 of the draft declaration provisionally adopted by the UN General Assembly's working group, included as Appendix B, which contains alternative language covering all aliens 'present' in a State. The latter, of course, covers only migrant workers and their families. See text at Chapter IV, note 69, and Article 1 of the draft convention included as Appendix C.
10 See generally Chapter V.
11 See text at Chapter V, note 39.
12 See generally text at Chapter III, notes 5-30.
13 The United States Supreme Court, for instance, has construed the Equal Protection Clause of the Fourteenth Amendment to prevent States from discriminating against aliens in so far as welfare benefits and admission to the Bar are concerned. See *Graham* v. *Richardson*, 403 U.S. 365 (1971) and *In re Griffiths*, 413 U.S. 717 (1973). For a compilation of cases on aliens and equal protection under the US Constitution, see P. Mutharika, *The Alien under American Law*, ch. II (1980).
14 See, e.g., the use of the word throughout the revision of the Elles draft declaration provisionally adopted by the UN General Assembly's working group, included as Appendix B. Compare text at Chapter III, note 52, for the UN's earlier avoidance of the term.
15 R. Rist, *Guestworkers in Germany*, xi (1978).
16 *International Herald-Tribune*, 23 February 1982, at 1. The article reports that '[b]y the government's count there are 4·65 million foreigners in West Germany, or 7·5 percent of the total population, an increase of 16 percent over the last three years. The largest group are Turks, about 1·5 million, who live mostly in the big cities'. See also 'Gastarbeiter in the ghetto', *The Times* (London), 16 August 1982, at 4; 'Bonn dilemma as foreign workers overstay their welcome,' *The Guardian* (London), 23 October 1982, at 5; 'No more their guests,' *The Daily* (Bombay), 9 January 1983, at 9. The Bundestag recently approved legislation offering migrant workers from non-EEC States 10,500 Deutschmarks to return home. *International Herald-Tribune*, 12-13 November 1983, at 2. Compare text at Chapter VI, note 10.
17 *New York Times*, 15 August 1983, at A2. The article reports that '[o]ut of a French

population of some 54 million, there are an estimated 4·3 million foreigners, up about 90,000 from last year. Roughly 4 in 10 of the foreigners live in and around Paris ... but it is the 1·5 North Africans, about half of them from Algeria, who loom large in the public mind'. Compare text at Chapter VI, note 10.

18 See, e.g., 'Second-class citizens in egalitarian Sweden', *The Times* (London), 18 August 1982, at 6.

19 See, e.g., 'High hurdles among the Alps', *The Times* (London), 17 August 1982, at 5.

20 See, e.g., 'Expulsions anger China', *The Times* (London), 4 June 1983, at 6: 'China has protested to Mongolia about the expulsion of nearly 1,800 Chinese citizens and the confiscation of their property by the Mongolian customs. The Foreign Ministry said in a Note to the Mongolian Embassy here that the departing Chinese had been "stripped and subjected to insulting examination"'.

An Indian scholar, moreover, recently invoked the law of State responsibility for injuries to aliens in protesting the ill-treatment of Indians in the Middle East and Pakistan. S. Chandra, *Civil and Political Rights of Aliens*, 12-13 (1982), rejecting *sub silentio* an Indian jurist's frequently cited attack on this body of law, made two decades ago. S. Guha Roy, 'Is the law of responsibility of States for injuries to aliens a part of universal international law?,' 55 *A.J.I.L.* (1961), 863.

It is interesting to note that India also recently announced the construction of a $450 million barbed wire fence along its 1,365 mile border with Bangladesh to keep out illegal aliens. *International Herald-Tribune*, 15 August 1983, at 5. One need not speculate long as to how India would react should the US adopt current ill-advised proposals to fence out Mexicans!

21 As Professor Bishop predicted would occur some years ago. See W. Bishop, 'General course of public international law', 115 *Recueil des Cours* (Hague Academy of International Law) (1965–II), 147, at 422.

22 A. Swart, 'The legal status of aliens: clauses in Council of Europe instruments relating to the rights of aliens', 11 *N.Y.I.L.*, (1980), 3, at 27-8.

23 *Id.* at 47-8.

24 On 'Human Rights of Aliens in Europe', 'The Admission of Aliens to the Territory of the Host Country and his Residence There', 'The Participation of the Alien in Public Affairs (Political and Associative Life)', and 'The Fact that Aliens Belong to Various Cultures and the Tensions which this Creates'.

25 R. Plender, 'Human rights of aliens in Europe', *Council of Europe* H/Coll (83) 2 (1983), at 16.

26 *Id.*

27 A. Evans, 'Development of European Community law regarding the trade union and related rights of migrant workers', 28 *I.C.L.Q.* (1979), 354, at 365.

28 R. Plender, *supra*, note 25, at 19.

29 *Id.*

APPENDIX A

The Draft Declaration on the Human Rights of Individuals who are not Citizens of the Country in which they Live

[This declaration is contained in *International Provisions Protecting the Human Rights of Non-citizens:* Study prepared by the Baroness Elles: Special Rapporteur of the Sub-commission on the Prevention of Discrimination and Protection of Minorities, U.N. Doc. E/CN. 4/Sub. 2/392/Rev.1 (1980).]

The General Assembly.

Considering that the Charter of the United Nations encourages the promotion of universal respect for and observance of the human rights and fundamental freedoms of all human beings,

Considering that the Universal Declaration of Human Rights proclaims that all human beings are born free and equal in dignity and rights and that everyone is entitled to all the rights and freedoms set forth in the Declaration, without distinction of any kind, such as race, colour, sex, language, religion, political or other opinion, national or social origin, property, birth or other status,

Considering that the Universal Declaration of Human Rights proclaims further that everyone has the right to recognition everywhere as a person before the law and aims at ensuring that all are equal before the law and are entitled without any discrimination to equal protection of the law, and that all are entitled to equal protection against any discrimination in violation of the Declaration and against any incitement to such discrimination,

Being aware that the States parties to the International Covenants on Human Rights now in force undertake to guarantee that the rights enunciated in these covenants will be exercised without discrimination of any kind as to race, colour, sex, or language,

Conscious that, with improving communications and the development of peaceful contacts and friendly relations between countries, individuals increasingly reside and work in countries of which they are not citizens,

Reaffirming the principle of the sovereign equality of States,

Noting that the International Convention on the Elimination of All Forms of Racial Discrimination provides that States may make certain distinctions, exclusions, restrictions or preferences between their own citizens and the citizens of other countries,

Noting further that existing international instruments need to be supplemented in order to protect the human rights of individuals who are residing and may be working in countries of which they are not citizens,

Proclaims this Declaration:

Article 1

For the purposes of this Declaration, the term 'non-citizen' shall apply to any individual who lawfully resides in a State of which he is not a national.

Article 2

1. Non-citizens shall observe the laws in force in the State in which they reside and refrain from illegal activities prejudicial to the State.

2. Every State is entitled to expect that non-citizens will respect the customs and traditions of the people of the State.

Article 3

Every State shall make public any laws, regulations or administrative measures which distinguish between citizens and non-citizens or affect the rights of non-citizens.

Article 4

Notwithstanding any distinction which a State is entitled to make between its citizens and non-citizens, every non-citizen shall enjoy at least the following rights, always respecting the obligations imposed upon a non-citizen by article 2, and subject to the limitations provided for in article 29 of the Universal Declaration of Human Rights:

  (i) The right to security of person and protection by the State against violence or bodily harm, whether inflicted by government officials or by any individual, group or institution;

 (ii) The right to equal access to and equal treatment before the tribunals and all other organs administering justice, and to have the free assistance of an interpreter if he cannot understand or speak the language used in court;

(iii) The right to freedom of movement and to choice of residence within the borders of the State, subject to such restrictions as are absolutely necessary for compelling reasons of public policy, public order, national security, or public health or morals;

 (iv) The right to leave the country and return to his own country;

  (v) The right to marriage and choice of spouse;

(vi) The right to own property alone as well as in association with others;
(vii) The right to freedom of thought, conscience and religion;
(viii) The right to freedom of opinion and expression;
(ix) The right to freedom of peaceful assembly and association;
(x) The right to retain his own language, culture, and traditions.

Article 5

No non-citizen shall be subjected to arbitrary arrest or detention.

Article 6

No non-citizen shall be subjected to torture or to cruel, inhuman or degrading treatment or punishment.

Article 7

1. No non-citizen shall be subjected to arbitrary expulsion or deportation.

2. A non-citizen may be expelled from the territory of a State only in pursuance of a decision reached in accordance with law and shall, except where compelling reasons of national security otherwise require, be allowed to submit reasons against his expulsion and to have his case reviewed by and be represented for the purpose before the competent authority or a person or persons especially designated by the competent authority.

3. Collective expulsion of non-citizens is prohibited.

Article 8

Notwithstanding any distinction which a State is entitled to make between its citizens and non-citizens, every non-citizen shall enjoy at least the following economic and social rights, always respecting the obligations imposed on a non-citizen by article 2:

(i) The right to just and favourable conditions of work, to equal pay for equal work, and to just and fair remuneration;
(ii) The right to repatriate earnings and savings, in accordance with national laws in force;
(iii) The right to join trade unions and participate in their activities, subject to national laws in force;
(iv) The right to public health, medical care, social security, social service and education, provided that the minimum requirements for participation in national schemes are met and that undue strain is not placed on the resources of the State.

Article 9

1. No non-citizen shall be subjected to arbitrary confiscation of his lawfully acquired assets.

2. Any non-citizen whose assets are expropriated in whole or in part in accordance with national laws in force shall have the right to just compensation.

Article 10

Any non-citizen shall be free to communicate with the consulate or diplomatic mission of his country or, in their absence, with the consulate or diplomatic mission of any other State entrusted with the protection of his own country's interests in the State where he resides.

APPENDIX B

Text of articles of the Draft Declaration on the Human Rights of Individuals who are not Citizens of the Country in which they Live adopted by the open-ended working group of the UN General Assembly

[These articles are contained in U.N. Doc. A/C.3/38/11 (1983). Material in normal type has been adopted by the working group. Material in parentheses has been provisionally adopted by the working group. Material in brackets has been proposed to the working group.]

The General Assembly,

Considering that the Charter of the United Nations encourages the promotion of universal respect for and observance of the human rights and fundamental freedoms of all human beings, without distinction as to race, sex, language or religion,

Considering that the Universal Declaration of Human Rights proclaims that all human beings are born free and equal in dignity and rights and that everyone is entitled to all the rights and freedoms set forth in the Declaration, without distinction of any kind, such as race, colour, sex, language, religion, political or other opinion, national or social origin, property, birth or other status,

Considering that the Universal Declaration of Human Rights proclaims further that everyone has the right to recognition everywhere as a person before the law, that all are equal before the law, are entitled without any discrimination to equal protection of the law, and that all are entitled to equal protection against any discrimination in violation of the aforementioned Declaration and against any incitement to such discrimination,

Being aware that the States parties to the international covenants on human rights now in force undertake to guarantee that the rights enunciated in these covenants will be exercised without discrimination of any kind as to race, colour, sex, language, religion, political or other opinion, national or social origin, property, birth or other status,

Conscious that, with improving communications and the development of peaceful and friendly relations among countries, individuals increasingly live in countries of which they are not citizens,

Reaffirming the purposes and principles of the United Nations Charter,

Recognizing that the protection of human rights and fundamental freedoms provided for in international instruments should also be ensured for individuals who are not citizens of the country in which they live,

Proclaims this Declaration:

(Article 1)

(For the purposes of this declaration, the term 'alien' shall apply to any individual who [lawfully] [resides] [is present] in a State of which he is neither a national nor a citizen.)

Article 2

Aliens shall observe the laws of the State in which they reside or are present and regard with respect the customs and traditions of the people of that State.

Article 3

Every State shall make public the national legislation or regulations affecting aliens.

Article 4

(1) Aliens shall enjoy in accordance with domestic law in particular the following rights:

(a) The right to life, liberty and security of person;
(b) The right to protection against arbitrary or unlawful interference with privacy, family, home or correspondence;
(c) The right to equal access to, and equal treatment before courts, tribunals and all other organs and authorities administering justice and, when necessary, to free assistance of an interpreter in criminal proceedings and when prescribed by law other proceedings;
((d) The right to choose a spouse, to marry, to found a family; [or to be joined by his or her family] [and to be reunited with his or her spouse, unmarried minor children, and if permitted by domestic law, other family members];)
(e) The right to freedom of thought, opinion, conscience and religion;
(f) The right to retain their own language, culture and traditions.

((2) Subject to such restrictions as are prescribed by law and which are necessary in a democratic society in the interests of national security, [national development] or public safety, public order (*ordre public*), public health or morals or the protection of the rights and freedoms of others, and are consistent with the other rights recognized in this declaration, aliens shall enjoy:

(a) The right to liberty of movement and freedom to choose their residence within the borders of the State;

(b) The right to leave the country;

(c) The right to freedom of expression;

(d) The right to manifest one's religion or whatever belief;

(e) The right to peaceful assembly and the right to freedom of association;

(f) The right to own property alone as well as in association with others in accordance with domestic law.)

[(3) The provisions of this article shall apply to individuals lawfully resident within a State.]

Article 5

No alien shall be subjected to arbitrary arrest or detention; no alien shall be deprived of his liberty except on such grounds and in accordance with such procedures as are established by law.

Article 6

No alien shall be subjected to torture or to cruel, inhuman or degrading treatment or punishment and, in particular, no alien shall be subjected without his free consent to medical or scientific experimentation.

(Article 7)

([An alien [lawfully] [residing] in the territory of a State may be expelled therefrom only in pursuance of a decision reached in accordance with law and shall except where compelling reasons of national security otherwise require, be allowed to submit the reasons against his expulsion and to have his case reviewed by, and be represented for the purpose before, the competent authority or a person or persons especially designated by the competent authority. [The [collective] expulsion [of groups] of aliens on the ground of criteria of race, religion, culture or any other discriminatory criterion is prohibited.]])

(New article)

(No provision of this Declaration shall be interpreted as restricting the right of any State to establish differences between nationals and aliens. However, such differences shall not be incompatible with the specific provisions of applicable international legal instruments in force for that State.)

(Article 8)

([Aliens [who find themselves] [lawfully] [residing] in the territory of a State shall enjoy, in accordance with the national laws, the following economic and social rights], subject to their obligations referred to in article 2:

(i) The right to safe and healthy working conditions, to fair wages and equal remuneration for work of equal value without distinction of any kind, in particular, women being guaranteed conditions of work not inferior to those enjoyed by men, with equal pay for equal work;

(ii) The right to transfer abroad earnings, savings or other personal monetary assets, [in accordance with] [subject to] national laws in force.

(iii) The right to join trade unions and other organizations or associations, and to participate in their activities, subject only to the rules of the organizations concerned [and national laws in force].

(iv) [The right to health protection, medical care, social security, social service, education, [professional training], rest and leisure,

[providing that they fulfil the requirements under the relevant schemes for the participation of nationals residing in that State] [and that undue strain is not placed on the resources of the State.]

[providing that they fulfil the requirements under national law for the receipt of such benefits and that undue strain is not placed on the resources of the State.]]

2. With a view to protecting the basic rights of non-nationals carrying on lawful paid activities in the country in which they find themselves, such rights may be specified by the Governments concerned in multilateral or bilateral conventions.)

(Article 9)

(1. No alien shall be arbitrarily deprived of his lawfully acquired assets.

2. Any alien whose assets are expropriated in whole or in part in accordance with national laws in force shall have the right to [prompt, adequate, effective and] [prompt, adequate and effective] [just] compensation [subject to national laws and regulations in force] [in accordance with international law] [in accordance with the recognized principles of international law].)

(Article 10)

(Any alien shall be free [in all circumstances] to communicate with the consulate or diplomatic mission of the State of which he is a citizen or a national or, in their absence, with the consulate or diplomatic mission of any other State entrusted with the protection of the interests of the State of which he is a citizen or a national in the State where he resides.)

APPENDIX C

The Draft International Convention on the Protection of the Rights of all Migrant Workers and their Families

[The author collated the material below from the following documents: U.N. Doc. A/C.3/36/10 (1981); U.N. Doc. A/C.3/37/1 (1982); U.N. Doc. A/C.3/37/7 (1982); U.N. Doc. A/C.3/38/1 (1983); Governing Body, International Labour Office, 225th Session of the International Organisations Committee apps. I, II, ILO Doc. GB/225/IO/1/1 (1984). The material in normal type has been provisionally adopted by the UN Working Group. The material in brackets has been proposed to but not provisionally agreed upon by the UN Working Group.]

Preamble

The States Parties to this Convention,

(1) [*Reaffirming*] [*Taking into account*] the [permanent validity] [the importance] of the principles [and standards] [norms] embodied in the basic instruments of the United Nations concerning human rights, in particular the Universal Declaration of Human Rights, the International Covenant on Economic Social and Cultural Rights, the International Covenant on Civil and Political Rights, the International Convention on the Elimination of All Forms of Racial Discrimination, and the Convention on the Elimination of All Forms of Discrimination Against Women,

(2) [*Reaffirming also*] [*Taking into account*] the principles [and standards] [set forth in the relevant instruments] elaborated within the framework of the International Labour Organisation, especially the Conventions concerning Migration for Employment (No. 97) and Migrations in Abusive Conditions and the Promotion of Equality of Opportunity and Treatment of Migrant Workers (No. 143) and the Recommendations concerning Migration for Employment (No. 86) and Migrant Workers (No. 151),

(3) *Reaffirming* the importance of the principles contained in the Convention Against Discrimination in Education of the United Nations Educational, Scientific and Cultural Organization,

(4) *Recalling* [the Declaration on the Protection of All Persons from Being Subjected to Torture and Other Cruel, Inhuman, or Degrading Treatment

or Punishment,] the Declaration of the Fourth United Nations Congress on the Prevention of Crime and the Treatment of Offenders, the Code of Conduct for Law Enforcement Officials, and the Slavery Conventions,

(5) *Recognizing* the importance of the work carried out in connexion with [migrant labour] [migrant workers and their families] in various organs of the United Nations system, in particular in the Commission on Human Rights, the Commission for Social Development, the Food and Agriculture Organization of the United Nations, the United Nations Educational, Scientific and Cultural Organization and the World Health Organization, and in various regional organizations,

[(6) *Recognizing* that the principal objective of the International Labour Organisation, as stated in its Constitution, is the protection of the interests of workers when employed in countries other than their own, [that the ILO has thus been vested with special authority and responsibility to deal with the subject of migrant workers and that the ILO possesses unique competence, expertise, and experience in migrant worker matters]

[(6) *Recognizing* the importance of the International Labour Organisation in the defence of the interests of migrant workers,]

[and that the ILO has made a significant contribution to the promotion of the interests of migrant workers,]]

(7) *Recognizing* the progress made by certain countries on a regional or bilateral basis, as well as the importance and usefulness of bilateral and multilateral agreements for the protection of the rights of migrant workers and their families,

(8) *Realizing* the importance and extent of the migration phenomenon which involves millions of people and affects a large number of countries in the international community,

[(9) *Aware* of the [positive] impact that the flows of migrant workers have on [the process of regional integration] and of the [important] role that such flows may play in the organization of the new international economic order,]

[(10) *Considering* that international flows of migrant workers originate in differences in degree of development and level of income between States of origin and States of destination, and that such flows are a reflection and part of the supply of and demand for labour at the international level,]

(11) *Considering* the situation of [vulnerability] in which migrant workers find themselves in the receiving societies [for reasons relating, among other

things, to their absence from their country of origin and to the difficulties of their [insertion] [adaptation] [presence] in the receiving society] [for various reasons],

[(12) *Bearing in mind* the beneficial effects that labour mobility on an international scale has had and will continue to have on the economy of both States of origin and States of destination,]

[(13) *Bearing [also] in mind* on one hand the contribution of migrant workers to the economy of the receiving countries and on the other hand the social costs connected with the migratory process,]

(14) *Recognizing* the necessity to promote a balanced international economic development in order to minimize the [need for and] problems linked with international migration,

(15) *Convinced* that the status and fundamental rights of migrant workers and their families have not been sufficiently recognized everywhere and therefore require appropriate international protection,

(16) *Taking into account* that often migration is the cause of serious problems for the families of migrant workers as well as for the workers themselves, in particular because of the scattering of the family,

[(17) *Considering, therefore,* that the fundamental human rights and labour rights of all migrant workers and their families, including the rights of undocumented workers, who are even more defenceless because of their irregular status, require appropriate protection at the international level,]

[(17) *Bearing in mind* that the human problems involved in migration are even deeper in the case of illegal migration and that therefore appropriate action should be reinforced also at the international level in order to prevent and suppress illegal and clandestine movements and traffic of migrant workers, while at the same time assuring the protection of their fundamental human rights,]

(18) *Considering* that in most cases workers who are undocumented or in an irregular situation are employed under worse conditions of work than other workers including migrant workers in a regular situation, and that certain employers find this an inducement to seek such labour in order to reap the benefits of unfair competition,

[(19) *Considering* that the widest recognition of the rights of all migrant workers and the effective safeguarding of these rights will accordingly tend to discourage the seeking of migrant workers who are undocumented or in an irregular situation and to contribute to a reduction in irregular migration flows,]

[(20) *Considering* however that, in order not to discourage prospective migrants for employment from respecting the normal procedures established by the competent authorities of the country concerned the recognition of certain rights ought to be limited to migrant workers in a regular situation, including those whose situation has been regularized,]

(21) *Convinced therefore* of the need to bring forth the international protection of the rights of all migrant workers and their families reaffirming and establishing basic norms in a comprehensive Convention which could be applied universally,

Have agreed on the following articles:

PART I
Scope and definitions

Article 1

This Convention is applicable to all migrant workers and members of their families, except as otherwise provided hereafter and without distinction on grounds such as sex, race, colour, language, religion or convictions, political or other opinion, national, ethnic or social origin, nationality, age, economic position, [property], birth, marital or any other status.

[*Article 2*]

[(1) The term 'migrant worker' refers to any person who, in a State of which he is not a national, is to engage, is engaged or has been engaged in an economic activity for an employer or on his own account.

(2) For the purpose of this Convention:

(a) Frontier workers shall be considered migrant workers when they engage in work in one State but retain their permanent residence in a neighbouring State to which they normally return every day.

(b) Seasonal workers shall be considered migrant workers when they are employed or engaged in work which, by its character, is dependent on seasonal conditions and can therefore be performed only during part of the year.

(c) Seafarers, including fishermen, shall be considered migrant workers when they are engaged in any function whatsoever on board a vessel other than a warship registered in a State of which they are not nationals.

(d) Migrant workers on a permanent offshore installation shall be considered migrant workers when the installation on which they are engaged falls under the jurisdiction of a State of which they are not nationals.

(e) Itinerant workers shall be considered migrant workers when, having their permanent residence in one State, they have to go for purposes of their occupation to another State for a short period.

(3) The term 'migrant worker' excludes:

(a) persons employed by international organisations and agencies and persons employed by a State outside its territory whose admission and status are regulated by general international law or by specific international agreements or conventions;

(b) persons employed on behalf of a State outside its territory for the execution of programmes of co-operation for development agreed with the receiving State and whose admission and status are regulated by specific international agreements or conventions.]

Article 3

For the purposes of this Convention, the term 'members of the family' includes the spouse [or the companion who lives matrimonially with the worker if such a relationship is recognised by the laws] [governing the personal status of the worker] [of the State of employment or the State of origin], [the dependent [minor, unmarried] children], [the dependent parents of the worker or the spouse] and other persons who are recognised as members of the family for the purposes of this Convention by the relevant laws and regulations of the State of employment or relevant bilateral or multilateral agreements between the States Parties concerned.

Article 4

For the purpose of this Convention, migrant workers and members of their families, as defined in the preceding articles:

(a) are considered as documented or in a regular situation if they possess the requisite authorisations in respect of admission, stay and economic activity;

(b) are considered as undocumented or in an irregular situation if they do not possess the authorisations of the State in whose territory they are that are required by law in respect of admission, stay or economic activity, or if they cease to fulfil the conditions to which their admission, stay or economic activity are subject.

Article 5

The rights as set forth in this Convention, shall be recognised and guaranteed during the entire migration process, that is, during the preparation for emigration, on leaving from the State of departure, in the course of transit through a State, during the journey, during the entire period of stay, residence, employment or work in the State of employment and on return to the State of origin or the State of normal residence.

Article 6

For the purpose of this Convention:

(a) The term 'State of origin' means the State of which [the migrant worker or the members of his family, as the case may be] [any persons to which this Convention is applicable], are nationals;

(b) The term 'State of employment' means the State where the migrant worker is for the purpose of [employment] [or work] [and where members of his family have accompanied or joined him];

(c) The term 'State of return' means the State to which the migrant worker [or members of his family] decides to return, whether it be his State of origin or the State in which he is normally resident;

(d) The term 'State of transit' means any State through which the migrant worker [or members of his family] pass on their departure or return.

PART II
Fundamental human rights of all migrant workers and members of their families

Article 7

Each State Party to this Convention undertakes to respect and to ensure to all migrant workers and members of their families within its territory and subject to its jurisdiction the rights recognised in this part of the Convention without distinction of any kind on the basis of race, colour, sex, language, religion, political or other opinion, national [ethnic] or social origin, nationality, age, property, birth [marital] or other status.

Article 8

(1) Migrant workers and members of their families shall be free to leave any country, including their country of origin. This right shall not be subject to any restrictions except those which are provided by law, are necessary to protect national security, public order (*ordre public*), public health or morals or the rights and freedoms of others, and are consistent with other rights recognised in this Convention.

(2) Migrant workers and members of their families shall have the right at any time to re-enter their country of origin.

Article 9

The right to life of migrant workers and members of their families shall be protected by law [under the same conditions as for citizens of the State concerned].

Article 10

Migrant workers and members of their families shall not be subjected to torture or to cruel, inhuman or degrading treatment or punishment.

Article 11

(1) Migrant workers and members of their families shall not be held in slavery or servitude.

(2) Migrant workers and members of their families shall not be required to perform forced or compulsory labour.

(3) Paragraph (2) shall not be held to preclude, in countries where imprisonment with hard labour may be imposed as a punishment for a crime, the performance of hard labour in pursuance of a sentence to such punishment by a competent court.

(4) For the purpose of this article the term 'forced or compulsory labour' shall not include:

(a) any work or service, not referred to in paragraph (3), normally required of a person who is under detention in consequence of a lawful order of a court, or of a person during conditional release from such detention;

(b) any service exacted in cases of emergency or calamity threatening the life or well-being of the community [in cases provided for by law];

(c) any work or service which forms part of normal civil obligations so far as it is imposed also on citizens of the State concerned.

Article 12

(1) Migrant workers and members of their families shall have the right to freedom of thought, conscience and religion. [This right shall include freedom to have [or not to have] or to adopt [or not to adopt] a religion or beliefs of their choice, and freedom, whether individually or in community with others and in public or private, to manifest their religion or belief in worship, observance, practice and teaching.]

[(2) Migrant workers and members of their families shall not be subject to coercion which would impair their freedom to have [or not to have] or to adopt [or not to adopt] a religion or beliefs of their choice.]

(3) Freedom to manifest one's religion or [beliefs] [convictions] may be subject only to such limitations as are prescribed by law and are necessary to protect public safety, order, health, or morals or the fundamental rights and freedoms of others.

(4) The States Parties to this Convention undertake to have respect for the liberty of migrant workers [to practise their religion and] to ensure the religious and moral education of their children, including children over whom they have legal guardianship, in conformity with their own convictions.

Article 13

(1) Migrant workers and members of their families shall have the right to hold opinions without interference.

(2) Migrant workers and members of their families shall have the right to freedom of expression; this right shall include freedom to seek, receive and impart information and ideas [of all kinds], regardless of frontiers, either orally, in writing or in print, in the form of art, or through any other media of their choice.

(3) The exercise of the rights provided for in paragraph (2) of this article carries with it special duties and responsibilities. It may therefore be subject to certain restrictions, but these shall only be such as are provided by law and are necessary:

(a) for respect of the rights or reputations of others;
(b) for the protection of national security or of public order (*ordre public*), or of public health or morals.

Article 14

Migrant workers and members of their families shall not be subjected to arbitrary or unlawful interference with their privacy, family, home, correspondence, or other communications nor to unlawful attacks on their honour and reputation. They shall have the right to the protection of the law against such interference or attacks.

Article 15

Migrant workers and members of their families shall not be arbitrarily deprived of property, whether owned individually or in association with others. Where, under the legislation in force in the country of employment (receiving country), their assets are expropriated in whole or in part, they shall have the right to just compensation.

Article 16

(1) Migrant workers and members of their families shall have the right to liberty and security of person.

(2) Migrant workers and members of their families shall be entitled to [normal police] protection by the State against violence, physical injury, threats and intimidation, whether by public officials or by private individuals, groups or institutions.

(3) Any verification by law enforcement officals of the identity of migrant workers or members of their families shall be carried out in accordance with procedures established by law.

(4) Migrant workers and members of their families shall not be subjected individually or collectively to arbitrary arrest or detention, nor be deprived of their liberty except on such grounds and in accordance with such procedures as are established by law.

(5) Migrant workers and members of their families who are arrested shall be informed at the time of arrest and, so far as possible in a language which they understand, of the reasons for their arrest and shall be promptly informed in a language which they understand of any charges against them.

(6) Migrant workers and members of their families who are arrested or detained on a criminal charge shall be brought promptly before a judge or

other officer authorized by law to exercise juridical power and shall be entitled to trial within a reasonable time or to release [in accordance with the penal procedure of the receiving State]. [It shall not be the general rule that while awaiting trial, they shall be detained in custody, but release may be subject to guarantees to appear for trial, at any other stage of the judicial proceedings and, should the occasion arise, for the execution of the judgement.]

(7) (a) In the case of arrest or detention of a migrant worker or a member of his family [on a criminal charge], if he so requests, the diplomatic or consular authorities of his country of origin, or representing the interests of that country, shall be informed without delay of the arrest or detention and that of the reasons therefor. Any communication addressed to the said authorities by the person concerned shall also be forwarded to them without delay;

(b) The person concerned shall be informed without delay of the above-mentioned rights;

(c) The said diplomatic or consular authorities shall have the right to visit the person concerned during any period of detention [on a criminal charge] or imprisonment, to converse and correspond with him and to arrange for his legal representation [in accordance with the terms of the Vienna Convention relating to consular relations].

(8) Migrant workers and members of their families who are deprived of their liberty by arrest or detention shall be entitled to take proceedings before a court, in order that that court may decide without delay on the lawfulness of their detention and order their release if the detention is not lawful. [In taking such proceedings, they shall have the free assistance of an interpreter if they cannot understand or speak the language used.]

(9) Migrant workers and members of their families who have been victims of unlawful arrest or detention [shall have an enforceable right to compensation] [shall have the right to bring an action for compensation] [for damages caused] [subject to domestic legislation].

Article 17

(1) Migrant workers and members of their families who are deprived of their liberty shall be treated with humanity and with respect for the inherent dignity of the human person and for their cultural identity.

(2) If they are detained in custody while awaiting trial, they shall, [whenever possible,] [save in exceptional circumstance,] be segregated from convicted persons and shall be subject to separate treatment appropriate to their status as unconvicted persons. Accused juvenile persons shall be separated from adults and brought as speedily as possible for adjudication.

[(3) Any migrant worker or a member of his/her family who is detained in a country of transit or in a receiving country [pending on a charge of] [for] violation of provisions relating to migration, shall be housed, in so far as practicable, separately from persons in detention pending trial for other offences.]

[(3) Any migrant worker or member or member of his family who is detained in the State of destination for infraction of the provisions concerning migration shall be housed in suitable accommodation [under judicial control] separate from the prisons or other centres of detention or imprisonment for offenders or criminals.]

(4) During any period of imprisonment in pursuance of a sentence imposed by a court of law, the treatment of a migrant worker or a member of his family shall be aimed at his reformation and social rehabilitation. Juvenile offenders shall be segregated from adults and be accorded treatment to their age and legal status.

[(5) During detention or imprisonment, migrant workers or members of their families shall enjoy the right to visits by members of their families.]

[(6) In any case of application of sanctions, including pending proceedings for the expulsion or deportation of migrant workers or their families, the competent authorities of the State of destination shall pay special attention to the problems posed by the families of such workers, with particular reference to the specific needs of women and minor children.]

[(7) The fundamental human rights and the labour rights of migrant workers or their families shall not, in the event of their being subjected to any form of detention or imprisonment provided for by the laws in force in the State of destination, be limited or impaired merely because such workers or their families lack the required migration documentation. This provision shall apply at all times, including during any expulsion or deportation proceedings.]

[(8) All costs arising from the detention of migrant workers or their families shall be borne by the competent authorities of the State of destination.]

Article 18

[(1) Migrant workers and members of their families shall have the right to equality with citizens of the State concerned as regards access to and treatment by the courts and tribunals. In the determination of any criminal charge against them, or of their rights and obligations in a suit at law, they shall be entitled to a fair and public hearing by a competent, independent and impartial tribunal established by law.]

(2) Migrant workers and members of their families who are charged with a criminal offence shall have the right to be presumed innocent until proved guilty according to law.

(3) In the determination of any criminal charge against them, migrant

workers and members of their families shall be entitled to the following minimum guarantees:

(a) to be informed promptly and in detail in a language which they understand of the nature and cause of the charge against them;

(b) to have adequate time and facilities for the preparation of their defence and to communicate with counsel of their own choosing;

(c) to be tried without undue delay;

(d) to be tried in their presence, and to defend themselves in person or through legal assistance of their own choosing; to be informed, if they do not have legal assistance, of this right; and to have legal assistance assigned to them, in any case where the interests of justice to require, and without payment by them in any such case if they do not have sufficient means to pay for it;

(e) to examine, or have examined, the witnesses against them and to obtain the attendance and examination of witnesses on their behalf under the same conditions as witnesses against them;

(f) to have the free assistance of a [qualified] interpreter if they cannot understand or speak the language used in the proceedings;

(g) not to be compelled to testify against themselves or to confess guilt.

(4) In the case of juvenile persons, the procedure shall be such as will take account of their age and the desirability of promoting their rehabilitation.

(5) Migrant workers and members of their families convicted of a crime shall have the right to their conviction and sentence being reviewed by a higher tribunal according to law.

(6) When migrant workers or members of their families have by a final decision been convicted of a criminal offence and when subsequently their conviction has been reversed or they have been pardoned on the ground that a new or newly discovered fact shows conclusively that there has been a miscarriage of justice, the persons who have suffered punishment as a result of such conviction shall be compensated according to law, unless it is proved that the non-disclosure of the unknown fact in time is wholly or partly attributable to them.

(7) Migrant workers and members of their families shall not be liable to be tried or punished again for an offence for which they have already been finally convicted or acquitted in accordance with the law and penal procedure of each country.

Article 19

(1) Migrant workers and members of their families shall not be held guilty of any criminal offence on account of any act or omission which did not constitute a criminal offence, under national or international law, at the time when the criminal offence was committed [nor shall a heavier penalty be imposed than the one that was applicable at the time when the criminal offence

was committed]. If, subsequent to the commission of the offence, provision is made by law for the imposition of a lighter penalty they shall benefit thereby.

[(2) In accordance with the principle of proportionality of penal sanctions, courts shall have regard, in imposing any sentence for criminal offences committed by migrant workers or members of their families, to any incidental sanctions or consequences affecting their rights of residence or work including expulsion.]

(3) Nothing in this article shall prejudice the trial and punishment of any person for any act or omission which, at the time when it was committed, was criminal according to [the general principle of law recognised by the community of nations] [the legislation of the receiving State].

Article 20

[Migrant workers and members of their families shall not be imprisoned, deprived of their authorisation of residence or work permit, or expelled merely on the ground of [inability] [failure] to meet a contractual obligation.]

Article 21

It shall be unlawful for anyone, other than a public official duly authorised by law, to confiscate identity documents, documents authorising entry to or stay, residence or establishment in the national territory, or work permits. No authorised confiscation of such documents shall take place without delivery of a detailed receipt. [It shall be a [serious] offence, and punishable accordingly, unlawfully to confiscate such documents or to destroy or attempt to destroy them.]

Article 22

[(1) Migrant workers and members of their families shall not be subject to measures of [collective] [mass] expulsion.]

'[(1) Each case of expulsion be examined and decided individually.]'

[(2) Migrant workers and members of their families may be expelled from the territory of a State Party to this Convention only in pursuance of a judicial or administrative decision reached or dictated in accordance with law and stating the reasons for the decision.]

[(3) The decision shall be communicated to them in writing.]

[(4) Except where the decision is pronounced by a judicial authority the person concerned shall have the right to appeal [to press its examination by a higher authority] against it. If the [appeal] [review] is not to be examined by a judicial authority, it shall stay the execution of the decision except where the reasons stated therefor involve substantial requirements of national security or public order. If a decision which has been the subject of such immediate execution is subsequently annulled, the person concerned shall have the right to compensation according to the law.]

[(5) In case of expulsion, the person concerned shall be allowed a reasonable opportunity to obtain the settlement of any claims for wages and other entitlements due to him by his employer, to settle any contractual liabilities, [and where this appears necessary for reasons of personal security, to seek entry to a country other than his country of origin.] Account shall also be taken of the person's family circumstances.]

[(6) Expulsion or departure from the receiving country shall not in itself prejudice any rights acquired under the law of a migrant worker or a member of his/her family.]

[(7) In any case of expulsion or deportation, the authorities of the State of destination [shall bear the costs incurred and] [shall refrain from exerting pressure on the persons concerned in any manner in order to obtain their agreement to summary procedures such as 'voluntary exit', when such agreement is not spontaneously forthcoming from the persons concerned.]]

Article 23

(1) Migrant workers and members of their families shall have the right to seek consular [and diplomatic] protection [and appropriate assistance] from the authorities of their country of origin or those representing the interests of that country [and to receive from them legal advice and counsel] whenever the rights recognised in this Convention or their rights under the legislation of the country of employment [receiving country] are impaired.

[(2) The consular [or diplomatic] authorities of the country of origin or those representing the interests of that country shall be notified of any decision to expel a migrant worker or a member of his/her family [legally present in the State of destination] at least 48 hours before the expulsion is to take effect.]

Article 24

Every migrant worker and every member of a migrant worker's family shall have the right to recognition everywhere as a person before the law.

Article 25

(1) All migrant workers shall enjoy treatment not less favourable than that which applies to nationals of the receiving State in respect of remuneration and:

(a) other conditions of work, that is to say overtime, hours of work, weekly rest, holidays with pay, safety, health, termination of the employment relationship, and any other conditions of work which, according to national laws or practice, are covered by this term;

(b) other terms of employment, that is to say minimum age of employment, restriction on home work and any other matter which, according to national laws and practice, are considered a term of employment;

(2) It shall not be lawful to derogate from the principle of equality of treatment referred to in paragraph 1 above.

(3) The States Parties to the present Convention shall take all appropriate measures to ensure that migrant workers are not deprived of any rights derived from this principle by reason of any irregularity in their stay or employment. In particular, employers shall not be relieved of any legal or contractual obligations, nor shall their obligations be limited in any manner, by reason of any such irregularity.

Article 26

(1) The States Parties to the present Convention recognise the right of all migrant workers and members of their families:

(a) to take part [freely] in [peaceful] meetings and activities of trade unions and of other associations [apart from political parties and organisations] [legally] established for the protection of economic, social, cultural and similar interests [subject only to the rules of the organisation concerned];

(b) to join any trade union and any such association as aforesaid [, subject only to the rules of the organisation concerned];

(c) to seek the aid and assistance of any trade union and of any such association as aforesaid.

(2) No restrictions may be placed on the exercise of these rights other than those which are prescribed by law and which are necessary in a democratic society in the interests of national security, public order (*ordre public*) or the protection of the rights and freedom of others.

Article 27

[(1) (a) Migrant workers and members of their families shall enjoy equality of treatment with nationals of the receiving State in respect of social security. As regards migrant workers and members of their families who are undocumented or in an irregular situation, States Parties may limit these rights to social security protection arising out of employment or to contributory benefits, [that is, benefits the grant of which depends on direct financial participation by the migrant workers or their employer or on a qualifying period of economic activity.]

(b) Where the application of the preceding paragraph requires the conclusion of multilateral or bilateral agreements, such agreements shall, inter alia, make provision for the maintenance of acquired rights and of rights in the course of acquisition and for the payment of benefits outside the national territory including provisions for transfer of pension, continuity of social benefits and accumulation of contributive rights. Where such agreements are required, the States Parties to the present Convention shall spare no effort to conclude them.

(c) In so far as migrant workers and members of their families are not specifically entitled to receive contributory social security benefits or to continue to receive such benefits, they shall be entitled to the reimbursement of the whole or such part of the contributions paid as may be appropriate.

(2) Migrant workers and members of their families shall be entitled to claim compensation from an employer for any loss of social security benefits due to his omission to give the notices and to make the payments required by the social security scheme or schemes by which they should normally have been covered.]

Article 28

[(1) All migrant workers and members of their families shall have the right to receive any medical care which is urgently required for the preservation of their life or the restoration of their health.

(2) Such emergency medical care shall not be refused to them by reason of any irregularity in their situation or in that of their parents with regard to stay or employment or by reason of the absence of any guarantee as to the payment of the expenses involved.]

[Emergency medical care required for the preservation of the life or the restoration of the health of migrant workers and the members of their families shall not be refused to them by reason of the irregularity of their situation or that of their parents with regard to stay or employment or by reason of the absence of a guarantee as to the payment of expenses involved.]

Article 29

[[Children of all migrant workers shall have the basic right of access to education.] [Access by children of any migrant worker to pre-school educational institutions or schools shall not be refused or limited by reason of the irregular situation with respect to stay or employment of either parent or by reason of the irregularity of their own stay in the receiving State.]]

Article 30

[The irregularity of its own situation or of that of its parents shall not have the effect of depriving a child of its right to a name, to registration, or of the right to a nationality, with a view to reducing cases of statelessness.]

Article 31

[The States Parties to the present Convention shall ensure respect for the cultural identity of all migrant workers and their families and shall permit them to maintain their cultural links with their State of origin.]

[All migrant workers and their families shall enjoy the right to maintain their cultural dignity.]

[The States to the present Convention shall recognise the right of all migrant workers and their families to maintain their cultural identity.]

Article 32

Upon termination of their stay in the receiving State all migrant workers and members of their families shall have the right to transfer any savings and to take with them all personal effects, working tools and other belongings.

Article 33

(1) Migrant workers and members of their families shall have the right to be informed by both the State of origin and the State of employment concerning:

(a) their rights arising out of this Convention;

(b) the conditions of admission, their rights and obligations under the law and practice of the receiving State and such other matters as will enable them to comply with administrative or other formalities in that State.

(2) Each State Party to this Convention shall take the appropriate measures to disseminate the said information or to ensure that it is provided by employers, trade unions or other appropriate bodies or institutions. As appropriate, it shall co-operate with other States concerned.

(3) The said information shall be provided to migrant workers and to members of their families, wherever possible free of charge, upon request and in their own language or in a language which they are able to understand.

Article 34

None of the provisions of Part II of this Convention shall have the effect of relieving migrant workers and the members of their families from either the obligation to comply with the laws and regulations of any State of transit and the State of employment or the obligation to respect the cultural identity of the inhabitants of such States.

[Article 34bis]

[Nothing in Part II of this Convention shall be interpreted as implying the recognition of the legality of the situation of a migrant worker or a member of his family who is undocumented or in an irregular situation or any right to the regularisation of his situation, nor should it prejudice the measures intended to ensure sound and equitable conditions for international migration as provided in Part V.]

PART III
Additional rights of migrant workers and members of their families in a [regular situation] [legal status]

Article 35

Migrant workers and members of their families who are in a [regular situation] [lawful status] in the State of employment as regards their admission, [duration of] stay and [type of] employment [or other economic activity] [and other matters related to their immigration and employment status], as well as those whose situation has [been regularised,] [become lawful since entry into the State of employment] shall enjoy the rights set forth in Part III, in addition to those set forth in Part II.

Article 36

[Each State Party to the present Convention shall be free to establish in its national legislation the criteria governing admission, duration of stay, type of employment [or other economic activity] of migrant workers and members of their families and to decide in each case whether to grant any such authorisation, subject to no limitations other than those provided for in this Convention. Any conditions subject to which the admission, stay, [and] employment [or other economic activity] of migrant workers and members of their families is authorised shall not be such as to impair, nor be applied so as to impair, the rights and guarantees provided for in this Convention.]

[Nothing in the present Convention shall affect the right of each State Party to establish in its national legislation the legal criteria governing the admission, duration of stay, type of employment or other economic activity, and all other matters relating to the immigration and employment status of migrant workers and members of their families] [subject to such limitation as imposed on it by this Convention or other rules of international law].

Article 37

Before their departure, or at the latest at the time of their admission to the State of employment, migrant workers and members of their families shall have the right to be fully informed by the State of origin and the State of employment of all conditions applicable to their admission and particularly those concerning the duration of the stay authorised, employment which they may take up and economic activities in which they may engage as well as of the requirements which they must satisfy in the State of employment and the authority to whom they must address themselves for any modification of those conditions.

Article 38

1. States of employment shall make every effort to authorise migrant workers and members of their families to be temporarily absent [for reasonably long periods] without effect upon their authorisation to stay or to work, as the case may be. In doing so, States of employment shall take into account the special needs and obligations of migrant workers and members of their families [in particular those obligations stemming from their links with the State of origin].

2. Migrant workers and members of their families shall have the right to be fully informed of the terms on which such temporary absences are authorised.

Article 39

(1) Migrant workers and members of their families in a [regular situation] [lawful status] shall have the right to liberty of movement in the territory of the State of employment [and freedom to choose their place of residence there.]

(2) The above-mentioned right shall not be subject to any restrictions except those which are provided by law, are necessary to protect national security, public order (*ordre public*), public health or morals, or the rights and freedoms of others, and are consistent with the other rights recognised in the present Convention.

Article 40

1. Migrant workers and members of their families in a [regular situation] [lawful status] shall have the right to freedom of association with others in the State of employment, including the right to form associations and trade unions, for the promotion and protection of their economic, social, occupational, cultural and other similar interests, [including the preservation of their [national identity], cultural identity and cultural and other similar links with the States of origin.]

2. No restrictions may be placed on the exercise of these rights other than those prescribed by law and which are necessary in a democratic society in the interests of national security or public order (*ordre public*), [public health and morals] or for the protection of the rights and freedoms of others.

Article 41

[States of origin and States of employment shall collaborate with a view to facilitating, [without unreasonable restrictions,] [as provided for in their national legislation] the exercise by migrant workers and members of their families in a [regular situation] [lawful status] of the right:

(a) to take part in the conduct of public affairs of their country of origin, directly or through freely chosen representatives;

(b) to vote and to be elected at elections in their country of origin;

(c) to have access, on general terms of equality, to public services in their country of origin.]

Article 42

(1) States Parties to the present Convention shall consider the establishment of procedures or institutions through which account may be taken, both in States of origin and in States of employment, of the special needs, aspirations and obligations of migrant workers and members of their families.

(2) [States of employment shall facilitate the consultation or participation of migrant workers and members of their families in decisions concerning the life and administration of local communities.]

(2) [States of destination reserve the right to permit or not to permit, to the extent provided for in their internal legislation, the participation of migrant workers in public activities or in administrative decision-making.]

(3) [Migrant workers shall enjoy political rights in the State of destination only to the extent that that State, in the exercise of its sovereignty, may grant them such rights.]

Article 43

[(1) Migrant workers in a [regular situation] [lawful status] shall enjoy equality of treatment with nationals of the State of employment, subject to no limitations other than those provided for in the present Convention, in respect of:

[(1) Migrant workers in a [regular situation] [lawful status] shall enjoy [equality of treatment with nationals of the State of employment] [subject to the national legislation of the State of employment] [subject to no limitations other than those provided for in the present Convention], [in particular in Article 50, para. 2 (a)] in respect of:

(a) access to educational facilities and institutions;

(a) access to educational facilities and institutions, subject to the admission requirements and other regulations of the facilities and institutions concerned;

(b) access to vocational guidance and placement services;

(b) access to vocational guidance and placement services, subject to the resources of the State of employment;

(c) access to vocational training and retraining facilities and institutions;

(c) access to vocational training and retraining facilities and institutions, subject to the resources of the State of employment;

(d) access to housing, [including social housing schemes,] and protection against exploitation in respect of rents;

(e) access to social and health services, [provided that the requirements for participation by nationals in schemes of the State of employment are met;]

(f) The exercise of trade union rights, including eligibility for office in trade unions, in bodies of an occupational, economic or social character, and in labour-management relations bodies, including bodies representing workers in undertakings;

(g) access to co-operatives and self-managed enterprises;

(h) access to and participation in cultural life.

(2) States Parties to the present Convention shall promote conditions to ensure effective equality of treatment to enable migrant workers to enjoy the above-mentioned rights whenever the terms of their stay, as authorised by the State of employment, meet the appropriate requirements.]

(d) access to housing, [including social housing scheme,] and protection against exploitations in respect of rents;

(e) [access to social and health services,] [provided that the requirements for participation in schemes of the State of employment are met;]

(f) the exercise of the right of freedom of association with others;

(g) access to and participation in cultural life.

(2) States Parties to the present Convention shall endeavour to facilitate effective equality of treatment to enable migrant workers in a lawful status to enjoy the above-mentioned rights subject to the terms of their stay under the national legislation of the State of employment [including opportunities for advancement] [wherever the terms of their stay, as authorised by the State of employment, meet the appropriate requirements.]]

Article 44

(1) States Parties to the present Convention [, recognising that the family is the natural and fundamental group unit of society and is entitled to protection by society and the State,] shall take appropriate measures to ensure the protection of the unity of families of migrant workers in a [regular situation] [lawful status], equal to that given to nationals.

(2) Spouses and minor dependent unmarried sons and daughters [of migrant workers] shall be authorised to accompany or join migrant workers

and to stay in the State of employment for a duration not less than that of the worker, subject to [procedures prescribed by] the [national] legislation of the State of employment or [applicable] international agreements. States of employment may make this authorisation subject to the condition that the migrant worker has available appropriate accommodation and resources to meet the needs of the persons concerned. The process of varifying that such conditions are met shall be completed within a reasonable period.

(3) States of employment shall [favourably] consider the admission of other [dependent] family members on humanitarian grounds.

Article 45

(1) Members of the family of migrant workers in a [regular situation] [lawful status] shall enjoy equality of treatment with nationals of the State of employment, subject to no limitations other than those provided for in the present Convention, in respect of:

(a) access to educational facilities and institutions;
(b) access to vocational guidance and training facilities and institutions;
(c) access to social and health services;
(d) access to and participation in cultural life.

(2) States of employment, [provided that the requirements for partici-pation in schemes of the State of employment are met,] [in accordance with their national circumstances and legal systems] shall pursue a policy, where appropriate in collaboration with the States of origin, aimed at [facilitating the integration of children of migrant workers in the local school system, particularly in respect of the teaching of the local language] [securing the same rights and opportunities enjoyed by children of the State of employment concerning access to all systems, forms and degrees of education by facilitating the learning of the local language].

(3) States of employment shall endeavour, as far as practicable and [where appropriate] in collaboration with States of origin, to facilitate for the children of migrant workers the teaching of their mother tongue and culture.

[(4) States of employment shall provide, as far as practicable, special schemes of education in the mother tongue of children of migrant workers, at least at the primary level.]

Article 46

[(1) At the time of their admission to the territory of the receiving country or of the regularisation of their situation, migrant workers and members of their families in a regular situation shall enjoy exemption from customs

[(1) At the time of their initial admission to the territory of the State of employment, migrant workers and members of their families shall, subject to the applicable laws and regulations of the State of employment as

duties in respect of their personal effects and in respect of portable hand tools and portable equipment of the kind normally required for the carrying out of their trade or occupation.] well as relevant international agreements, enjoy exemption from customs duties in respect of the equipment necessary to perform the trade or occupation for which they are admitted to the State of employment.]

(2) [The same exception to migrant workers and members of their families shall be accorded by the State of return at the time of their final return.]

Article 47

[The States Parties to the present Convention, shall, as far as possible and in accordance with the arrangements laid down in their legislation and applicable agreements, authorise and provide facilities for the transfer to the country of origin or the country of normal residence of migrant workers and members of their families of such parts of their earnings and savings as they may wish to transfer. The transfer of sums required for the maintenance of members of the migrant worker's family shall on no account be prevented or restricted.]

[Migrant workers shall have the right, subject to applicable currency laws and regulations, to transfer their earnings and savings from the State of employment to other States, in particular those funds necessary for the support of their families, and States of employment shall take appropriate measures to facilitate such transfers in accordance with procedures established by law.]

Article 48

Subject to agreements on double taxation, migrant workers and members of their families shall not be liable to taxes, duties or charges of any description whatsoever higher or more onerous than those imposed on nationals in similar circumstances. [They shall be entitled, under conditions no less favourable than those applicable to nationals, to deductions or exemptions from taxes or charges and to all allowances, including allowances for dependants.]

Article 49

(1) Where a separate authorisation to reside is required by national legislation, the States of employment shall issue to migrant workers authorisation of residence for at least the same period of time as their authorisation to engage in employment [or other economic activity]. [This provision does not apply to frontier workers.]

(2) [In States of employment where migrant workers are free to choose any type of employment for any employer] without prejudice to Article 36 of the present Convention, migrant workers shall neither be regarded as in an

irregular situation, nor shall they lose their authorisation of residence, by the mere fact of the loss of employment [or the termination of their economic activity] prior to the expiry of their working permits or similar authorisations.

[(3) In order to allow migrant workers referred to in paragraph (2) above sufficient time to find alternative employment, the authorisation of residence shall not be withdrawn, at least for a period corresponding to that during which they may be entitled to unemployment benefits.]

Article 50

[(1) Without prejudice to Article 36 of the present Convention, loss of employment shall not in itself imply the withdrawal of the authorisation to work.

[In States of employment where migrant workers are admitted for an indefinite period of time and are free to choose any type of employment for any employer, loss of employment shall not in itself imply the withdrawal of the authorisation to work without prejudice to Article 36 of the present Convention.]

(2) Migrant workers shall accordingly enjoy equality of treatment with nationals, particularly in respect of guarantees of security of employment, the provision of alternative employment, relief work and retraining during the remaining period of their authorisation to work.]

Article 51

[(1) States of employment shall permit migrant workers in a [regular situation] [lawful status] freely to choose their employment [or other economic activity], subject only to such restrictions or conditions as are authorised by the following paragraphs of this article.

[In States of employment whose laws and regulations provide that migrant workers lawfully present may freely choose their employer or employment after a certain period of lawful employment, only the restrictions or conditions set forth in the following paragraphs of this article shall be applicable.

(2) States of employment may:

(1) A State of employment may:

(a) restrict access by migrant workers to limited categories of employment, functions, services or activities where this is necessary in the interests of the State;

(a) restrict access by migrant workers to certain categories of employment and certain geographical regions where this is provided by national laws and regulations;

(b) restrict free choice of employment [or other economic activity] in accordance with regulations

(b) restrict free choice of employment in accordance with its laws and regulations concerning recognition of

governing the conditions of recognition of occupational qualifications acquired outside its territory. A State Party shall endeavour to provide for recognition of such qualifications, wherever possible;

(c) determine the conditions under which a migrant worker who has been admitted to take up employment may be authorised to engage in work on his own account and vice versa. In this connection, account shall be taken of the period during which the worker has already been employed or engaged in work on his own account.

(3) In the case of migrant workers in a [regular situation] [lawful status] whose permission to work is limited in time, States of employment may also:

(a) make the right of free choice of employment [or other economic activity] subject to the condition that the migrant worker has lawfully worked in its territory for a continuous period not exceeding two years;

(b) limit access by a migrant worker to employment [or other economic activity] in pursuance of a policy of granting priority to workers who are 'its nationals or who are assimilated to its nationals for these purposes by virtue of legislation or bilateral or multilateral agreements. Any such limitation shall cease to apply to a migrant worker who has lawfully worked for a continuous period exceeding five years;

(c) if the State of employment is a developing country, impose such

occupational qualifications acquired outside its territory. A State Party shall endeavour to provide for recognition of such qualifications, wherever possible;

(c) determine the conditions under which a migrant worker who has been admitted to take up employment may be authorised to engage in work on his own account and vice versa. In this connection, account shall be taken of the period during which the worker has already been employed or engaged to work on his own account.

(2) In the case of migrant workers lawfully in the territory of a State or employment whose permission to work is limited in time, a State of employment may in addition to the provisions of paragraph 1:

(a) make the right of free choice of employment and employer subject to the condition that the migrant worker has lawfully worked in its territory continuously for a prescribed period;

(b) limit access by a migrant worker to employment in pursuance of a policy of granting priority to workers who are its nationals or who are assimilated to its nationals for these purposes by virtue of legislation or bilateral or multilateral agreements. Any such limitation shall cease to apply to a migrant worker who has lawfully worked continuously for a prescribed period;

(c) if the State of employment is a developing country, impose such restrictions as may be called for by a policy aimed at meeting requirements for qualified manpower with its own nationals.]

restrictions as may be called for by a policy aimed at meeting requirements for qualified manpower with its own nationals.]

Article 52

[(1) The spouse and children of a migrant worker whose authorisation of residence or admission is without limit of time shall be permitted free choice of employment or [other economic activity] under the same conditions as are applicable to the migrant worker in accordance with Article 51.

(2) In respect of the spouse and children of any migrant worker admitted in accordance with Article 44, the States Parties to the present Convention shall pursue a policy aimed at granting priority in respect of employment or [other economic activity] over other workers who seek admission to the receiving country.]

[(1) If specifically authorised by the State of employment, the spouse and children of a migrant worker lawfully present in the State of employment shall be permitted to engage in employment;

(2) In respect of the spouse and children of any migrant worker admitted in accordance with Article 44, the States Parties to the present Convention shall, subject to national laws and regulations and applicable bilateral and multilateral agreements, consider granting priority in respect of employment over other workers who seek admission to the State of employment.]

Article 53

[Without prejudice to the terms of their authorisation of residence, migrant workers as defined in Article 2(1) who are [in a regular situation] [lawful status] shall, in addition to the rights provided for in Articles 25 and 43, enjoy equality of treatment with nationals of the receiving State in respect of:

(a) security of employment;

(b) access to relief work organised by a public authority;

(c) subject to any conditions or restrictions imposed in pursuance of Article 51, the provision of alternative employment in the event of loss of work; in that event they shall be given priority over other workers who seek admission to the receiving country.]

Article 54

[Migrant workers as defined in Article 2(1) who are in [a regular situation] [lawful status] shall be

[Migrant workers as defined in Article 2(1), who are in a regular situation, shall be entitled to equality

entitled to equality of treatment with
nationals of the State of employment
in the exercise of their occupation or
profession.]

of treatment with nationals of the
State of employment in the exercise of
their occupation or profession, except
as provided otherwise by the laws
and regulations of the State of
employment.]

[*Article 55*]

[(1) States Parties shall apply the following provisions to migrant workers
in a regular situation who have been admitted to the receiving country for a
period of time on the basis of a work contract with an enterprise or employer
carrying out in that country specific projects that by their nature are limited
in time:

(a) The said migrant workers shall be admitted and authorised to work for
the entire period of time required for the carrying out of the duties or assignments concerned;

(b) The receiving country shall facilitate the installation by the enterprise
carrying out the specific project of any necessary facilities for the said migrant
workers and their families, such as housing, schools, medical and recreational
services. The application of this provision shall not entail additional costs for
the receiving State, unless this is provided for in specific agreements;

(c) Subject to any provisions contained in specific agreements, the said
migrant workers shall have the right to have their earnings paid in or transferred to their country of origin or the country of their normal residence:

(d) The said migrant workers shall be entitled to be accompanied or joined
by the spouse and dependent children for the duration of their duties or
assignments, in accordance with Article 47, paragraphs (1) and (2), except
where this is not possible on account of considerations of safety.

(2) The provisions of Articles 38 to 45, Article 46, paragraphs (e) to (g),
Article 49, Article 51 and Article 58 shall also apply to the said migrant
workers. The other provisions of Part III shall not apply to them.

(3) Subject to the provisions of this Convention applicable to the said
migrant workers, the States concerned shall endeavour, whenever appropriate,
to establish by agreement specific provisions on social and economic matters
relating to these migrant workers.]

Article 56

[(1) Migrant workers and members of their families in [a regular situation]
[lawful status] may not be expelled from a receiving country except:

(a) for reasons of national security, public order, or morals;

(b) if they refuse, after having been duly informed of the consequences of such refusal, to comply with the measures prescribed for them by an official medical authority with a view to the protection of public health;

(c) if a condition essential to the issue or validity of their authorisation of residence or work permit is not fulfilled;

[(d) in accordance with the applicable laws and regulations of the State of employment.]

(2) [In accordance with applicable laws] any such expulsions shall be subject to the procedural safeguards provided for in Part II of this Convention.

[(3) Before any expulsion or deportation may be carried out, all fundamental rights of migrant workers must be legally safeguarded.]

PART IV
Provisions applicable to particular categories of migrant workers and members of their families

[*Article 57*]

[The particular categories of migrant workers and members of their families specified below who are in a regular situation as regards their admission, stay and employment or other economic activity, shall enjoy the rights referred to in Part IV.]

[*Article 58*]

[(1) Frontier workers, as defined in Article 2(2)(a) shall be entitled to all of the rights provided for in Parts II and III of this Convention which can be applied to them by reason of their presence and work in the territory of the State of employment, excluding rights relating to or arising out of residence and rights arising out of Article 44.

(2) The preceding paragraph shall be subject to any contrary provisions in agreements for the time being in force between the State of employment and the State of origin or of normal residence of the migrant worker concerned.

(3) Frontier workers shall have the right freely to choose their employment or other economic activity subject to Article 51. This right shall not affect their status as frontier workers.]

[*Article 59*]

[(1) Seasonal workers, as defined in Article 2(2)(b), shall be entitled to all of the rights provided for in Parts II and III of this Convention which can be applied to them by reason of their presence and work in the territory of the State of employment.

(2) A seasonal worker who, not counting seasonal interruptions, has been lawfully employed or working in the State of employment for an aggregate period of 24 months shall be entitled to take up other employment or economic

activity, subject to any conditions or limitations imposed in accordance with Article 51.]

[*Article 60*]

[(1) Seafarers as defined in Article 2(2)(c), workers on permanent offshore installations, as defined in Article 2(2)(d), and members of their families shall enjoy the following rights:

(a) If the said workers have been authorised to take up residence in the State of employment, they and the members of their families shall be entitled to the rights provided for in Parts II and III of this Convention.

(b) If the said workers have not been authorised to take up residence in the State of employment, they shall be entitled to all of the above-mentioned rights which can be applied to them by reason of their presence and work in the State of employment, excluding rights relating to or arising out of residence and rights arising out of Article 44.

(2) The preceding paragraph shall be subject to any contrary provisions in agreements for the time being in force between the State of employment and the State of origin or of normal residence of the migrant worker concerned.

(3) For the purpose of this article, the State of employment means the State under whose flag or jurisdiction is operated the ship or installation on which the migrant worker is engaged.]

[*Article 61*]

[Itinerant workers, are defined in Article 2(2)(e) shall be entitled to all of the rights provided for in Parts II and III of this Convention which can be applied to them by reason of their presence in the territory of the State of employment, excluding rights relating to or arising out of residence or employment and rights arising out of Article 44.]

PART V
Promotion of sound, equitable and humane conditions in connection with lawful international migration of workers and their families

Article 62

Without prejudice to the provisions of Article 36, regarding the freedom of each State to determine the criteria for authorising the admission, duration of stay, [type or choice of] employment [or other economic activity] of migrant workers and members of their families, the States of employment shall consult and co-operate with other States concerned with a view to promoting sound, equitable and humane conditions in connection with lawful international migration of workers and their families.

[In this respect due regard should be paid not only to manpower needs and resources, but also the social, economic, cultural [and political] and other consequences for migrant workers involved in such migration, as well as for the community or States concerned.]

Article 63

(1) The States Parties to the present Convention shall maintain appropriate government [agencies] [institutions] [entities] [and promote other services] to deal with questions concerning international migration of workers and their families. Their functions [shall] [should] include, inter alia:

(a) the formulation of policies regarding such migration;

(b) exchange of information, consultation and co-operation with the competent authorities of other States involved in such migration.

(c) [the provision of information, [particularly to employers and their organisations as well as [to workers and] workers' organisations] on policies, laws and regulations relating to migration and employment, on agreements concluded with other States on migration for employment and other relevant topics and on conditions of work and life of migrant workers and members of their families in the States of employment;]

(d) the provision of information and assistance to migrant workers and members of their families regarding requisite authorisations and formalities and arrangements for departure, travel, arrival, stay, employment [and other economic activities] exit and return to the State of return as well as on conditions of work and life in the State of employment and on customs, currency, tax and other relevant laws and regulations;

[(e) other measures which are necessary to facilitate the implementation of the present Convention.]

[(e) the recommending of legislation, regulations and other measures which are necessary to facilitate the implementation of the present Convention and to deal with matters relating to international migration and migrant workers.]

[(2) The States Parties to the present Convention shall co-operate in the provision of adequate consular and other services which are necessary to meet the social, cultural and other needs of migrant workers and their families.]

Article 64

[(1) Subject to the following paragraph, the right to undertake operations with a view to the recruitment [or placing] of workers in employment in another country shall be restricted to:

[The recruitment [or placement] of workers for employment in another State may be carried out [in conformity with] [subject to] national laws and regulations and in accordance with applicable international agreements [solely] by:

(a) public services or bodies of the country in which such operations take place;

(b) public services or bodies of the receiving country, if authorised by agreement between the States concerned;

(c) a body established by virtue of a bilateral or multilateral agreement.

(2) National laws and regulations and bilateral or multilateral agreements may also permit the said operations to be undertaken, subject to the approval and supervision of the authorities of the country concerned, by:

(a) the prospective employer of a person in his service acting on his behalf;

(b) private agencies.]

(a) governmental bodies of the State in which such recruitments takes place;

(b) governmental bodies of the State;

(c) a body established by virtue of a bilateral or multilateral agreement;

(d) a prospective employer or a person in his/her service, or private agencies, provided that [any required] approval and supervision for such operations is [solely] granted by the appropriate competent authorities of the State concerned.]

Article 65

(1) States Parties concerned shall co-operate in the adoption of measures regarding the orderly return of migrant workers and their families to the State of return [and their re-establishment in that State,] when they decide to return or their authorisation of residence or employment expires, or when they are in the State of employment in an irregular situation.

(2) In this respect, States concerned may agree on specific measures and modalities for the easing of the process of final return and, whenever possible, the promotion of appropriate conditions in the State of return.

(3) States Parties concerned may also co-operate with a view to ensuring the durable economic, social and cultural reintegration of migrant workers and members of their families in the State of origin on terms agreed upon by the States concerned.

Article 66

(1) The States Parties to the present Convention, including countries of transit, shall collaborate with a view to preventing and eliminating [illegal or] clandestine movements and employment of migrant workers in an irregular situation. The measures to be taken to this end within the jurisdiction of each State concerned shall include:

(a) appropriate measures against the dissemination of misleading information relating to emigration and immigration;

(b) measures to detect and eradicate illegal or clandestine movements of migrant workers and members of their families and to impose effective sanctions on persons or entities who organise, operate or assist in organising or operating such movements;

(c) measures to impose effective sanctions on persons, groups or entities who use violence, threats or intimidation against migrant workers or members of their family in an irregular situation.

(2) States of employment shall take all adequate measures that might be effective in eliminating employment in their territory of migrant workers in an irregular situation, including sanctions on persons or entities employing such workers wherever appropriate. The rights of migrant workers vis-à-vis their employer arising from employment shall not be impaired by these measures.

Article 67

States Parties to the present Convention undertake that, when there are migrant workers and members of their families in an irregular situation on their territory, they [will not permit that situation to persist] [shall endeavour to ensure that such a situation does not persist]. In considering the possibility of regularising the situation of such persons in accordance with applicable national legislation and bilateral or multilateral agreements, appropriate account shall be taken of the circumstances of their entry, the duration of their stay in the State of employment and other relevant considerations, in particular those relating to the family [and social] situation of the workers. If it is decided not to permit a migrant worker or a member of his family to stay in the State of employment, their orderly return to their State of return, or any other State in which their admission is guaranteed, shall be ensured as well as their protection during the period pending their departure and during their journey, as stipulated in Part II of the present Convention.

Article 68

[(1) The States Parties shall, if not yet provided for in their legislation, [in the same manner as they do for national workers] provide measures to establish and ensure that working and living conditions of migrant workers and members of their families are in keeping with the standards of fitness, safety, health and principles of human dignity. Such measures shall include inspection of the working and living premises of migrant workers and members of their families by such competent authorities as designated by each State Party concerned. The said authorities shall also make recommendations for the improvement in the quality of these conditions.

(2) The States Parties shall ensure that, wherever necessary, assistance is provided for the repatriation to the State of origin of the bodies of deceased migrant workers or members of their families and that death compensation matters are promptly settled.]

PART VI
[*Article 69*]
Application of the Convention

[(1) For the purpose of reviewing the application of the present Convention, there shall be established a Committee on the Protection of the Rights of All Migrant Workers and Their Families (hereinafter referred to as 'the Committee') consisting of 18 experts of competence in the field covered by the Convention.

(2) (a) Twelve members of the Committee shall be elected by secret ballot by the States Parties from a list of persons nominated by the States Parties, consideration being given to equitable geographical distribution of membership and to the representation of the different forms of civilization and of the principal legal systems. Each State Party may nominate one person.

(b) The remaining six members shall be appointed by the Governing Body of the International Labour Office.

(c) All members shall serve in their personal capacity.

(3) The initial election shall be held no later than six months after the date of the entry into force of the present Convention. At least three months before the date of each election the Secretary-General of the United Nations shall address a letter to the States Parties inviting them to submit their nominations within two months. The Secretary-General shall prepare a list in alphabetical order of all persons thus nominated, indicating the States Parties which have nominated them, and shall submit it to the States Parties not later than one month before the date of each election.

(4) Elections of members of the Committee shall be held at a meeting of States Parties convened by the Secretary-General at United Nations Headquarters. At that meeting, for which two thirds of the States Parties shall constitute a quorum, the persons elected to the Committee shall be those nominees who obtain the largest number of votes and an absolute majority of votes of the States Parties present and voting.

(5) The Secretary-General shall inform the Director-General of the International Labour Office of the result of the elections and shall invite the Governing Body of the International Labour Office to appoint the remaining members.

(6) The members of the Committee shall serve for a term of four years. However, the terms of six of the elected members and three of the appointed members shall expire at the end of two years; the names of these nine members shall be chosen by lot by the Chairman of the Committee.

(7) If an expert has ceased to function as a member of the Committee before the expiry of his term, the State Party which nominated the expert, or the Governing Body of the International Labour Office which appointed the expert, shall appoint another expert for the remaining part of the term. In cases where the new expert is appointed by the State Party, the appointment is subject to the approval of the Committee.

(8) The members of the Committee shall receive emoluments from United Nations resources on such terms and conditions as the General Assembly may decide, having regard to the importance of the Committee's responsibilities.

(9) The members of the Committee shall be entitled to the facilities, privileges and immunities of experts on mission for the United Nations as laid down in the relevant sections of the Convention on the Privileges and Immunities of the United Nations.

(10) The Secretary-General shall provide the necessary staff and facilities for the effective performance of the functions of the Committee.]

[*Article 70*]

[(1) States Parties undertake to submit to the Secretary-General of the United Nations, for consideration by the Committee, a report on the position of their law and practice in regard to the rights recognized in the Convention and to other privisions included herein:

(a) Within one year after the entry into force for the State Party concerned;
(b) Thereafter every four years.

(2) Reports shall indicate factors and difficulties, if any, affecting the implementation of the present Convention.]

[*Article 71*]

[(1) The Committee shall adopt its own rules of procedure.

(2) The Committee shall elect its officers for a term of two years.

(3) The Committee shall normally meet annually in order to consider the reports submitted in accordance with article 70 of the present Convention.

(4) The meetings of the Committee shall be held at United Nations Headquarters or at any other convenient place as determined by the Committee.]

[*Article 72*]

[(1) The Committee shall examine the reports submitted by each State Party to the present Convention and shall transmit such comments as it may consider appropriate to the State Party concerned. This State Party may submit to the Committee observations on any comments made by the Committee in accordance with this article.

(2) The Committee shall, through the Economic and Social Council, report annually to the General Assembly of the United Nations on its activities and

may make suggestions and general recommendations based on the examination of reports and information received from the States Parties. Such suggestions and general recommendations shall be included in the report of the Committee together with comments, if any, from States Parties.

(3) The Secretary-General shall transmit the reports of the Committee to the Commission on Human Rights of the United Nations and to the Governing Body of the International Labour Office.

(4) The Committee may invite the specialized agencies of the United Nations to submit information on such matters dealt with in the Convention as fall within their field of competence. The specialized agencies may participate, in an advisory capacity, in the consideration by the Committee of such matters.]

[*Article 73*]

[(1) If a State Party considers that another State Party is not giving effect to the provisions of this Convention, it may bring the matter to the attention of the Committee. The Committee shall then transmit the communication to the State Party concerned. This State shall, within three months, submit to the Committee written explanations or statements clarifying the matter and the remedy, if any, that may have been taken by that State.

(2) If within six months of the Committee's transmission of the initial communication to the State Party concerned the matter is not adjusted to the satisfaction of both parties, either State shall have the right to request the Committee to deal with the matter in accordance with the following paragraphs of this article.

(3) The Committee shall make available its good offices to the States Parties concerned with a view to a friendly solution of the matter on the basis of respect for the present Convention.

(4) The Committee shall hold closed meetings when examining communications under this article.

(5) In any matter referred to it, the Committee may call upon the States Parties concerned, referred to in paragraph 2, to supply any relevant information.

(6) The States Parties concerned, referred to in paragraph 2, shall have the right to be heard by the Committee and to make submissions in writing.

(7) The Committee shall, within 12 months after the transmission of the initial communication under paragraph 2, submit a report:

(a) If a solution within the terms of paragraph 3 is reached, the Committee shall confine its report to a brief statement of the facts and of the solution reached.

(b) If a solution within the terms of paragraph 3 is not reached, the Committee shall confine its report to a brief statement of the facts; the written submissions and record of the oral submissions made by the States Parties concerned shall be attached to the report.

The report shall be communicated to the States Parties concerned.]

[*Article 74*]

[The provisions of this Convention concerning the settlement of disputes or complaints shall be applied without prejudice to other procedures for settling disputes or complaints in the field covered by this Convention laid down in the constituent instruments of, or in conventions adopted by, the United Nations and its specialized agencies, and shall not prevent the States Parties from having recourse to other procedures for settling a dispute in accordance with international agreements in force between them.]

[*Article 75*]

[Nothing in the present Convention shall be interpreted as impairing the provisions of the Charter of the United Nations and of the constitutions of the specialized agencies which define the respective responsibilities of the various organs of the United Nations and of the specialized agencies in regard to the matters dealt with in the present Convention.]

PART VII
General provisions

[*Article 76*]

[(1) No provisions in this Convention shall affect any rights or freedoms afforded to migrant workers and members of their families by virtue of:

(a) the law [, legislation] or practice of a State Party; or
(b) any international treaty in force for the State Party concerned.

[(2) No provision in the present Convention may be interpreted as authorising any State, group or person to engage in any activity or perform any act that would impair any of the rights or freedoms recognised herein [or introduce limitations based on the present Convention].]

[(2) Nothing in this Convention may be interpreted as implying for any State, group or person any right to engage in any activity or perform any act aimed at the destruction of any of the rights and freedoms set forth herein or at their limitation to a greater extent than is provided for in the Convention.]]

[*Article 77*]

[The rights provided for in this Convention shall not be capable of renunciation. [It shall be unlawful to exert any form of pressure upon migrant workers and members of their families with a view to their relinquishing or foregoing any of the said rights.] [Any form of pressure upon migrant workers and members of their families with a view to their relinquishing or foregoing any of the said rights shall be subject to penalties.] [No form of pressure upon migrant workers and members of their families with a view to their relinquishing or foregoing of any of the same rights shall be permitted.] Any provision in any agreement or contract [the effect of which is] [implying] the relinquishment or foregoing of any of the said rights shall be void.]

[*Article 78*]

[Each State Party to the present Convention undertakes [in accordance with its constitutional processes and with the provisions of this Convention]:

(a) to ensure that any person whose rights or freedoms as herein recognised are violated shall have an effective remedy, notwithstanding that the violation has been committed by persons acting in an official capacity;

(b) to ensure that any person claiming such a remedy shall have his right thereto determined by competent judicial, administrative or legislative authorities, or by any other competent authority provided for by the legal system of the State, and to develop the possibilities of judicial remedy;

(c) to ensure that the competent authorities shall enforce such remedies when granted.]

[*Article 79*]

[Each State Party undertakes [in accordance with its constitutional processes and the provisions of this Convention] to adopt the legislative and other measures that are necessary to implement the provisions of the present Convention.]

[*Article 80*]

[States Parties to the present Convention shall remain free to conclude bilateral or multilateral agreements, subject to no limitations other than those provided for in this Convention [with a view to:]

[(a) resolving such problems as may arise from its implementation, in particular situations in matters such as social security, model employment contract and the validity of certificates and documents;]

[(b) ensuring the fair and just treatment of all migrant workers and members of their families.]]

PART VIII
Final provisions

[*Article 81*]

[(1) This Convention shall be open for signature by ... It is subject to ratification, acceptance or approval.

(2) This Convention shall be open to accession by any State referred to in paragraph 1 of this article.

(3) Instruments of ratification, acceptance, approval or accession shall be deposited with the Secretary-General of the United Nations.]

[*Article 82*]

[(1) This Convention shall enter into force the first day of the month following a period of three months after the date of the deposit of the 15th instrument of ratification, acceptance, approval or accession.

(2) For each State ratifying this Convention or acceding to it after the deposit of the 15th instrument of ratification, acceptance, approval or accession, it shall enter into force the first day of the month following a period of three months after the date of the deposit of its own instruments of ratification, acceptance, approval or accession.]

[*Article 83*]

[(1) The provisions of this Convention shall extent to all parts of federal States without any limitations or exceptions.

(2) Any State may, at the time of signature, ratification, acceptance, approval or accession or at any other date, declare that the Convention shall extend to all territories for the international relations of which it is responsible or to one or more of them. Such declaration shall take effect at the time the Convention enters into force for the State or if made subsequently, on the first day of the month following the expiration of a period of three months after the date of the receipt of such declaration by the Secretary-General of the United Nations. Such declarations, as well as any subsequent extension and their withdrawal, shall be notified to the Secretary-General of the United Nations.]

[*Article 84*]

[At the time of signature, ratification, acceptance, approval or accession, any State may declare that it shall apply Articles 51, 52, 53, 54, and 55 of this Convention only in relation to nationals of other States Parties.]

[*Articles 85–8*]

[These articles will contain standard final provisions concerning denunciation, revision, notification, and authenticity of texts.]

INDEX